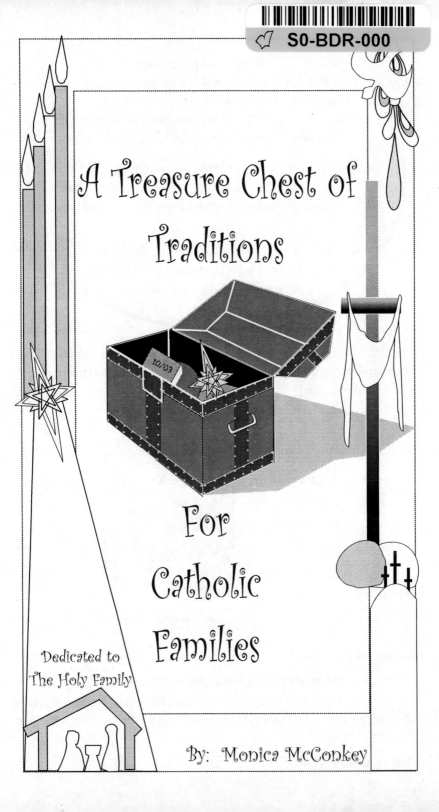

A Treasure Chest of Traditions

For Catholic Families

Dedicated to
The Holy Family

By: Monica McConkey

Many of the ideas in this book are original. Others are original adaptations of secular crafts, while others are original descriptions and often slight elaborations or variations of long-standing Catholic Traditions.

Every effort has been made to trace and contact original idea owners, acknowledging them through the **Experienced Mom Idea** Award.

We apologize for any inadvertent omissions or errors. All graphics are original work of the author and protected by copyright.

Contact Monica McConkey at **ArmaDei@aol.com** for additional copies and updates regarding this book and other Catholic products available through Arma Dei. Fund-raising plans for Churches, Schools and other Catholic organizations are available.

Thank-you for not photocopying without permission.

Ephesians 6:14

ARMA DEI
FAMILY
MINISTRY
equipping Catholic families

ISBN: **0-9689159-0-6**

A Treasure Chest of Traditions

A Treasure Chest of Traditions for Catholic Families offers ideas for activities, crafts and recipes to help families celebrate the various Seasons and Feast Days of the year. With fun-filled activities, we can build our own family traditions while passing on the richness of our Catholic Faith.

Guided by the Liturgical Calendar, the book journeys through the Seasons of Advent, Christmas, Lent, Easter and the 2 spans of Ordinary Time. The months of the Roman Calendar are woven in, providing the context for Feasts and Commemorations.

Suggested activities are intended to prompt families to actively practice their Faith, delving into Church Celebrations and allowing these festivities to spill back into home life.

 By celebrating the lives of the Saints, we become acquainted with models of holiness.

 By offering prayers and devotions and welcoming prayer petitions, we may spark a strong prayer life within our children.

 By providing reason to refer to Scripture, we encourage familiarity with the Bible and cultivate a deeper respect for God's Word.

 By providing an opportunity to better acquaint ourselves with the Catholic Catechism, we may find ourselves asking more questions, ultimately leading us to a deeper understanding of our Faith.

 By pursuing these themes at home, we pass on to our children the importance of our Catholic Tradition in our lives, while gaining a better understanding of Catholic Teaching.

Challenged to participate more deeply in our Faith, we will treasure our rich Catholic Tradition. We will also treasure our increasingly intimate relationship with Jesus; a result of a deeper commitment to our Faith.

For Catholic Families

4 Contents Guide

HAPPY NEW YEAR! 9 – 14

New Year's Eve Party, Decorations, Toast, Advent Wreath Punch Bowl, Chocolate Advent Wreath Cake, Pinata

December

St. Nicholas, St. Ambrose, Immaculate Conception, Our Lady of Guadalupe, St. Lucy, St. Abraham/St. Isaac/St. Jacob, St. Stephen, St. John, Holy Innocents

ADVENT 15 – 38

Letters to the Christ Child, Advent Decorations, Christ Kindl, Nativity Activities, Homemade Nativity, Decorative Prayer Chains, Advent Wreaths, Advent Calendars, Jesse Tree, Mini Gingerbread Manger, Christmas Eve Treats, A Gift Basket for The Christ Child

CHRISTMAS 39 – 50

A Gift for The Christ Child, Jesus: Light of the World (Ice Candles, Paper Bag Lanterns), Feast of the Holy Family (Felt Friends & Flat, Family Activities), Gift Tags/ Place Setting Tags, Bird Treat - Tree Decorations

EPIPHANY 51 – 58

Epiphany Centrepiece, Epiphany Box, Epiphany Party (Parade of the Kings, King's Cake, Blessing of the Home, Blessing of the Waters, A Holy Water Font, Water Appreciation)

January

Mary, Mother of God, St. Ita, St. Anthony, St. Sebastian, St. Frances de Sales, Conversion of St. Paul

ORDINARY TIME 59 – 84

Bapdays, Saints' Namedays, Prayer (Prayer Bank, Envelope Prayer Bank, Prayer Carousel, Angel of God, Act of Contrition, Daily Offerings, Grace before Meals, A Few Good Habits, Bedtime Prayers, Prayers with Gestures, Five Finger Prayers), Shrove Tuesday (Happy Cakes, Fruity Cakes, Fluffy Cakes), Mardi Gras (masks)

February

Presentation of the Lord, St. Blase, St. Veronica, St. Agatha, St. Scholastica, Our Lady of Lourdes, St. Valentine, Chair of St. Peter

The location of Feast Days may not directly correspond with this guide.

LENT 85-114

Intro, Our Lenten Share, Thirty Pieces of Silver, Simple Suppers, Pretzels, Friend of Jesus, Basket of Blessing Eggs, Daily Gifts to Jesus, Count Our Blessings Book, The Weight of the Cross, Lenten Calendar, Crown of Thorns, Resurrection Crown, Offering Cross, Sin Cross, Heart Cross Banner, Band-Aids for Christ

March

St. John of God, St. Frances of Rome, St. Dominic Savio, St. Patrick, St. Joseph, Annunciation, St. Joseph of Arimathea

April

St. John Baptist de la Salle, St. Mark, St. Zita, St. Catherine of Siena

HOLY WEEK 115-130

Preparation (for Holy Week), Spring Cleaning, Make a Paschal Candle (or Paschal Votive Candle), Easter Story Eggs, Simplified Seder Supper, Stations of the Cross, Easter Story Banner, Passion Play (Clothes Peg People, Paper Roll People), Empty Tomb Cookies, Coloured Jelly Easter Eggs

EASTER 131-137

Intro, Wafer Cross Cookies, Prayer Petal Flower Easter Baskets, Easter Mosaic, Melted Wax Stained Glass, Resurrection Rolls

MONTH OF MAY: 138-150 MONTH OF MARY

Mary Altar, May Crowning, The Angelus, Family Mantle of Protection, Mother's Day Breakfast Tray, Mary Garden, Stepping Stones to Mary's Heart (Mary Garden Markers), Modest Mary Dolls, Paper Dolls of Mary, Mary Collage

May

St. Joseph the Worker, St. Philip and St. James, St. Matthias, St. Isidore, St. Bernardine of Siena, St. Joan of Arc, the Visitation

ASCENSION / PENTECOST 151-159

Prep for Pentecost, Ascension of the Lord Kites, Ascension Bubble Blower (and Bubbles), Praises Phrases, Pentecost Pinata, Dough Doves, Holy Spirit Sweets, Catch the Spirit! Wind Catcher

Feast Days are woven in throughout the primary Liturgical Calendar ordering. Look for the corresponding Monthly Saints' Day pages.

6 Contents Guide

The location of Feast Days may not directly correspond with this guide as they are woven in throughout the primary Liturgical Calendar ordering.

June

St. Anthony of Padua, FATHER'S DAY
St. John the Baptist, St. Peter and St. Paul

160-171

TRINITY SUNDAY / IMMACULATE HEART OF MARY / CORPUS CHRISTI / SACRED HEART OF JESUS
Trinity Braid Pins, Trinity Bracelets, Woven Prayer Petition Heart, Jesus Tour, Father's Day Gifts, Woven Heart Gift

July

St. Thomas, St. Benedict, St. James, St. Christopher, St. Joachim and St. Ann, St. Martha, St. Ignatius

ORDINARY TIME 172-207
School's Out! Activities, CATHLETICS Intro, Medals, Cathletics Lingo Bingo, Catechism Cube, Trivia Tube, Flash Cards, Project: Definition (Def-A-Day, Definition Detail), Momentum Builder Grid, Jell-O Box Jeopardy, Jell-O Boxes Revisited, (Jig-Saw Jell-O Boxes, Four-in-a-Row), Catechism Playing Cards, Holy Rummoli!, Lists and Levels

August

St. John Vianney, St. Agatha (1/2 Feast), Transfiguration, St. Clare, Assumption of Mary, Queenship of Mary, St. Bartholomew, St. Monica, St. Augustine

ORDINARY TIME 208-219
EXTRAORDINARY EVENTS IN ORDINARY TIME (Fuss-Worthy Firsts, Family Journal of Firsts & Family Events, Memory Catcher Cards, Birthday Journal, Family Guestbook, Calendar Scroll, Family Tree, Family Treasure Chest, Birth of a Sibling (Baby Survival Kit), Death of a Loved One, Moving (House Swatch), Celebrating Sacraments (Sacrament Anniversary Party)

220-227

EVERYDAY IN ORDINARY TIME
Prayer Time and Mass Prep, Church Collector Cards, Mass Parts and Prayers, Family Blessings Mailbox, The God Box, Family Fridge Calendar (Cut-and-Paste Fridge Calendar, Special Event Markers, Build-Your-Own Fridge Calendar)

September

St. Gregory, Birth of Mary, Triumph of the Cross, Our Lady of Sorrows, St. Matthew, St. Vincent de Paul, the Archangels

ORDINARY TIME 228-240

Pass the Torch Party, Bible Bingo, Holy Heroes Felt Friends and Folder, Holy Heroes Puppets and Puppet Theatre, Holy Cards Intro, Holy Hero Album, Holy Card Memory Game, Holy Medal Bracelet 241-279

MONTH OF OCTOBER: MONTH OF THE ROSARY

Intro, Homemade Rosaries, Rose Bead Rosaries, Paper Beads, Spiritual Bouquet)

October

St. Theresa, Guardian Angels, St. Francis of Assisi Our Lady of the Rosary, St. Gerard, St. Luke, St. Simon and St. Jude

The location of Feast Days may not directly correspond with this guide as they are woven in throughout the primary Liturgical Calendar ordering.

ORDINARY TIME

Foil Kiss Roses, ANGEL CRAFTS (String of Guardian Angels, Spoon Angels, Jelly Bean Angel, Sweet Angel Treats, Telephone Book Angel, Paper Mache' Angel, Guardian Angel Mobile), Rosary Refresher, Spiritual Bouquet Cards, Rosary Gift Cards, Crown of Roses (Single Rosary Crown, Potato Stamping, 3-Rosary Crown), Crowns and Wreaths (Crown of Jewels), Special Intentions Candle, Picture Frame, Profile of Jesus, Painting and Paint Palette, Sin Pin Bowling, Fishers of Men Coin Toss, St. Jude Files (Fridge Frame of Prayer Postings, Mobile Prayer Posting Boards), Alternative Halloween Decorating (Simple Angels, Angel Pumpkin), Alternative Halloween Costumes

November

All Saints, All Souls, Churches of St. Peter and St. Paul, Presentation of Mary, St. Cecilia, St. Andrew

ORDINARY TIME 280-295

Dream Team of Saints (Intro, Family Litany of the Saints, Dream Team Photo, Dream Team Mobile) All Saints' Day Party (Intro, Liturgical Chairs, Armour of God, Works of Mercy Relay Race, Cathletics Competition, Saint Name Game, List and Twist, David and Goliath Bean Bag Toss, Sacramental Memory Game, Count the Rosaries in the Jar, Rosary Bee, Halo Toss, Holy Heroes' Halo Game, Sin Pinata) FEAST OF CHRIST THE KING (King's Crown, Royal Dinner)

296-299

Web of Catholic Resources, Magazine Rack, Bibliography

ARMA DEI
FAMILY
MINISTRY
equipping Catholic families

We would appreciate your feedback!
If you find any errors/omissions to be corrected, if you feel any instructions need further clarification or if you have any ideas or special tips to add, please respond to: ArmaDei@aol.com

You could be eligible for an Experienced Mom Idea award and have your idea and/or name published in the next edition!

Happy New Year!

We usually think of New Year's Day as occurring each January 1st, as defined by the secular calendar. For Catholics, our Church calendar begins with the Season of Advent, about one month earlier. How about entering the New Liturgical Year with a New Year's Eve Party?

If it is just unthinkable to keep the kids up until midnight, remember that sundown is a good alternative. Nightfall can be used to mark the beginning of the next day, as in Jewish tradition. Watch for sunset times on the weather channel or pick an arbitrary time (like 1 hour before bedtime!).

The Liturgical Year begins with Advent. Encompassing the 4 Sundays before Christmas, Advent begins between Nov.27-Dec.3.

Advent focuses on the arrival of Christ as our Messiah. It is a time of preparation and anticipation!

ADVENT

Decorations!

Make an ADVENT WREATH PUNCH BOWL to kick off the party and launch everyone into the season of Advent! Decorate with purple and pink, the official colours of Advent.

Loosely tape large pieces of purple and pink tissue paper over lamp shades and other lights to emit an Advent glow, (if appropriate coloured bulbs are not available).

MAKE SURE that the tissue paper does not touch the light fixture or bulb, and that there are sufficient gaps to allow venting. Alternate different light sources, to make sure no overheating occurs.

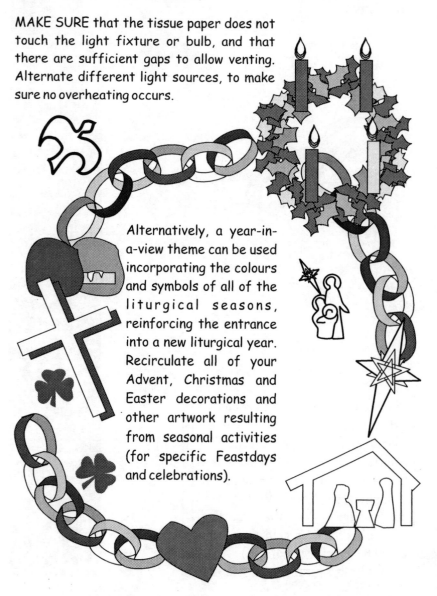

Alternatively, a year-in-a-view theme can be used incorporating the colours and symbols of all of the liturgical seasons, reinforcing the entrance into a new liturgical year. Recirculate all of your Advent, Christmas and Easter decorations and other artwork resulting from seasonal activities (for specific Feastdays and celebrations).

Have lots of favourite snacks and drinks to bring in the New Year and include a countdown and TOAST as close to midnight as the children can stay awake for.

The TOAST is an important aspect of the New Year Celebration. Punch or tailored drinks may entice your children. It can be a great opportunity to get creative with your children's favourite juice. Add gingerale or soda water if you think they would like it. Freeze pieces of fruit within colourful juice ice cubes for added colour.

Fruit and fruit juice blended with a cup of sherbert or ice cream in the blender froths up a tasty drink, even tastier!

Add a sliced orange by cutting a slit into it and clipping it onto the top of the glass. Little umbrellas are always a hit if they are available, but comparable little paper garnishes can be made with a little imagination!

11

Advent is that reflective time in which we Christians recall the truth that even in the dead of winter, even in the dark, God is always being born in the world, in our lives and in our hearts.

Fr. Daniel Homan prior of St. Benedict Monastery

ADVENT

Happy New Year!

ADVENT WREATH PUNCH BOWL

Create the juice-ice wreath with a tube cake pan. Improvise with a round cake pan and insert a glass or cup, half-filled with water, in the centre of the pan, before adding the juice to the rest of the pan. When frozen, remove from freezer, adding boiling water to the centre cup to ease the cup out of the mold. It may be necessary to warm the underside of the pan to ease the remaining ice ring from the pan.

Place 4 pineapple rings around the rim of the ice ring. Place a slice of orange on each pineapple ring. Thread a few maraschino cherries on each of 4 toothpicks and push one into each orange slice.

Alternatively, tealights can be used to add to the Advent Wreath effect. Just place them on the pineapple and orange slices. The inner hole of each pineapple slice could be enlarged to accommodate and secure the tealights in place. Remember to blow them out when the punch is being served!

CHOCOLATE ADVENT WREATH CAKE

This cake is made with a tube cake pan as well, but with regular cake batter! Decorate the cake with chocolate leaves, made by coating fresh rose, mint or gardenia leaves (which have been carefully washed and dried) with melted chocolate.

Melt semi-sweet chocolate chips in a double boiler or in microwave (2-3 minutes). Allow chocolate to cool and pour onto waxed paper. Dip the veined side of the leaf into the chocolate, holding the stem. Take care not to get chocolate on the other side of the leaf. Lay the chocolate coated leaf on wax paper to dry (chocolate side up). Cool in fridge for 15-30 minutes until chocolate is firm. Gently peel leaves off chocolate (beginning at the stem end).

Place 4 real candles or 4 crispy rolled cookies (dipped in chocolate) for the Advent candles.

Happy New Year!

The PINATA is a great activity to engage the whole family and build anticipation for the Advent season ahead!

A PINATA does not have to be filled with only CANDY. It is a great opportunity to build excitement around other objects such as stickers, friendly notes or Bible verses, holy medals and holy cards. Figures for the Nativity scene or objects representing and accompanied by Bible references could be included, to be used for the ADVENT CALENDAR or JESSE TREE.

Of course a little candy or a few treats are welcomed additions to the contents of the PINATA...

A PINATA can be made by covering a balloon with paper mache (strips of torn newspaper or scrap paper coated with watered down glue or wallpaper paste). By adding various other size balloons or scrunched up newspaper, covering them and connecting them to the balloon with paper mache, other shapes can be applied to create other animals or objects. Use your imagination (or your children's!) to come up with fun shaped pinatas to continue the theme of the celebration! See other PINATA ideas in the ALL SAINTS' DAY CELEBRATION.

Allow layers to dry before beginning another. The more layers, the stronger the pinata will be. Try winding string or yarn around the shape within one of the layers of paper mache, to add strength.

Don't forget to leave a hole in the paper mache so that the balloon can be poked (when the paper mache has dried sufficiently) and treats can be added. Cover the hole with more paper mache and allow to dry. Paint away!

The first 2 weeks of Advent continue the themes of the final weeks of Ordinary Time: Christ's return as part of the Final Judgement.

ADVENT

If a hole is left near the bottom of the hanging pinata, streamers can be used to wind around the treats before they are tucked into the pinata. Push more streamers into the hole to keep the treats in place. Allow the ends of all the streamers to dangle outside the pinata. When the time is right, everyone can grab hold of a streamer instead of beating the pinata with a stick!

Use your imagination!

This method works particularly well if the pinata resembles the children's favourite animated character. Children may become quite attached to a character-pinata during the process of making it! Beating your accomplishment with a stick may not be the best outcome! After the pinata is emptied (by pulling the streamers) hang the special party momento in the children's playroom!

The hole can be covered by a pouch or a "trap door" flap. The flap can be a piece of material, lightly tacked in place with glue.

If the flap is lightly tacked at points on all four corners, carefully wind the streamers around these fragile connection points. The flap should easily fall away as the streamers are pulled.

(pouch)

Streamers wound around glued points.

In a pinch, a paper bag can be used as a pinata. Just fill the bag with the loot, tie a string around the top of the bag to close it, and string it up! It may not be as appealing or elaborate as the homemade paper mache' pinata, but with a little paint and decoration...and a lot of fun stuff inside, it will still be a great event.

Letters to the Christ Child

On the First Sunday of Advent, encourage each child to write a letter to The Christ Child. Let them express their most deepest desires and conclude their letter with a personal promise to The Christ Child.

Traditionally, these letters are placed on the window sill for The Christ Child to retrieve. The letters often disappear on the first night. For those stubborn little ones who might need to improve their behaviour a little bit, the letters might not be retrieved right away! ...just a little incentive to clean up our act before Christmas!

Continuing with this tradition, gifts at Christmas are received from The Christ Child, rather than from Santa Claus. This distinction effectively focuses Christmas on the birth of Jesus rather than popular Santa culture. If Santa is an integral part of your Christmas celebration, explain that Santa gives gifts in honour of the joyous event of Jesus' birth. Celebrate the Feast of St. Nicholas, reaffirming Santa's roots to the holy hero.

Advent is the season that is meant to nurture our joyful and hopeful anticipation and longing for the Coming of the Lord.

Fr. Roger Vandenakker

Companions of the Cross

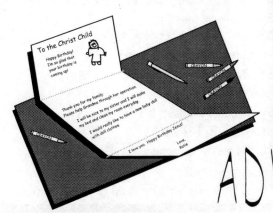

To the Christ Child

Happy Birthday!
I'm so glad that your birthday is coming up!

Thank you for my family.
Please help Grandma through her operation.
I will be nice to my sister and I will make my bed and clean my room everyday.
I would really like to have a new baby doll with doll clothes.

I love you. Happy Birthday Jesus!

Love,
Katie

ADVENT

Saints' Days

1. St. Florence, laywoman *
2. St. Bibiana, virgin, martyr *
3. St. Francis Xavier, priest   MEMORIAL
4. St. John Damascene, priest, doctor   OPTIONAL MEMORIAL
5. St. Gerald, bishop *
6. **St. Nicholas of Myra,** bishop   OPTIONAL MEMORIAL
7. **St. Ambrose,** bishop, doctor   MEMORIAL
8. **IMMACULATE CONCEPTION OF THE BLESSED VIRGIN MARY**   SOLEMNITY
9. St. Peter Fourier, priest *
9. Blessed Juan Diego, layman
10. St. Romaric, abbot *
11. St. Damasus I, pope   OPTIONAL MEMORIAL
12. **OUR LADY OF GUADALUPE**   FEAST
13. **St. Lucy,** virgin, martyr   MEMORIAL
14. St. John of the Cross   MEMORIAL
15. St. Nino, virgin *
16. St. Adelaide, queen *
17. St. Olympias, widow *
18. St. Gatian, bishop *
19. Blessed Urban V, pope *
20. **St. Abraham, St. Isaac, St. Jacob,** patriarchs *
21. St. Peter Canisius, priest, doctor   OPTIONAL MEMORIAL
22. St. Chaeremon, St. Ischyrion, martyrs *
23. St. John of Kanty, priest   OPTIONAL MEMORIAL
24. St. Adele, widow *
25. **CHRISTMAS**   SOLEMNITY
26. **St. Stephen,** first martyr   FEAST
27. **St. John,** apostle, evangelist   FEAST
28. **HOLY INNOCENTS,** martyrs   FEAST
29. St. Thomas Becket, bishop, martyr   OPTIONAL MEMORIAL
30. St. Anysius, bishop *
31. St. Sylvester I, pope   OPTIONAL MEMORIAL

The traditional Church Calendar assigned at least one Saint to each day of the year. It was decided in Vatican II that only certain Saints' Feastdays would be extended to the Universal Church; others could continue to be celebrated by individual Churches, nations, religious orders (or families!) of particular association.

*This Feast Day does not occur in the revised Roman Calendar.

Advent Decorations

Decorations of purple and pink could stay up for the entire Advent season, holding off the Christmas decorations until Christmas Eve or at least Gaudete Sunday. Gaudete Sunday is the third Sunday of Advent when we rejoice that the arrival of Jesus is drawing near and the wait is almost over.

As an alternative to the usual Christmas lights...invest in purple lights to decorate your house, shrubs or trees. Reserve a string or two of pink lights to illuminate the third and fourth Weeks of Advent, reflecting the end of Advent drawing near.

If you enjoy the atmosphere that a Christmas Tree brings to the home for the weeks building up to Christmas, how about decorating it in stages? Save the light effect and tinsel for Christmas Eve (or at least Gaudete Sunday). Just don't plug it in, until Jesus' arrival is immanent!

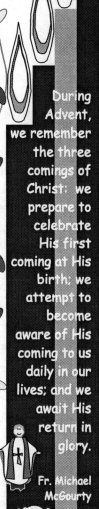

During Advent, we remember the three comings of Christ: we prepare to celebrate His first coming at His birth; we attempt to become aware of His coming to us daily in our lives; and we await His return in glory.

Fr. Michael McGourty

An Irish Catholic Tradition places candle lights in the windows (originally attracting fugitive priests to safe homes). Consider this lighting technique as a beacon for Mary and Joseph on their journey to Bethlehem! Look for candle-shaped electric lights to achieve this effect.

ADVENT

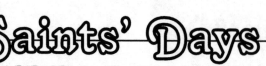

Saints' Days

DECEMBER 6: The Optional Memorial of St. Nicholas, patron of bakers

Santa Claus is the secular evolution of a holy hero in our Faith: St. Nicholas. As Austrian tradition holds, the bishop is allowed by God to continue the kindness to children that he is known for, by returning on his Feast day and visiting them. St. Nicholas gives little treats to good children who can answer catechism questions and recite their prayers.

In many countries, on the eve of this Feast, children set their shoes out in hopes that St. Nicholas will fill them with treats during the night. Some children leave hay and carrots for the horse traveling with St. Nicholas.

Make some homemade cookies from your favourite family recipes and enjoy them after a special family dinner. Perhaps these cookies could provide little rewards for those who can recite certain prayers and catechism answers. (See CATHLETICS in the summer months of this book.)

DECEMBER 7: The Memorial of St. Ambrose, patron of candle-makers

A legend recounts that as a baby, a swarm of bees once flew around Ambrose and landed on his tongue. Although his mother was terrified, the bees did not sting the baby, but left a bit of honey on his tongue. This was said to foretell his future as a great preacher, speaking with a "honeyed" tongue.

In light of his connection to bees and his role as patron of candlemakers, why not make some BEESWAX CANDLES? Check out your local craft store for beeswax sheets and candle wicks. These make great Advent candles, Christmas candles or Christmas gifts or can be personalized for birthday, NAMEDAY or BAPDAY celebrations.

Advent Decorations

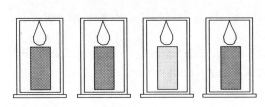

Create some window decorations that will witness to your neighbours and provide interesting light affects and ambiance within your home!

Choose a large window (or several adjacent ones), clearly visible at the front of your house. Cut out 3 purple rectangles and 1 pink rectangle out of tissue paper. The size of the rectangles will depend on your tissue supply and your window size. EACH rectangle could be 2/3 the height of the window and 1/4 or 1/2 the width. If it is preferred that substantial clear glass be visible, use smaller dimensions for the rectangles.

Tape 2 purple rectangles, 1 pink rectangle and the remaining purple rectangle on the lower portions of the windows. Start from right to left to ensure that they will be viewed in the right order from the outside. Cut out one flame (1/2 the height of a rectangle) out of yellow tissue paper. Add a flame on the appropriate rectangle (candle) each Sunday of Advent as the weeks progress, (starting from right to left).

"Prepare the way of the Lord" said St. John the Baptist. Advent is a time of spiritual preparation for the first coming of Christ. It is a season of joyful expectation!

Fr. Leslie Tamas

Saints' Days

DECEMBER 8: The Solemnity of the Immaculate Conception

The Feast of the Immaculate Conception does not celebrate Jesus' conception, but rather Mary's conception within the womb of her mother, St. Anne.

Many people begin offering novenas of prayers and Masses, 9 days before this feast.

In honour of this Feast celebrating Mary's conception, let's pamper pregnant mothers a little bit on this day. If you know of a pregnant mother, bake some cookies to satisfy those cravings.

Make some decorations to help prepare the baby's room (and help pregnant moms "nest"!):

Centre a HOLY CARD on coloured construction paper and fit it to a frame. Place it in the frame and decorate the frame with little angels. Angel stickers are always easy to apply, but a simple angel shape can be cut out of paper or modeled out of clay and painted.

Create a SPOON ANGEL and attach a little note with the Guardian Angel prayer and instructions to hang the angel well out of reach from the crib.

DECEMBER

To celebrate the sin-less-ness of Mary from the moment of her conception, how about a PURE WHITE DINNER?

Stick to white fish, white rice or white (oriental) rice noodles with white cream sauce and white cauliflower with white cheese sauce. Remember to leave out the dark spices from your recipes. Serve with a tall glass of white milk.

Dessert is the fun part! Look in your favourite cookbook for white cake with white icing or make meringue cookies (without nuts or dried fruit) and inject white whipped cream with a cake decorating syringe.

White cupcakes with white icing are always a hit, as is vanilla ice cream.

Other fun toppings include white chocolate flakes (made with a cheese grater). Use your imagination!

Christ Kindl

Let everyone draw another family member's name from a hat and encourage everyone to keep their selection secret.

Throughout Advent, each family member carries out special good deeds for their selected person, in secret.

Each day, sneak a special treat into a lunchbox, make the other person's bed when they are not looking or do other chores that they regularly do.

Quietly show your love for that person without giving away your identity until Christmas Eve!

ADVENT

Nativity Activities

The NATIVITY is a familiar scene to us all. The following traditions help to keep our focus throughout Advent, transforming a model of the Holy Family into an unfolding play...impacting our lives.

Mary and Joseph (and the donkey) trek around the house, arriving at the stable on Christmas Eve. The journey is tied to good deeds and sacrifices, moving the figures closer to the stable every time such a deed is done. The shepherd tends the sheep near the stable throughout the whole month. The 3 wise men begin their journey after Christmas, arriving on Epiphany.

The figures can be set up within the manger scene with the exception of Baby Jesus, who is added on Christmas Eve. Pieces of straw (or felt material representing blankets) are added to the Baby Jesus' bed as good deeds are performed within the home during the season of Advent. Explain that good deeds provide comfort for Baby Jesus.

Almost anything can be painted and accessorized to look like figures for a HOMEMADE NATIVITY. Egg cartons can be cut apart into single units and pushed together to form stout little people. Paint or material or coloured paper can be added to personalize each figure.

The top of a milk carton can become quite a stylized Biblical figure. Make cuts as illustrated. Stuff the open spout with paper towel, ensuring that one smooth surface (of paper towel) fills the opening. Paint or add fabric or paper to personalize.

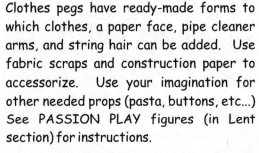

Clothes pegs have ready-made forms to which clothes, a paper face, pipe cleaner arms, and string hair can be added. Use fabric scraps and construction paper to accessorize. Use your imagination for other needed props (pasta, buttons, etc...) See PASSION PLAY figures (in Lent section) for instructions.

Toilet paper rolls can be used for figures as well, using pipe cleaner arms (poked through the paper roll) and paint and material scraps to personalize. Egg carton shapes can be used to round the head. String can be glued on for hair. See PASSION PLAY for more details.

Homemade Nativity

If you choose to MAKE your own NATIVITY, try popsicle sticks, cardboard or paper mache' for the stable. Just add figures, animals and straw!

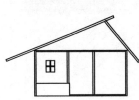

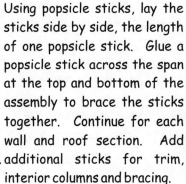

Using popsicle sticks, lay the sticks side by side, the length of one popsicle stick. Glue a popsicle stick across the span at the top and bottom of the assembly to brace the sticks together. Continue for each wall and roof section. Add additional sticks for trim, interior columns and bracing.

OR

Place a cardboard shoebox on it's long side. Add a long piece of cardboard, gently folded to create a pitched roof and glue this in place on top of the box. Make openings in the box for windows and cut additional cardboard pieces for trim and bracing details.

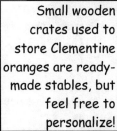

Small wooden crates used to store Clementine oranges are ready-made stables, but feel free to personalize!

OR

Create a more primitive cave-like setting out of wire and paper mache' or layer the cardboard version (with the pitched roof) with paper mache' and paint.

ADVENT

Saints' Days

DECEMBER

December 12: The Feast of Our Lady of Guadalupe

An imprinted image of Our Lady of Guadalupe was found with out-of-season roses, in the cloak of Juan Diego. The Blessed Virgin Mary had appeared to Juan and encouraged him to convince the authorities to build the Shrine of Our Lady of Guadalupe, now a popular pilgrimage site.

Prepare to have some Mexican food for dinner. Prepare the fixings for soft or hard tacos and let everyone build their own!

Decorate the family dinner table with fancy homemade roses made out of coloured tissue paper.

Cut pieces of tissue paper into 6" squares. Use 5-10 squares for each flower. Place in a pile, lining up the edges, and alternating the colours.

Fold accordion style, making $\frac{1}{2}$ " pleats. When completed, staple the folded accordion in the centre (or tie with string or a twist tie). Gently peel one layer at a time, pulling the edges of the paper toward the centre.

These flowers can be displayed as is, or sprayed lightly with spray paint and/or perfume.

Decorative Prayer Chains

At the beginning of Advent, cut 1"x8" strips of wrapping paper or coloured paper (maybe purple and pink for Advent?). On each strip write a different prayer, a name of a person to pray for or a good deed to do. Get the children involved by getting them to prepare some or at least give some ideas for the messages. Create one strip for each day of Advent, for each member of the family. The strips are kept in a bag or bowl or ADVENT CALENDAR.

Each day of Advent, each member of the family randomly selects a strip. At the end of the day (after the good deeds are carried out), the strip is formed into a loop and stapled, through the previous link. By Christmas Eve, the family has created a long decorative chain to offer as a gift to Jesus and decorate the tree or other prominent spot in the house.

The same idea can be used (in reverse!) to create the ANTICIPATION PRAYER CHAIN. The strips (complete with prayers or good deed messages) are immediately linked into chains at the beginning of Advent. Each member of the family has a chain with one loop for each day of Advent.

Take on someone else's chore today.

Each morning, everyone carefully rips one link from their chain and carries out the message on the strip. The shrinking chain provides a countdown to Jesus' birthday!

The links can be saved in the GIFT FOR THE CHRIST CHILD gift box, once they are removed from the shrinking ANTICIPATION CHAIN.

Compliment someone today.

Pray for Grandma today.

ADVENT

26 Advent Wreaths

Wreaths are an ancient symbol of victory. Advent wreaths symbolize the victory of Christ's coming and the glory of His Birth.

There are 4 candles in the advent wreath, representing the 4 weeks of Advent. The three purple candles represent our waiting, repentance, hoping and longing expectation for the arrival of Christ. The pink candle representing the 3rd week, reminds us that the time of Christ's arrival is approaching fast, and we must prepare!

A simple Advent wreath can be made from an artificial evergreen wreath. Others may prefer to form a circle out of real evergreen branches, tied with wire.
Four matching candle holders are placed within the wreath to hold the candles. Candle holders can even consist of slightly flattened balls of playdough: just push a candle into each ball. (Ensure the ball has a diameter about twice the size of the diameter of the candle.)

Decorate the wreath, tying purple bows around the candle bases. Add sprigs of artificial holly, pine cones or dry herbs.

Set the wreath on the dinner table or similarly visible place throughout Advent. Mount the wreath on a green-painted styrofoam ring, for extra stability. If the candles are carefully secured, the wreath can even be suspended from a chandelier or ceiling in the dining room or front hall. Allow the wreath to hang high enough so that it does not interfere with regular usage of the space or create a fire hazard, but low enough to accommodate regular and safe candle-lighting.

Each week of Advent, the appropriate candles of the family Advent Wreath are lit. Advent readings and prayers are said. Family discussion could take place, reflecting on themes of waiting (week 1), hoping (week 2), preparing (week 3) and celebrating (week 4).

As a dining table centrepiece, angels could be placed in the centre of the wreath, to be replaced by the Holy Family on Christmas Eve. Alternatively, a white candle could be placed within the centre of the wreath, representing Jesus, the Light of the world. It could be present throughout Advent, but only lit after Christmas Eve.

The purple and pink candles can be replaced by white ones to transform the Advent Wreath into an EPIPHANY CENTREPIECE.

A FELT BOARD ADVENT WREATH allows the children to build the wreath throughout Advent. Each numbered leaf is added as each day passes. Each candle flame is added on the corresponding Sunday.
Velcro can be used to secure the pieces more permanently.

This format can also be combined with the ADVENT CALENDAR. The separate leaves and candles could be hidden in the pockets of the ADVENT CALENDAR.

Alternatively, the ADVENT CALENDAR could take the shape of the ADVENT WREATH. The leaves and candles could be secured in place (sewn or glued on three sides). An Advent treat or Nativity piece could be hidden under each leaf (within the pocket). The felt flames could be added to the candles on corresponding Advent Sundays.

28 Advent Calendars

As an alternative to the Advent Calendars filled with chocolate, create a calendar with pockets to hold other objects. A material calendar could be made with felt strips sewn on the sides and bottom with dividers creating separate pockets. (Smaller pieces can be glued or sewn on three sides to create separate pockets). Squares of paper could be secured on three edges to cardboard to create a paper version. Little envelopes could be used for a similar effect.

Plastic pill organizers (found at the dollar store) offer individual compartments for every day of the week. Other versions of calendars use wood with screws or nails to hang different objects for each day of Advent.

Get creative with the shapes of the pockets. Each pocket could be a house or landmark on a path to the manger scene or an ornament on an outline of a tree. Check out ADVENT WREATHS for an alternate layout, with pockets in the form of leaves, creating a wreath.

Fill the pockets with stickers (from Christian stores) of Bible heroes or Bible verses. Other pockets could hold notes with positive messages written on them; activities to do that day (paper snowflakes, bake cookies), prayer intentions or good deeds to do, or links for a PRAYER CHAIN. If the pockets contain ornaments, little hooks or velcro pieces could be secured throughout the banner to display the objects as they are revealed day by day.

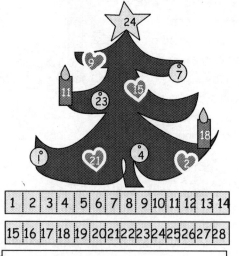

Notes of prayers, good deeds and encouragement can be saved in the GIFT FOR THE CHRIST CHILD gift box, once they are removed from the ADVENT CALENDAR, to be shared on Christmas Day.

The Advent Calendar could also be combined with the JESSE TREE. Objects could be collected or made to represent various things in Scripture, accompanied with the appropriate Bible reference. As they are removed from the calendar, they could be added to the JESSE TREE.

The Advent Calendar can also be combined with the NATIVITY. If you can find a small plastic Nativity set, perhaps a figure could fit in each pocket with the Christ Child in the last pocket, slowly assembling a manger scene in your child's room. Extra items to fill remaining pockets could include straw for the crib, tinsel to decorate the manger, the Star of Bethlehem, trees to surround the manger and handmade animals or angels...check your local craft store for ideas.

Figures could be drawn or created out of paper or cut from saved Christmas cards and mounted to cardboard. They could then be lightly taped to a cardboard manger or pinned on a bulletin board within a picture of a manger. Nativity figures could also be made out of felt and secured to a felt manger banner. Other fabric can be used, positioning the components with velcro.

Having a manger to place the figures in, prevents small pieces from being dangerous and getting lost.

30 The Jesse Tree

The Jesse Tree encourages us to reflect on many of the Biblical characters who contributed to the events leading to the arrival of our Messiah. The Advent tradition, named after the father of David, consists of symbols hung on a tree branch. This tree represents the Family Tree of Jesus, tracing His Lineage to Jesse, either in faith or bloodline. This lineage establishes Christ as the proper fulfillment of the many prophecies concerning the coming Messiah.

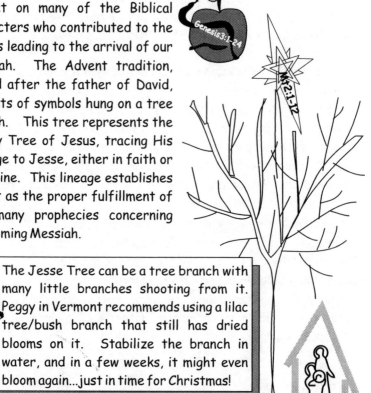

Genesis 3:1-24

Mt 2:1-12

Lk 2:1-20

The Jesse Tree can be a tree branch with many little branches shooting from it. Peggy in Vermont recommends using a lilac tree/bush branch that still has dried blooms on it. Stabilize the branch in water, and in a few weeks, it might even bloom again...just in time for Christmas!

EMI

The tree could be made out of wire and paper mache', painted and propped up in a base of styrofoam or playdough / clay. It could be constructed out of cardboard and mounted on the wall, with symbols pinned to or hung from the branches. The tree and symbols could also be made out of felt, for a felt board version. If other fabrics are used, velcro could be used to secure the different pieces in place.

The symbols can be drawn, cut from Christmas cards, created out of felt or construction paper, homemade playdough or clay. They can be as simple or elaborate as you choose. The Biblical reference allows us to easily read about the character or event and perhaps choose a unique symbol to capture the essence.

The Jesse Tree can allow us to refocus our Advent season, shifting our attention from presents under a Christmas tree to the Jesse Tree's focus of the arrival of Christ. Try to postpone putting up the Christmas tree until a few days before Christmas, allowing the Jesse Tree to be even more meaningful for the season of Advent. If you prefer, decorate the Christmas tree with Jesse Tree ornaments only, adding Christmas tree ornaments on Christmas Eve.

The next 2 pages offer many suggestions for characters or events and symbols. Do not limit yourself to these. As long as the Christ Child is the crowning ornament, any combination of other Biblical figures or events can be included. Work together with your family to choose which characters or events will be included and what symbols best represent them.

If anyone in your family has a Biblical name, ensure that you include that Bible character in your Jesse Tree.

This tradition is one that can grow. Start by creating a few symbols each year and really reflect on the Biblical references with your family. Over the years you will have quite the collection!

To combine the Jesse Tree with the ADVENT CALENDAR, it is recommended that there are enough symbols for each day of Advent. As you build your collection however, the symbols could be dispersed throughout the calendar as one of many activities (or treats!) involved throughout the Advent season.

The last 2 weeks of Advent focus on the Coming of the Son of God as a human!

ADVENT

The Jesse Tree

Creation (Gen. 1:1-27) earth
Adam & Eve in the Garden (Gen. 3:1-24)
fig leaf/apple with snake
God saves Noah & animals (Gen. 6,7,8:1-9) Noah's ark, rainbow
God's covenant with Abraham
(Gen. 12:1-3, 13:2-18, 18:1-5)
Abraham's tent, camel, stars

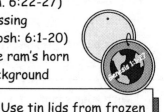

Abraham's sacrifice (Gen. 22:1-24)
a ram with an altar
Jacob's dream (Gen. 27:41 - 28:22)
Jacob's ladder going up to Heaven
Joseph and his brothers (Gen. 37:3-4, 12-28)
Joseph's many coloured coat
God calls Moses (Ex. 2:23-24; 3; 4:1-20)
the burning bush

Heavenly food (Ex. 16:1-36)
a woman gathering manna
Gen 27:41-28:22
God gives His Laws (Ex. 19, 20:1-21)
the Ten Commandments on tablets
Blessing of Aaron (Num. 6:22-27)
hand raised in blessing
Joshua/Jericho falls (Josh: 6:1-20)
Sword and trumpet, large ram's horn
with fallen walls in background

Ruth & Naomi (Ruth 1-4)
a sheaf of wheat standing in a field
God calls Samuel (1Sam. 3:1-21)
young boy sleeping / oil lamp
Jesse / Jesse's family chosen by God
(Is. 11:1, 1Sam. 16:1-13)
shepherd's crook / dead tree stump
with sapling growing from it /
branch with leaves

> Use tin lids from frozen juice containers for matching ornaments. Push a snug-fitting circle of construction paper into each disk for a colourful background.

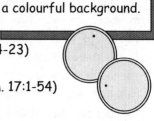

David (1 Sam. 16:14-23)
harp / star
David & Goliath (1 Sam. 17:1-54)
a slingshot

Psalm 23
    shepherd's crook
Wisdom of Solomon (1 Kings3:3-28)
    2 women with child between them / crown
    scales of justice
Elijah (1 Kings 17:1-16, 2 Kings 2:1-13)
    man with raven, chariot in a whirlwind of fire
Elisha (2 Kings 5:1-27)
    hand and dove
Nehemiah (Neh. 2:17-18)
    city walls
Angels (Tobit 12:15-20, Heb. 1:1-14)
    angels
Esther (Esther 2)
    crown
Isaiah (Is. 6:1-8, 9:1-7)
    scroll, tongs, lit candle   1Kings3:3-28
Jeremiah (Jer. 31:31-34)
    Stone
Daniel in the Lions' Den (Dan. 6:1-28)
    Daniel and lions
Jonah & the whale (Jonah 1&2)
    huge fish
Zechariah & Elizabeth (Lk. 1:5-25, 57-80)
    angel, altar
Blessed Virgin Mary (Mt. 1:23, 26-56, Is. 7:14)
    a pure white rose, lily, heart
Gabriel appears to Mary (Lk. 1:26-38)
    woman and angel
John the Baptist (Lk. 1:57-80)
    shell and water
Joseph (Mt. 1:18-25)
    carpenter tools
Mary & Joseph (Lk. 2:1-5)
    Joseph walking beside Mary on a donkey
Nativity (Lk. 2:1-20)
    manger with baby
Wise men follow the star (Mt. 2:1-12)
    great star with silhouette of
    3 wise men on camels

Psalm 23

Jonah1,2

33

During Advent, we hear how God promised to send Jesus and how the people of the Old Testament waited in hope for Jesus to come. This reminds us that God always keeps His promises and gives us hope as we wait to get ready for Jesus to come again.

Fr. Scott McCaig
Companions of the Cross

ADVENT

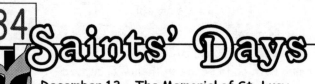

**December 13. The Memorial of St. Lucy,
patroness of the blind**

St. Lucy was a young Christian who vowed at an early age to be a bride of Christ. She was reported to the government for the crime of being a Christian, by a suitor she had turned away.

One legend reports that she plucked out her own eyes because their beauty attracted unwanted attention from suitors. Her eyes miraculously healed.

In many countries on this day, young girls dress in white dresses with red sashes (symbolizing martyrdom). They carry palms and wear crowns (or wreaths) with candles sticking out of them.

Transform the ADVENT WREATH for a day, into a St. Lucy crown. Replace the coloured advent candles with 7 white ones and scatter glitter or cutouts of stars on the table to remind us of St. Lucy, whose name means "light".

A longstanding tradition is to serve special buns or cookies called "Lucia Cats".

Make some shortbread cookies with cat cookie cutters or form the cat shape by hand. Alternatively a cat face can be added to store bought cookies, using raisins or chocolate chips for eyes and icing to create the other details.

A Hungarian custom on this day involves planting a few grains of wheat which sprout up right around Christmas...a great symbol of new life.

Originally inspired by gingerbread houses made and described by Karen on *The Catholic Mothers Email Discussion List*, this EMI is shared with Sue Conrad of Christ the King School in Richmond Hill, Ontario. Sue's class glues graham crackers to small milk cartons (with white glue) for the house shape.

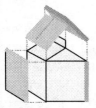

If the manger is to be eaten later, use the milk carton as formwork only, removing the carton once the melted sugar or icing has secured the shape.

MINI Gingerbread Manger

How about an alternative to the Gingerbread House? Create a miniature manger instead of a house. Use animal crackers for the animals. Jesus, Mary and Joseph could be cut from Christmas cards, mounted on cardboard and set into icing to stand within the manger. Alternatively, small cookie cutters could be used to make figures and animals out of cookie dough. Personalize with icing.

Miniature manger scenes can be made using graham crackers. Use sugar as the "glue". Just melt sugar slowly in a frying pan, stirring continuously as it changes from white to golden to brown.

Dip the side of a graham cracker evenly into the melted sugar. Quickly press this side into place against another cracker until it sets in place. Use icing and candy decorations to personalize the little graham cracker stable into a winter scene.

ADVENT

Saints' Days

December 20: St.Abraham, St.Isaac and St.Jacob*
Although this Feast is no longer part of the revised Liturgical Calendar, take this opportunity to read about these great figures in the Old Testament, focusing on Genesis 12, 17, 21, 22, 25:19-34, and 27.

Skim through the chapters in Genesis 12-25, and draw a family tree beginning with Abraham and finishing with Jacob's son, Joseph. In contrast to the FAMILY TREE described in the *Extraordinary Events in Ordinary Time* section of the book, use a different method to construct this tree, building upward instead of down. Begin with Abraham as the trunk of the tree assigning branches for the next generations. Fill in the various names given in the Bible.

* not in revised Church Calendar

Christmas Eve Treats

Instead of leaving cookies out for Santa, consider leaving a thoughtful gift for the Holy Family on the eve of Jesus' birth. Light a votive candle or tealight as the children go to bed, explaining that it is meant to help illuminate the Holy Family's path as they travel to the inn. Hopefully, it can be safely left on a table near a window (away from drapes or blinds!), visible from outside. Snacks, prayerful messages, homemade encouragement, congratulations or birthday cards can be left to accompany the candle, for the hungry and tired couple and the impending birth of the Messiah.

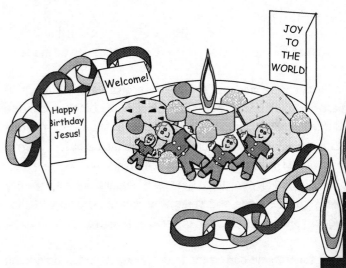

JOY TO THE WORLD

Welcome!

Happy Birthday Jesus!

I expect a visit from God - I must prepare!

Fr Tom Mohan

Congregation of the Priests of St. Basil

This EMI goes to Lynette Collins of Matamata, New Zealand. Her family decorates a "sand saucer" (by filling a saucer with sand and then covering the sand with flowers). They light a candle in the middle of the sand saucer after Midnight Mass, just before the children go to bed.

They leave some food as well, for the Holy Family or perhaps Angels who might be in the area.

ADVENT

This is an activity that is a great preparation for Christmas, taking place during Advent. Although it would be nice to have it displayed under your tree on Christmas Day, representing Jesus' present, it would bring even more joy in time for Christmas for a family in need.

A Gift Basket for The Christ Child

Create a gift basket for a newborn. Include gifts that can be made at home.

Receiving blankets can be made by sewing a hem on a 24" x 36" piece of flannel. An extra special double thickness receiving blanket is made by sewing 2 (24" x 36") pieces of flannel together (right sides together). Leave a 4" opening to turn the fabric inside out. Finish it off by sewing around the complete edge, a 1/4" seam.

Face cloths can be made by sewing a hem on 6" square pieces of terry cloth. Blankets can be made the same way, sewing a hem on a 36" square (or bigger) piece of fleece or other comfy material found at a fabric store.

A decorated picture frame can be made by gluing objects and adding paint to an unpainted wooden frame.

Packages of diapers, wipes, Qtips, small bottles of shampoo, lotion and soap always come in handy and are a welcomed addition to any baby gift basket.

Decorate the gift creatively with ribbons and bows and enclose all the presents within a basket or baby bath. Enclose the gift-filled container in clear wrap, tied with ribbons and bows. An alternative wrapping involves using a receiving blanket, bath towel or fleece blanket to enclose the gifts, secured tightly with a sturdy ribbon.

Give the gift basket away at the first opportunity to a family (with a newborn) in need...or drop it off at an organization accepting these items for unwed mothers or poor families.

A Gift for The Christ Child

While wrapping up all the special gifts for the family, take special care to wrap up a present for The Christ Child.

Wrap a medium sized box and wrap the lid separately so that the lid can still be used to open and close the box. Make the wrapping as fancy as possible...fit for a King!

Let everyone in the family add to the contents of the box, contributing the little messages of prayer, thanksgiving and encouragement written to each other throughout the other activities (ANTICIPATION CHAIN / DECORATIVE CHAIN, ADVENT CALENDAR...).

> The box can be saved from year to year, even used as a type of mailbox, adding positive prayer, thanksgiving, encouragement or secret good deed messages throughout the season of Advent.

The Season of Christmas begins with Christmas Eve and extends to the Sunday after Epiphany, celebrating the Baptism of our Lord.

The wrapped present represents our gift to Jesus: our love and love-filled actions towards our family members. After the chaos of opening the material gifts under the tree, take the time as a family, to open these precious messages and share them with each other.

Leave the box displayed under the tree...it has another special use for the Feast of Epiphany!

Christmas

December 26: The Feast of St. Stephen

St. Stephen was a great preacher who was filled with the Holy Spirit. He was also the first martyr, dying for his faith in Jesus. His last words are familiar. Read Acts 7:54-60 and Luke 23:33-34.

In his preaching, St. Stephen gave a great summary of our ancestors and their persecution. Read Acts 7.

December 27: The Feast of St. John

St. John was the "beloved disciple" of Jesus who is credited with writing the 4th Gospel, 3 Epistles and the Book of Revelation. He remained with Jesus at the foot of the cross and was asked by Jesus to take care of Mary, the Mother of God.

Have a SCRIPTURE SEARCH! Dig out all the Bibles in the house. Take turns calling out specific passages written by St. John, (including the chapter and verse) and see who can find the Scripture the fastest! Remember to refer to the number before John's name for the First, Second or Third Letter of John, not to be confused with his Gospel. Here are a few to get you started:

1 John 4:11-12   John 10:14-15   Revelations 4:11

3 John 11   Revelations 7:11-12   John 3:16

Look for ways to celebrate an APOSTLE PARTY! Check out the other Apostle Feast Days!

JESUS: LIGHT of the WORLD!

ICE CANDLES

Fill a round balloon with water to the size of a grapefruit. Blow a little air into the balloon before tying it. Set the water balloon in a clean 500mL plastic container (sour cream or yogurt container). Allow to freeze for 4-5 hours.

In this time, a thick layer of ice should be formed within the balloon. The centre of the balloon should still be liquid or slush.

Burst and discard the balloon. If there is not already an opening at the top, tap the ice shell until there is one. Allow the water to pour out. Freeze the shell again, to ensure it is frozen throughly.

Place a tea light within the round shell. Display outside to announce that

JESUS,
THE LIGHT OF THE WORLD,
HAS ARRIVED!

For a larger variation, rub oil on the inside of a small bucket. Fill with water to $\frac{3}{4}$ full. Allow to freeze for 5-6 hours. After this time, the form should be partially frozen. Scoop out the slush remaining in the centre, leaving the ice shell. Re-freeze it until you are ready to light the tea light inside it.

Experiment with other shaped containers, perhaps inserting glass jars at different stages of the freezing process and adding additional water to envelop the glass. Food colouring added to the water will create special coloured ice effects.

God, who is so big, bigger than the universe itself, became so small, small enough to dwell in the womb of Mary!

Fr. Roger Vandenakker Companions of the Cross

Christmas

JESUS:
LIGHT of the WORLD!

The lighting of candles is a great illustration of how Jesus brings light into the world. Using everyday objects, celebrate Jesus' light in our lives with these special light effects.

PAPER BAG LANTERNS
Collect a series of paper lunch bags. Carefully draw a design on the outside of each bag. Each bag can have a special design or the bags can be placed together to spell JESUS, with one letter on each bag.

Cut out the design or letter on the surface of the bag. Glue coloured tissue paper on the inside surface of the bag, over the cut-out design.

Place some sand in the bottom of the bag and stand the bag upright. Place a tealight in the sand and enjoy the coloured light emitted from the series of bags while the design is illuminated.

These PAPER BAG LANTERNS can even be set outside to witness to the neighbourhood. Just make sure there is enough sand in the bottom of the bags to weigh them down.

Feast of the Holy Family

The Feast of the Holy Family occurs on the first Sunday after Christmas. On this Feast, we celebrate the family life of Jesus, Mary and Joseph.

Consider the child Jesus, Mary and Joseph as models for all children, mothers and fathers. What do we imagine their home life to have been like as Jesus grew up? What can we learn and what can we strive for?

FELT FRIENDS

Consider making the members of the Holy Family out of felt. Sketch simple figures on paper. Cut and trace the pattern onto peach-coloured felt and cut the figures out. Create simple undergarments out of white felt and glue them in place (underwear, undershirt...)

3D FELT FRIENDS

Sew 2 identical figure-shaped pieces of felt together, over a pipe-cleaner skeleton. A little piece of a cotton ball will add to the shape of the head. No need to sew inside-out to hide the seams...a simple overcast stitch adds to the appeal of the homemade figures!

Personalize the figures by adding hair and facial features. Use "googly eyes" (found in a craft store) or draw the eyes with a marker or fabric paint. Alternatively, eyes can be made with small cut pieces of felt, buttons, beads, or sequins. Experiment for the look you desire.

Create modest garments out of different colours of felt, measured to fit the felt people.

With Mary and St. Joseph, we cherish this precious Gift of Jesus, in our hearts and in our families.

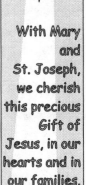

Fr. Scott McCaig
Companions of the Cross

Christmas

FELT FRIENDS' FLAT

The house or "flat" for the FELT FRIENDS is made out of a pizza box. Paint or line the outside of the box with decorative paper or material. Line the inside of the box with flannel or felt. The material can be carefully secured in place with double-sided tape.

If desired, "props" can be made to create different settings in front of a neutral black, grey, tan or brown lining. Use your imagination to create the inside of the Holy Family's home with simple furniture, windows to the outside, simple kitchen tools (and carpentry tools for St. Joseph!).

For extra durability, stitch through the material and cardboard with a heavy duty needle and thread. Alternatively, brass fasteners can be poked through the corners of the material-covered cardboard box.

The FELT FRIENDS' FLAT can be used much like a puppet theatre, providing a backdrop to stage events for the Holy Family figures. Imagine how the family members interacted and what their daily routine might have been...compared to our own!

Feast of the Holy Family

It may be a time to evaluate our own family life. Do we take time to be present as a family? Do we make family time a priority?

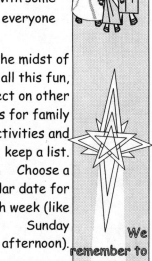

This may be a time to make a stronger commitment to family time. Kick off this new promise with some family fun. Decide on an activity that everyone would enjoy.

GO TOBOGGANING	MAKE A SCRAPBOOK OF FAMILY EVENTS	HAVE A BOARDGAME BONANZA!
CHECK OUT A TOURIST ATTRACTION	PLAY HIDE AND SEEK	MAKE HOMEMADE COOKIES
ADD TO FAMILY PHOTO ALBUMS	HAVE A PICNIC (INSIDE OR OUTSIDE)	CREATE AND GO ON A SCAVENGER HUNT

In the midst of all this fun, reflect on other ideas for family activities and keep a list. Choose a regular date for each week (like Sunday afternoon).

Activities don't have to take a long time. If something else comes up, make every effort to squeeze some family time in later in the week or make the following FAMILY DATE extra special!

GO TO A DRIVE-IN MOVIE AS A FAMILY	TAKE CLOSE-UP FAMILY PHOTOS	GO FLY A KITE
HAVE DINNER AND DESSERT FONDUES	GO BOWLING	MAKE A BLANKET FORT AND READ STORIES
TAKE TURNS GIVING EACH OTHER BACKRUBS	WATCH FAMILY HOME VIDEOS	TAKE SOME CANDID FAMILY PHOTOS

We remember to celebrate the Birth of Jesus. The God-made-man convinced us of His love.

Fr. Leslie Tamas

Christmas

December 28: The Feast of the Holy Innocents

On this Feast, we remember the male children under 2 who were killed, by orders of King Herod at the time of Jesus' birth. Moses was saved from a similar ordeal, when Pharoah ordered the deaths of the male children.

The children of Jesus' day who died in this way are considered to be martyrs not because they believed in Christ, but because they died instead of Jesus.

Choose this day to say prayers for the victims of abortion. Support a pro-life organization by offering time or money to their cause. Support groups helping mothers to choose life.

This day may also be a consolation to those who have lost children to miscarriage or other death. Be sure to continue prayers for these little ones by name, as you pray for your other family members.

On a lighter note, some families celebrate this day by honouring the youngest member of the family: the one closest in age to the little martyrs. Explain the significance of this day while enjoying a special treat, dinner or dessert favoured by the youngest child.

Gift Tags & Place Setting Tags

Be sure to save those religious Christmas cards. These beautiful images can help to create future JESSE TREE figures, Christmas Tree ornaments, ADVENT CALENDAR pieces and NATIVITY sets, GIFT TAGS and PLACE SETTING TAGS.

Simple Christmas tree ornaments can be made by cutting out pictures and gluing them to clean frozen juice lids. Both sides can be used and decorated with ribbons, pearls, beads or glitter glued around the edge. Mounting several of these ornaments vertically along a length of ribbon creates a special wall decoration.

Use a hammer and nail to create a hole at the top of the lid, if desired. Carefully file or hammer out any jagged edges created by the hole, on the back.

By mounting cut-out images from Christmas cards on frozen juice lids or cardboard or construction paper, GIFT TAGS and PLACE SETTING TAGS can be made. Leave a little room on the cut-out images to write the name or layer the image on coloured paper with room to spare for writing names.

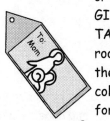

Christmas

Christmas Card Bookmarks

Other more elaborate GIFT TAGS can be made which will be treasured as BOOKMARKS for years to come. Collect billing envelopes; the kind of envelopes with little windows in them. Crop the envelope free from the post markings and return address, leaving the same amount of space on either side of the window, and keeping the pocket intact.

CUT HERE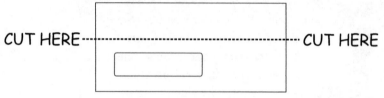CUT HERE

Crop a Christmas card until it is positioned well behind the window. Seal the only open side with glue or tape. Decorate the edge on all four sides (disguising the glue or tape used). Carefully print the name of the person who will receive the BOOKMARK. If desired, carefully record a favourite passage of Scripture or a Scriptural reference, preferably linked to the image.

To: DAD

Luke 2:1-14

Pictures on Christmas cards can be mounted or placed in small frames for display. Images of the Holy Family and angels make great framed pictures all year round, reinforcing Jesus' Presence in the home.

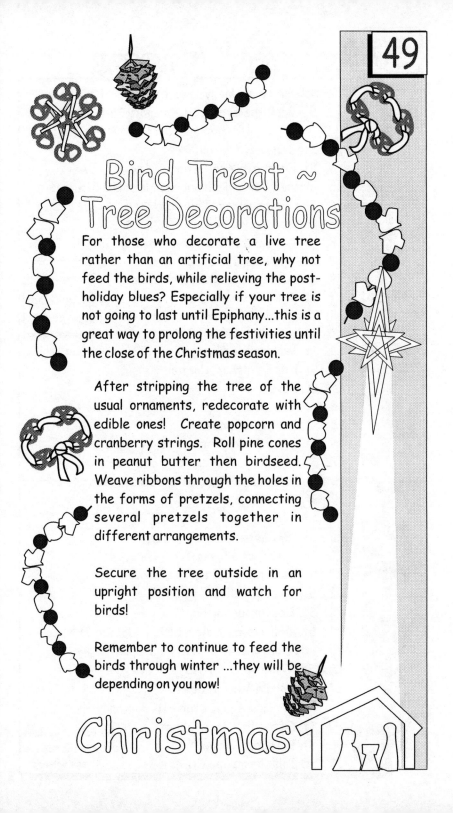

Bird Treat ~ Tree Decorations

For those who decorate a live tree rather than an artificial tree, why not feed the birds, while relieving the post-holiday blues? Especially if your tree is not going to last until Epiphany...this is a great way to prolong the festivities until the close of the Christmas season.

After stripping the tree of the usual ornaments, redecorate with edible ones! Create popcorn and cranberry strings. Roll pine cones in peanut butter then birdseed. Weave ribbons through the holes in the forms of pretzels, connecting several pretzels together in different arrangements.

Secure the tree outside in an upright position and watch for birds!

Remember to continue to feed the birds through winter ...they will be depending on you now!

Christmas

1. **Solemnity of Mary, Mother of God** Solemnity
2. St. Basil the Great, St. Gregory Nazianzen, bishops, doctors Memorial
3. St. Genevieve, virgin *
4. St. Elizabeth Ann Seton, widow   Memorial
5. Blessed John Nepomucene Neumann, bishop Memorial
6. **The Epiphany of The Lord** Solemnity
6. Blessed Andre Bessette Optional Memorial
7. St. Raymond of Penyafort, priest Optional Memorial
8. St. Apollinaris, bishop *
9. St. Adrian of Canterbury, abbot *
10. St. William, bishop *
11. St. Paulinus, patriarch of Aquileia *
12. St. Benedict Biscop (Bennet), abbot *
12. St. Marguerite Bourgeoys, religious Memorial
13. St. Hilary, bishop, doctor Optional Memorial
14. St. Sava, bishop *
15. **St. Ita (Ida)**, virgin *
16. St. Marcellus, pope *
16. St. Berard and Companions, martyrs *
17. **St. Anthony**, founder of monasticism Memorial
18. St. Volusian, bishop, St. Deicolus, abbot *
19. St. Wulstan, bishop *
20. St. Fabian, pope, martyr Optional Memorial
20. **St. Sebastian**, martyr Optional Memorial
21. St. Agnes, virgin, martyr Memorial
22. St. Vincent of Saragossa, deacon, martyr Optional Memorial
22. St. Vincent Pallotti, priest *
23. St. Ildefonsus, bishop *
24. **St. Francis de Sales**, bishop, doctor Memorial
25. **The Conversion of St. Paul**, apostle Feast
26. St. Timothy, St. Titus, bishops Memorial
27. St. Angela Merici, virgin Optional Memorial
28. St. Thomas Aquinas, priest, doctor Memorial
29. St. Gildas the Wise, abbot *
30. St. Bathildis, widow *
31. St. John Bosco, priest Memorial

Jan. 1
World Day
of Peace

*This Feast Day does not occur in the revised Roman Calendar.

JANUARY

Epiphany Centrepiece

Transform your ADVENT WREATH into an Epiphany centrepiece by replacing the purple and pink candles with white ones.

Wrap up 3 small boxes (raisin boxes / jewellery boxes or wooden building blocks) with decorative wrapping paper and bows and ribbons. Different size boxes add nice variety. Display the gift boxes on or around the wreath, representing the Kings' gifts for Jesus.

If Nativity figures had replaced angels within your ADVENT WREATH at Christmas, add 3 Kings slowly. Allow them to circle the outer edge of the wreath (as days pass) until they join the centre on Epiphany.

At Christmas, we celebrate that the Son of God became one of us. He didn't come to our planet just for a visit, He came to stay. Bethlehem was just the beginning: now He lives in you and me!

Fr. Daniel Homan
Prior of
St. Benedict
Monastery

Christmas

January 1: Solemnity of Mary, Mother of God

On this special day, we celebrate Mary's motherhood. Jesus was able to enter human history by Mary's surrender to the Will of God.

As Jesus died on the cross, He established a bond of mother and son, between Mary and His beloved disciple John. Jesus offers His mother to all of us, so that we may be drawn closer to Him, through Mary.

The Memorare is a special prayer asking help from Mary, as our mother.

Remember, O most gracious Virgin Mary, that never was it known that anyone who fled to your protection, implored your help, or sought your intercession, was left unaided.

Inspired by this confidence I fly to you, O virgin of virgins, my Mother. To you I come, before you I stand, sinful and sorrowful.

O Mother of the Word Incarnate, despise not my petitions, but in your mercy, hear and answer me. Amen.

(Assumed Public Domain)

Encourage the children to make a Mother's Day card for Mother Mary. Thank her for helping to bring Jesus into our world, and thank her for looking over us as our mother.

The Epiphany Box: The Fourth Gift

Now for the second use for the carefully wrapped GIFT FOR THE CHRIST CHILD box.

Remove the special messages from the wrapped box. (You might want to save those precious little notes in a safe place to look back on in the years to come).

Explain to the children how the 3 Kings brought gifts to Jesus on the Feast of the Epiphany. They represented people from different lands and confirmed Jesus' identity as The Messiah. They brought special gifts to Jesus, testifying to His Royalty, His Divinity and foretelling His Important Death for our sins.

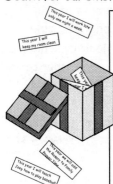

The wrapped box will represent our gift to Jesus; our promise to be faithful to Him. This activity comes at a convenient time, meshing nicely with the popular New Year's Resolutions that people like to make for the new year beginning on January 1.

We renew our decision to follow Jesus, whether it is easy or not, as His faithful disciples and friends.

Fr. Scott McCaig Companions of the Cross

Take the days before Epiphany to express your own resolutions that will bring you closer to Jesus (and closer to others) in the coming year. Record them and place them in the box to be reviewed on Epiphany of the following year! Store the box carefully with these resolutions. Even if the box is used as THE GIFT FOR THE CHRIST CHILD, ensure these resolutions remain untouched until Epiphany by keeping them in a separate labeled envelope within the box.

Christmas

Epiphany Party!

These ideas are variations of various customs surrounding the Feast of the Epiphany.

PARADE OF THE KINGS.

Create crowns out of pieces of construction paper, decorating them with other coloured paper cut into shapes of jewels.

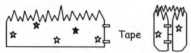

Crowns can also be made by cutting the bottom out of a margarine or sour cream container. (See the Feast of Christ the King). Cut a serrated edge or special peaks to create the look of a crown. Paint by brush or spray paint. (A solid black or white coat of paint may be necessary to eliminate patterns or text from the surface. Experiment with a light spray coat of gold or silver on top of a black or white base coat, adding paint until the desired look is achieved.) Sequins, buttons, coloured glass pebbles or construction paper can be attached for jewels.

Drape sheets or towels around the shoulders for cloaks. (A ROBE can be used as well. See ALTERNATIVE HALLOWEEN COSTUMES.)

Create a large star out of construction paper or foil and fasten it to the end of a stick or broom handle.

Parade around the house, with all the kings following the leader who holds the pole with the star elevated in front of them.

MAY YOUR PRAYERS BE ANSWERED!

JESUS LOVES YOU!

GOD BLESS YOU!

KING'S CAKE

Use a tube (ring) cake mold to create a crown-shaped cake. Add smarties and other candies to represent the jewels on the crown. Suckers or cut wafer cookies can be used to make peaks in the crown for additional detail.

Also called the Twelfth Cake (for the 12th day of Christmas), according to tradition, the Epiphany cake has charms baked into it, foretelling future events for those who find them. A coin could indicate wealth, a ring; marriage.

How about baking little messages of hopes and aspirations, prayers and blessings into the cake?

As part of the tradition, bake a bean into the cake. The one who finds the bean gets to be the King or Queen of the party. Let them have a special chair at the table, a crown, a cloak and let them order everyone around a little bit!

Christmas

20+C+M+B+04

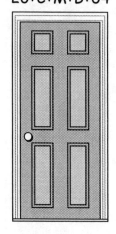

BLESSING OF THE HOME

This is a special activity for the new year. Take a piece of chalk to your parish priest to be blessed. (You may need to explain what you are doing!) Record this message on the interior surface over the main entrance or on the most visible doorway at the entrance of the house.

Write:

(the first 2 numbers of the current year)

+ C + M +B +

(the last 2 numbers of the current year).

The numbers remind us of the current year, while the letters correspond to the 3 Kings: Caspar, Melchior and Balthazar. Join hands together and say some family prayers including a request to bless the house and those who live in it.

A special reading from scripture corresponding to the visit of the 3 Kings will connect the activity to the Feast of Epiphany.

BLESSING OF THE WATERS

Don't forget to take the opportunity to bring some Holy Water home from Church. Perhaps the fashioning of a homemade HOLY WATER FONT is in order...

A HOLY WATER FONT can be fashioned out of clay and baked and painted. Make sure to poke out two holes before baking, so that it can be secured to the wall.

If you have a small decorative bowl that can be used, use the clay to create a shelf or cradle for the bowl.

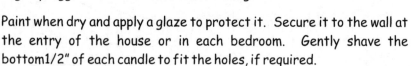

Two additional forms could be created on the horizontal surface to hold candles. Be sure to test the forms by placing the bowl and candles in. Make the openings slightly bigger to combat effects of baking.

Paint when dry and apply a glaze to protect it. Secure it to the wall at the entry of the house or in each bedroom. Gently shave the bottom1/2" of each candle to fit the holes, if required.

FISHING FOR BLESSINGS!

In Greek traditions, there was a procession to the sea, where the priest would throw a cross into the water. Youth would dive in after the cross. The one who retrieved the cross would receive gifts and blessings.

As a variation of this tradition, attach a magnet to a cross. Take turns trying to retrieve it using a pole with a magnet attached to it by a string. Alternatively, a cross can be painted on a frozen juice lid and thrown face down into a water-filled tub with blank frozen juice lids. (A layer of varnish over the painted cross will prevent the paint from peeling.) A pole with a magnet can be used to retrieve the frozen juice lids...preferably the one with the cross!

WATER APPRECIATION

In honour of traditions of the Blessing of the Waters and celebration of our Lord's Baptism, have some fun with water! Remember that our celebrations don't always have to be dignified and holy...we just need to remember why and Who we are celebrating!

Put bathing suits on and play in the bathtub...as many as can fit safely in there!

Fill clean squeeze bottles or spray bottles and have a good old fashioned water fight if there is a safe place to have one.

Paint on construction paper with brushes dipped in water.

Christmas

January 15: St. Ita (Ida)*

St. Ita founded a convent which became a famous training school for boys; two of these boys, Brendan and Mochoemoc went on to become saints.

When asked what 3 things God loves,
St. Ita replied,
"True faith in God with a pure heart,
a simple life with a religious spirit,
and an open hand inspired by charity."

When asked what 3 things God hates,
St. Ita replied,
"A scowling face,
obstinacy in wrong doing,
and arrogant trust in the power of money."

Talk about what these things mean, giving examples. Encourage drawing to express these ideas. Perhaps 2 banners or posters could be made and displayed as a reminder of how we can strive to please God.

OR

Take 2 blank sheets, and fold them in half. Place them together and staple at the crease, creating a little booklet. Allow the first page to be the cover page.

Open the book and number the pages 1 through 6. Draw a picture on each page representing each of the 6 "things" outlined by St. Ita. Identify each drawing by the words of St. Ita for each of the 6 "things". Use the little booklet as a colouring book.

* This Feast Day does not occur in the revised Roman Calendar.

LOTS OF REASONS TO CELEBRATE! 59

Just as a birthday is the anniversary of our birth, a BAPDAY is the anniversary of our Baptism; the day of our birth IN THE LORD. Celebrate this special day as a birthday with a favourite meal or dessert, decorating the table with pictures of the Baptism. Invite Godparents, friends and relatives and renew the Baptismal Vows while the Baptismal Candle is lit.

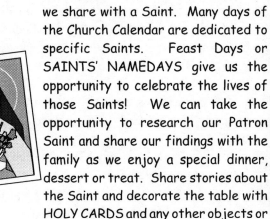

Ordinary Time

SAINTS' NAMEDAYS

Most of us have at least one name that we share with a Saint. Many days of the Church Calendar are dedicated to specific Saints. Feast Days or SAINTS' NAMEDAYS give us the opportunity to celebrate the lives of those Saints! We can take the opportunity to research our Patron Saint and share our findings with the family as we enjoy a special dinner, dessert or treat. Share stories about the Saint and decorate the table with HOLY CARDS and any other objects or symbols associated with him or her.

Holy cards or medals are great little gifts for these NAMEDAYS and can be collected and displayed each year on the Feast day. (See HOLY CARD activities in the other Ordinary Time section.)

Explain how we are all members of God's family, just as the Saints. We should aspire to their holiness in our daily lives.

As the Church Calendar includes many Feast days throughout the year, many of these occur during the season of Ordinary Time. Feast Days celebrate important events in our Catholic Faith as well as the lives of Saints and Martyrs throughout our Church History.

JANUARY

January 17: The Memorial of St. Anthony,
    patron of basket makers

St. Anthony was a hermit, devoted to silence, prayer and manual labour. He spent 20 years in isolation, relying on a simple diet of bread and water, once a day.

St. Anthony suffered and overcame many temptations from the devil, by making the sign of the cross. We make the sign of the cross to enter and complete an act of prayer. It helps to remind us to focus. It helps to strengthen us. It also represents a sign to God that we offer to Him our mind (gesture to our forehead), our will (gesture to our heart), and our entire body (gesture from left to right). We need to remind ourselves of the significance of this sign and concentrate on our actions as we use it with prayer.

St. Anthony often stopped throughout his work to pray and think of God. This helped to bring him closer to God. Small prayers can easily be incorporated into our day. Try to stop regularly throughout the day saying:

"Jesus, I trust in you",
"Jesus, Mary, Joseph",
"My Jesus, mercy",
"Blessed be the name of the Lord"
or
"Mother of mercy, pray for us".

Check out PRAYER HABITS in the first section of Ordinary Time.

JANUARY

Saints' Days

Try to remember to say a few of these little prayers while making a BREAD BASKET.

Make some pretzel dough. Roll out the dough and cut 1/4" strips. Place in a spiral form within a round baking dish, working from the centre outward, and building up the sides. Spaces between the strips are fine, as the dough will expand. Do not allow too much time for the dough to rise or the shape will be lost.

Bake in the oven according to pretzel recipe instructions. Baking time may vary from the recipe, so watch carefully to ensure that they are baked sufficiently.

Alternatively, roll the dough out into flat circles. Press the circles onto the sprayed underside of a clean muffin pan, allowing each circle to take the inverted forms. Place the muffin pan in the oven (upside-down) and bake until browning begins.

The basket can be filled with a mix of popcorn, CHEX or other snack-able cereal, pretzel sticks, and goldfish crackers.

The basket can also be left empty, and shared as a meal of bread with water, in honour of St. Anthony's simple diet.

PRAYER

Prayer is such an important part of our lives. Throughout our daily activities we are provided with countless opportunities to introduce prayer to our children. By making the time to say prayers throughout our day (and explaining why we say them) important prayerful habits and traditions will continue to play an integral part in our children's lives.

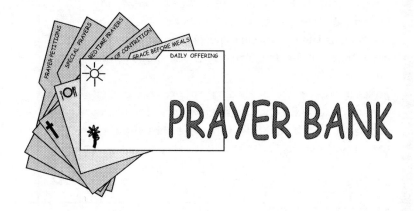

Collect simple prayers which can be easily learned by children. Look through prayerbooks for classic prayers or make up your own!

Record the prayers on index cards and decorate them. File them to be easily retrieved for mealtime, bedtime, other times of the day or special occasions. Help the children decorate the cards. Children will enjoy being able to choose from the various prayers...help them take ownership of their prayerlife early!

An alternate way of storing the prayers for easy retrieval is to make an ENVELOPE PRAYER BANK.

ENVELOPE PRAYER BANK

Ordinary Time

Select 10 envelopes of the same size.

Use a hole punch to make two holes on one edge of each of the envelopes (at precisely the same location). Decorate the envelopes, one for each time of day or type of occasion.

Make cardboard front and back covers, punching holes to match the envelopes. Decorate the covers.
Assemble the book of envelopes tying string or ribbon through the holes.

Store specially recorded prayers (on note paper) or holy cards (with prayers on them) within the envelopes. Keep in a handy location for easy access!

The two periods of Ordinary Time comprise 33-34 weeks of the year...that's almost 2/3 of the Liturgical Calendar!

The PRAYER CAROUSEL is another form of PRAYER BANK, used to collect and display various prayers to be said throughout the day. Each box within the carousel can carry either a set of prayers for a different day of the week or a different category of prayers.

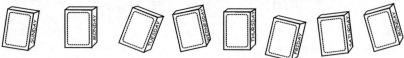

Cut three 12" diameter circular disks from corrugated cardboard. Use a string and pencil to create the circles (see St. Sebastian BEAN BAG ARROW GAME). Collect Jell-O or pudding boxes of the same size. Cut a window out of both the "front" and "back" of the box as well as one of the long sides. Poke a hole in the exact centre of both short sides of each box, feeding one straw through these holes in each box. (Straws should be pre-cut to be 1/4" shorter than the length of a toilet paper roll.)

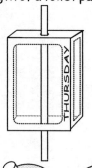

Decorate the boxes, perhaps recording the category of prayer (or day of the week).

Trace one end of a toilet paper roll at the centre of all three disks. Cut a slightly larger circle out of 2 of the disks, setting the third disk aside. The 2 disks should fit loosely, when threaded onto the toilet paper roll. Decorate the disks with paint or coloured paper.

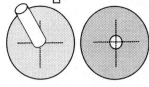

Mark dots at equal intervals, 3/4" from the edge of one of the cardboard disks. Using a hole punch, create holes at each of these markings. Using this disk as a template, mark and hole punch a second disk at precisely the same places. Match the disks together so that the holes are lined up

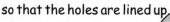

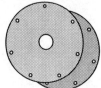

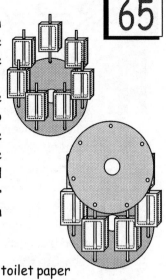

Each box (with a straw inserted through the centre) is inserted by the end of the straw into one of the holes around the edge of the disk.

When all of the boxes are in place, the second disk is carefully placed on top gently pushing the other ends of the straws into the matching holes. If the straws fit loosely through the punched holes, tape may be required on the outer face of the disk to keep the straws in place.

Glue one end of the toilet paper roll to the exact centre of the third disk. Allow to dry. The rest of the carousel should slide easily onto the toilet paper roll.

Cut a 14" diameter circle out of heavy decorative paper, bristol board or construction paper. Make one straight cut from the centre to the edge. Overlap these radius edges and staple in place to create a cone-shaped roof to set on top of the carousel.

Ordinary Time

The overall theme of Ordinary Time is our Salvation, made possible by Jesus.

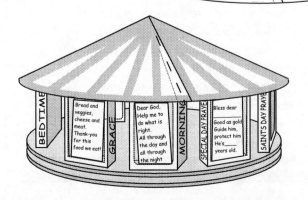

JANUARY

January 20: The Optional Memorial of
St. Sebastian, patron of athletes

St. Sebastian was condemned to be killed by arrows. He was shot down, but restored to health by St. Irene. When discovered, he was again condemned and this time killed by clubs. He is remembered for his strength and endurance.

Create a safe obstacle course within the house. Include climbing, jumping, running, push-ups, sit-ups or choose a modified version of a favourite family sport (mini-putt, bean-bag throw, beach ball bowling).

For an outdoor version, create an obstacle course in the snow. For extra challenge, strap on homemade snow shoes by tying large pieces of cardboard securely to the boots.

C.F. and her family play Disk Hockey...a homemade version of Air Hockey! They use old CDs especially free sampler CDs of software or music that they don't want anymore. They create the playing field and goal box with duct tape or masking tape on a carpet or smooth textured floor. (Remove the masking tape promptly after use to avoid difficult removal).

An empty margarine or sour cream container (with lid) can be used to push the CD across the floor attempting to get a goal in the opposite tape-marked net! (A smaller container might be more easily gripped by small hands.)
To more closely resemble air hockey, tape a wooden metre stick on both long dimensions of the playing field so that the disk will rebound off the sides.

JANUARY

In light of St. Sebastian's experience with arrows, create a BEAN BAG ARROW game. Create a target. Cut 3 various sized circles out of 3 different colours of material. Suggested sizes are 12", 30", 48" diameters. (Tie a pencil to a string. Hold the other end of the string at the centre and draw steadily with the pencil at the extent of the string, **to create a circle**.)

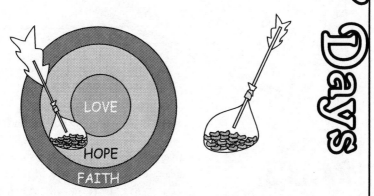

Create a bean bag arrow by filling a plastic baggy or piece of material with a handful of beans. Poke a straw into the opening of the baggy or material and tape the opening securely closed around the straw. If desired, add paper to the straw to look like a feather end tip of an arrow.

Place the circles, centred one on top of the other, with the smallest on top and the largest on the bottom, on the floor. Tack in place with a small amount of glue or tape.

If desired, label the concentric circles with the three theological virtues: faith, hope and love. Talk about the different virtues, referring to the Catechism (1812-1829).
Count points, assigning 5 points for hitting the outer ring (faith), 7 points for hitting the middle ring (hope) and 10 points for hitting the centre (love).

68 PRAYER

see p.256

DAILY PRAYERS
Angel of God,
my Guardian dear,
To whom His love commits me here.
Ever this day, be at my side,
To light and guard,
To rule and guide. Amen.
(Assumed Public Domain)

ACT OF CONTRITION

I'm sorry
for disappointing You.
I want to do what's right.
Help me, guide me
and love me still.
Watch over me day and night.

OUR FATHER

Our Father, Who art in heaven,
Hallowed be Thy Name.
Thy Kingdom come, Thy Will be done,
On earth as it is in heaven.
Give us this day our daily bread,
And forgive us our trespasses,
As we forgive those who trespass against us,
And lead us not into temptation,
But deliver us from evil. Amen.

ROSARY PRAYERS

HAIL MARY

Hail Mary, full of grace,
the Lord is with thee.
Blessed are thou among women,
and blessed is the fruit of thy womb, Jesus.
Holy Mary, Mother of God,
Pray for us sinners, now and at the hour of
our death. Amen.

GLORY BE...

Glory be to the Father,
and to the Son and to the Holy Spirit.
As it was in the beginning, is now and ever shall be,
world without end. Amen.

O MY JESUS...

O My Jesus, forgive us our sins, save us from the
fires of hell. Lead all souls to heaven, especially
those who have most need of Your Mercy.

see p.256
ROSARY
REFRESHER

ACT OF CONTRITION

O my God, I am heartily sorry for having offended You, and I detest all my sins because of Your just punishments, but most of all because they offend You, my God, Who are all good and deserving of all my love. I firmly resolve, with the help of Your Grace, to sin no more and to avoid the near occasion of sin. Amen.

Assumed Public Domain

DAILY OFFERING

Every morning,
as I wake
I offer my day,
for Jesus' sake.

Ordinary Time

DAILY OFFERING

Hold my hand
O Jesus, I pray.
Remind me to serve You,
Throughout the day.

During the first period of Ordinary Time, commencing immediately after the Feast of our Lord's Baptism, we focus on Christ's Baptism and the beginning of His preaching Ministry.

DAILY OFFERING

Good morning, dear Jesus
I give You this day.
Guide all my actions
And all that I say.

DAILY OFFERING

Thank You
for this day, dear Lord.
Help me follow You.
Help me understand Your Will,
And show me what to do.

DAILY OFFERING

O Jesus, I love You,
And this is my prayer.
Help me to please You,
And know You are there.

January 24: The Memorial of
St. Frances de Sales, patron of writers

St. Frances became a monk at the age of 9 years. He is best known for writing about holiness in everyday life in *Treatise on the Love of God* and *Introduction to a Devout Life*. As a family, discuss ways we can strive for holiness in our daily lives.

In honour of St. Frances' writings, write a family prayer. Keep it by the dinner table to recite before family meals. Add it to the PRAYER BANK.

January 25: The Feast of the Conversion of St. Paul

St. Paul was a strict Jewish man who did not accept the new Christians. He was a leader in the persecution of Christ's followers.

One day, he was thrown off his horse with a great flash of light. He heard the voice of Jesus saying "Why are you persecuting me?" He was left blind from the experience, yet transformed into a believer in Christ. His sight was restored and he met with the other Apostles and spent the rest of his life fearlessly preaching about Jesus. He is responsible for most of the Letters in the New Testament and is referred to as the Apostle of the Gentiles.

Help St. Paul get back up on his horse, to proclaim the message of Jesus. Create an image of a horse and a separate image of a figure riding the horse, on poster board. Colour it and cut it out. With a blindfold, reminiscent of St. Paul's temporary blindness, pin the figure of St. Paul on the horse, similar to the "pin the tail on the donkey" game.

A Few More Simple Prayers

GRACE BEFORE MEALS

Bread and veggies,
Cheese and meat.
We thank You
For this food we eat!

GRACE BEFORE MEALS

Bless us O Lord,
And these Thy Gifts
Which we are about to receive
From Thy Bounty,
Through Christ, Our Lord. Amen
(assumed public domain)

GRACE BEFORE MEALS

Thanks for this food,
It helps us to grow.
It helps us stay healthy
From head to toe.
Thanks for this food,
We are grateful indeed.
We pray for the hungry,
And all those in need.

Ordinary Time

Throughout the year, the entire Mystery of Christ is revealed. In contrast to the other seasons, Ordinary Time does not focus on a particular aspect of the Mystery, but rather on the fullness of the Mystery of Christ.

Saints' Days

1. St. Bridgid (Bride) of Ireland, virgin *
2. **Presentation of the Lord** Feast
3. **St. Blase**, bishop, martyr Optional Memorial
3. St. Ansgar, bishop Optional Memorial
4. **St. Veronica**, virgin *
5. St. Agatha, virgin, martyr Memorial
6. St. Paul Miki and Companions, martyrs Memorial
7. St. Richard of Lucca, King *
8. St. Jerome Emiliani, priest Optional Memorial
9. St, Apollonia, virgin, martyr *
10. **St. Scholastica**, virgin Memorial
11. **Our Lady of Lourdes** Optional Memorial
12. St. Saturninus and Companions, martyrs *
13. St. Catherine de Ricci, virgin *
14. St. Cyril, monk, St. Methodius, bishop Memorial
14. **St. Valentine**, priest, martyr *
15. Blessed Claude de la Colombiere, priest *
16. St. Onesimus, martyr *
17. Seven Founders of the Order of Servites Optional Memorial
18. St. Marie Bernadette Soubirous, virgin *
19. St. Conrad of Piacenza, hermit *
20. St. Eucherius, bishop *
21. St. Peter Damian, bishop, doctor Optional Memorial
22. **Chair of St. Peter the Apostle** Feast
23. St. Polycarp, bishop, martyr Memorial
24. St. Ethelbert, King of Kent *
25. St. Tarasius, bishop *
26. St. Porphyrius, bishop *
27. St. Gabriel of Our Lady of Sorrows, cleric *
28. St. Romanus, abbot *
29. St. Oswald, bishop *

* Not found in the revised Church Calendar

Feb. 1
World Day of
Consecrated
Life

Feb. 11
World Day of
the Sick

Prayer Habits

Simple prayers can be taught so easily to our children, by simple repetition. These are some great habits to get into...which can help all of us to grow closer to Jesus.

Ordinary Time

When you turn on a light,
say "**Jesus, Light of the World**"

While doing laundry, cooking, household chores, pray for those who will benefit from the work that you are doing.

When you can't sleep, pray.

When you pass a Catholic Church,
say "**Jesus, I believe You are truly present**"
and make the sign of the cross on your forehead.

If you hear someone use the Lord's name in vain,
say "**Blessed be the Name of the Lord**"

When you see an ambulance or fire engine racing or hear about a tragedy,
pray for the victims and for the safety of those coming to their aid.

When you are suffering physically or emotionally, try to offer it up for the Souls in Purgatory.

If at first you don't know what to say...just say an Our Father or Hail Mary or other favourite memorized prayer. The important thing is to SAY SOMETHING IN PRAYER and make an effort to remember God throughout your day.

Nothing is ever really ordinary for a Christian, for Christ is new everyday and so too the adventure of following Him as His Disciples.

Fr. Roger Vandenakker,

Companions of the Cross

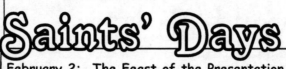

February 2: **The Feast of the Presentation of Our Lord**

This day is also called the Feast of the Purification of the Blessed Virgin, as well as Candlemas. It occurs 40 days after the birth of Jesus.

Consistent with Jewish Law, it was on this day that Mary and Joseph brought their offering to the Temple. It was only after these 40 days and the offering, that the mother was no longer excluded from public worship.

The offering brought by Mary and Joseph was two turtledoves; the offering of the poor. We know that Jesus and Mary were not in need of any purification, but this event shows us of their obedience.

This day is often celebrated with candlelight processions and the blessing of candles. The candles remind us that Jesus is the light of the world.

Be sure to light candles for the family dinner, remembering their significance on this day.

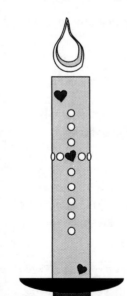

This day offers another opportunity to make family candles and get them blessed by your parish priest. Go to your local craft store for supplies and instructions for beeswax candles.

In Europe, if the weather is bad and skies are cloudy on this day, it is predicted that summer will arrive early. If it is a sunny day, there will be 40 more days of winter. It would seem that Groundhog day is an adaptation of this tradition.

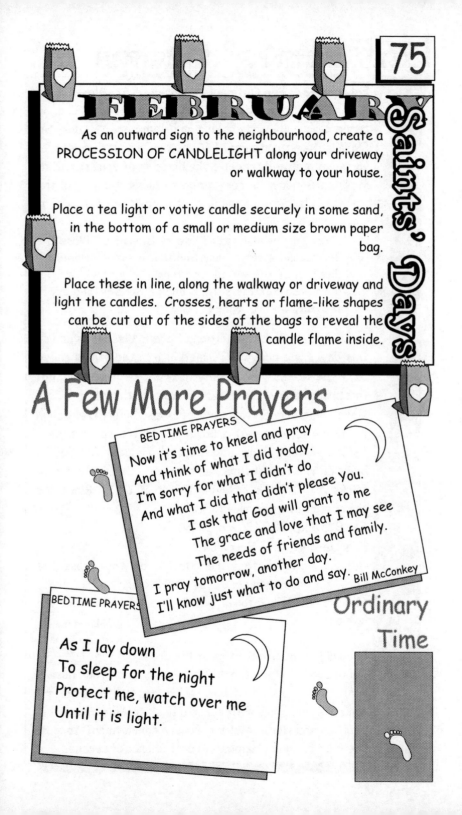

FEBRUARY

Saints' Days

As an outward sign to the neighbourhood, create a PROCESSION OF CANDLELIGHT along your driveway or walkway to your house.

Place a tea light or votive candle securely in some sand, in the bottom of a small or medium size brown paper bag.

Place these in line, along the walkway or driveway and light the candles. Crosses, hearts or flame-like shapes can be cut out of the sides of the bags to reveal the candle flame inside.

A Few More Prayers

BEDTIME PRAYERS

Now it's time to kneel and pray
And think of what I did today.
I'm sorry for what I didn't do
And what I did that didn't please You.
I ask that God will grant to me
The grace and love that I may see
The needs of friends and family.
I pray tomorrow, another day.
I'll know just what to do and say. Bill McConkey

BEDTIME PRAYERS

As I lay down
To sleep for the night
Protect me, watch over me
Until it is light.

Ordinary Time

February 3: The Optional Memorial of St. Blase

Legend has it that as St. Blase was taken to prison, he cured a boy who was choking on a fish bone. Today, St. Blase is the patron saint of those with throat diseases. If you did not already receive the blessing of your throat at Mass on Sunday, be sure to go to Mass today. As the priest holds two **unlit** candles in the position of a cross at your throat, he will say:

> "Through the merits and intercession of St. Blase, Bishop and Martyr, may God deliver you from all diseases of the throat, and from every other evil, in the name of the Father, and of the Son, and of the Holy Spirit. Amen"

In Europe there is a tradition of giving blessed bread on this day. The dough is formed into bread sticks called St. Blase sticks. According to this custom, people eat this bread when they suffer from a sore throat.

Make some bread sticks out of bread or pretzel dough today or buy some at a bakery. As you say a prayer before you eat them, add a special request for God to bless all the family throats this year. Share the bread sticks with friends, relaying the story of St. Blase and the custom of St. Blase sticks.

See BOUNCY BREAD (March 19)

February 4: St. Veronica *

As described in the 6th Station of the Cross, St. Veronica accompanied Jesus as He carried His cross. She offered Him a towel and the imprint of His face was left on it.

Read aloud the 6th Station of the Cross.

Talk about how we should have compassion for those in suffering. Talk about how we can make life easier for someone we know with chronic back trouble or another health condition. Make a family commitment to ease their suffering by helping out with chores or errands.

*Not in the revised Roman Calendar.

Prayers with Gestures Too!

Point at the body part or make a gesture for what it does!

With every step my FEET will take,
With everything my HANDS will make,
With my EYES, fixed on You,
I'll seek Your Will, in all I do.

Ordinary Time

With my EARS, I hear what You say,
With my KNEES bent, I'll kneel to pray,
With my LIPS, I'll sing Your praise,
With all my HEART and all my days.

THE FIVE FINGER PRAYER

(point to a finger with each line)

The Five Finger Prayer was inspired by an article written by Pamela Dowd in the Jan/Feb 1998 edition of Catholic Parent (p.17).

PRAISE YOU LORD   (thumb)
    For all You've done
THANK YOU LORD   (pointer)
    For everyone
FORGIVE ME LORD   (middle finger)
    For not being good
HELP ME LORD   (ring finger)
    To do as I should
HELP OTHERS LORD   (pinkie)
    I wish you would...   (Petitions to help others)

Saints' Days

February 5: The Memorial of St. Agatha
Celebrating the saint invoked against fire, take the opportunity to test fire alarms and carbon monoxide detectors. Host a SEMI-ANNUAL FAMILY FIRE DRILL, practicing a safe escape from the bedrooms, in the event of a fire.

Celebrate a successful FAMILY FIRE DRILL with hot chocolate around the family fireplace. If you don't have a fireplace, drink your hot chocolate by candlelight. Say a prayer for victims of house fires.

February 10: The Memorial of St. Scholastica
St. Scholastica was the twin sister of St. Benedict. She was the founder of a Benedictine Order of Nuns, while he was the founder of a Benedictine Order of Monks.
To honour these twin saints, serve a dinner in twin portions. Cut meat servings in two, for twin pieces on each plate. Arrange vegetables and rice or pasta in 2 equal mounds on each plate. Finish with a twin scoop serving of ice cream.
If there are twins in the family, make a special fuss over them today with a special treat or favourite meal. Collect some holy cards of the twin saints and talk about the lives of St. Benedict and St. Scholastica.

This is another version of the FIVE FINGER PRAYER. This prayer focuses on praying for others. When we focus on the needs of others, sometimes our own concerns are put into perspective.

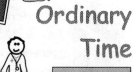

FIRST, my THUMB, nearest to me
I PRAY for my FRIENDS
and FAMILY.

Ordinary Time

NEXT, my POINTER, I PRAY for my
TEACHER
My DOCTOR, my DENTIST,
my PRIEST and PREACHER

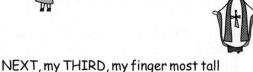

NEXT, my THIRD, my finger most tall
I pray for our LEADERS
who lead us all

NEXT, my FOURTH, my finger most weak
I PRAY for the SICK, POOR,
YOUNG, OLD and MEEK

NOW, the PINKIE, the LAST and the SMALL
I pray for these others,
then ME last of all.

Don't let the word "ordinary" fool you. This important part of the Liturgical Calendar is intended to remind us that Jesus is with us throughout all of our daily trials and triumphs. We must strive to reflect Jesus' teaching with our actions every day.

This Five Finger Prayer was inspired by a prayer submitted to Gene Gordon by D. Stephens for the Daily Devotion sent out by *Global Wide Web 4 Christ*.

**February 11: The Optional Memorial of
Our Lady of Lourdes**

Our Blessed Mother appeared to fourteen year old Bernadette Soubirous, eighteen times from February 11-July 16, 1858. The water that still flows from the site is accredited with over 5000 recorded cures! Lourdes remains to be a popular pilgrimage site.

The first apparition occurred at a shallow cave (or "grotto"). Build a LITTLE GROTTO FOR MARY. If a statue is not available, cut an image of Mary from a Christmas card, to be placed within.

The cave can be made out of paper mache', using a balloon as the formwork. Partially cover the balloon with paper mache' (leaving an opening for the grotto) and allow to dry. Pop the balloon and add substantial paper mache' to anchor the partial balloon form to a solid base of cardboard. Paint.

FEBRUARY

LITTLE GROTTO FOR MARY SHRINE

Fill a large, empty plastic dish detergent bottle with hot water for 10 minutes. This will soften the plastic of the bottle, before you begin to cut it.

Make a hole with a knife and then continue the cutting with scissors. Cut the neck of the bottle out and continue the cut as illustrated, on one flat side of the bottle.

Make a hole at the end of both top pieces and thread a wire or brass fastener through the holes, fastening the pieces together to form the arch.

The remaining side which extends beyond the arch will be pierced to allow for hanging on the wall.

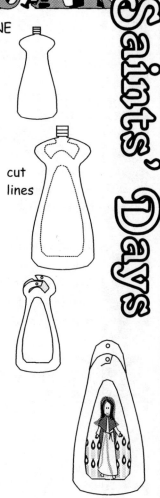

cut lines

Cut out the arch opening as illustrated. Spray paint if desired, before lining the inside of the bottle with material or cardboard. Add lace, glitter and other decorations as desired. Create small votive candles (and flames!) out of construction paper, to line the inside of the arch. Place the statue or cardboard-mounted image of Mary, inside the arch.

LITTLE GROTTO FOR MARY SHRINE (simpler version!)

Less cutting is required for this method.

Cut only the opening of the grotto on the face of the bottle.

Remove the cap of the bottle and insert a candle. The candle may need some shaving down (with a carrot peeler or sharp knife) to help it fit into the bottle. Shave only the bottom 1" of the candle.

Cut and hem material to create a skirt for the candle which may also drape over the opening of the grotto. Decide on the length of the curtain: either creating trim around the top edge of the grotto opening or actually covering the opening to peak curiosity.

Decorate with paint or construction paper as described in the other version of the LITTLE GROTTO FOR MARY SHRINE.

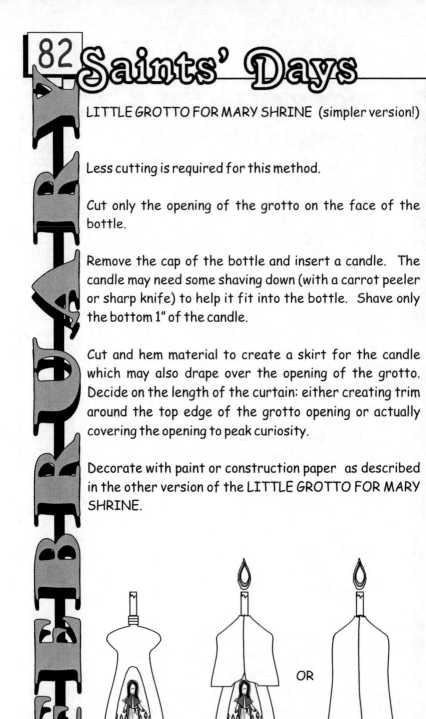

OR

Shrove Tuesday

Shrove Tuesday is the last day before Lent. There is a tradition of going to confession on this day, in preparation for Lent.

Other names for this day include "Fat Tuesday" or "Pancake Tuesday", tied in with the tradition of Mardi Gras. This celebration represented the last day of feasting and fun before Lent (beginning the next day on Ash Wednesday). Practically, it was a good time to finish up all the food that would be forbidden during Lent.

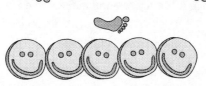

Ordinary
Time

HAPPY CAKES

Happy Cakes are pancakes made with happy faces imprinted on them. Pour the batter into the heated frying pan in the shape of 2 eyes and a smiling mouth. Allow these little forms to cook slightly before pouring a circle of batter over them. The eyes and smiling mouth forms will be slightly darker in colour as the pancake cooks, maintaining the happy face.

FRUITY CAKES

Mix fruit bottom yogurt with water to replace the quantity of milk within the batter ingredients. Cook as usual with this extra fruity batter!

FLUFFY CAKES

Use Club Soda in place of the milk or water called for in your batter recipe. The result will be light and fluffy pancakes!

This Experienced Mom Idea award goes to Gwen Wise for her pancake recipes!

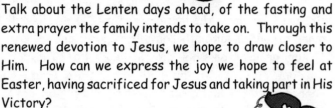

Talk about the Lenten days ahead, of the fasting and extra prayer the family intends to take on. Through this renewed devotion to Jesus, we hope to draw closer to Him. How can we express the joy we hope to feel at Easter, having sacrificed for Jesus and taking part in His Victory?

Why not take advantage of the masquerade party tradition of Mardi Gras and make some fun masks to wear for your last celebration before Lent?

Make joyful masks, reflecting a more intimate relationship with Jesus: something we can aspire to throughout the Lenten days ahead! Use paper plates, cutting shapes for eyes. Add vibrant colours with paint, tissue paper, string and other found objects, adding glitter and sequins for extra sparkle.

Other masks can be made using a corner of a cardboard box. Turn the box upside down and choose a corner with 3 solid sides. Trace the template on adjacent sides of the box. Join the outer edges with one line on the 3rd side of the corner, creating a triangular top to the mask. Poke holes where the eyes, mouth and tie-string will be (while the box is still intact).

Cut the 3 sided mask from the box. Use scrunched up paper or tissue to build up the features of the face (eyebrows, nose, mouth...). Layer paper mache' or tissue paper to smooth and strengthen the mask. Coloured tissue will create an interesting base on which less paint may be required for an interesting and colourful result.

Display the masks throughout Lent as reminders of the joy we will feel as we rejoice with Jesus at Easter, at the end of this Lenten period of sacrifice.

Lenten Practices

Lent is a time of reflection and prayer. It is a time of voluntary penance, choosing to join in the suffering of Jesus and bringing us closer to Him.

We can choose to give up something like candy or TV, remembering each time we deny ourselves of the huge sacrifice that Jesus made for OUR sins.

We may also choose to ADD something to our daily routine that will bring us closer to Jesus. Some families choose this time for renewed diligence in family prayer or scripture reading.

> Ask each member what they plan to do for Lent and keep each other accountable during Lent. A resolution to "be nice to my brother/sister" is a nice gesture...but should not really be limited to only this time of year! Encourage realistic expectations. It is better to fulfil one resolution wholeheartedly than to be discouraged and give up on an ambitious set of promises.

Don't give up! It is a good lesson to our children, that even if we slip from our resolution, we should keep on trying. A perfect record may not be as valuable as perfect intentions. Strive for something challenging rather than carrying out something easy, perfectly!

> Theresa M. of Columbia, South Carolina celebrates a Seder meal with her family **after** the Ash Wednesday night Mass "with hearts filled with the Presence of Jesus and heads marked with the ashes".

"Remember, you are dust and to dust you shall return" (Genesis 3:19)

We receive ashes on our foreheads on Ash Wednesday, recognizing our sin and remembering the Original Sin we inherited from Adam and Eve.

We are challenged to "Turn away from sin and be faithful to the Gospel" (Mark 1:15)

Lent

February 14: St. Valentine *

St. Valentine was arrested and later martyred for his faith. According to legend, he left a farewell note for the jailer's daughter who had been his friend. The note was signed "from your Valentine".

There are many traditions surrounding this day in which boys and girls exchange "valentines". It is a day to celebrate love.

BE MINE!

Make some valentines for friends and family members. Make special ones for Jesus and Mary, expressing your love for them. Send a valentine to someone who might be lonely on this day.

VALENTINE CAKE: Make a heart shaped cake out of one 9" square cake tin and one 9" round cake tin. Cut the circular cake in two and arrange each half on an adjacent side of the square, to form a heart. Write messages of love on little pieces of paper, fold them and gently "fold" them into the cake batter. Read the messages aloud as they are discovered while enjoying the cake. Decorate with pink and red icing, expressing messages of love and valentines.

JESUS LOVES ME!

VALENTINE COOKIES: Make shortbread cookies with heart shaped cookie cutters or make large round cookies and write messages on them with icing.

I LOVE YOU!

* Does not occur in the revised Roman Calendar.

"Sweetheart" candies with the messages on them are great for decorating Valentine cakes and cookies!

Our Lenten Share

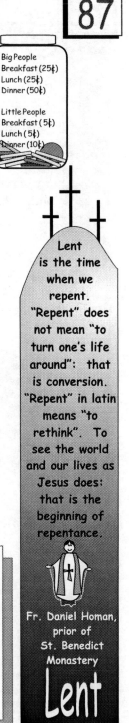

Big People
Breakfast (25¢)
Lunch (25¢)
Dinner (50¢)

Little People
Breakfast (5¢)
Lunch (5¢)
Dinner (10¢)

Find (and clean) a jar and matching lid. Hammer a slit into the lid by tapping a flat screwdriver with a hammer. Make sure that the slit is large enough for all sizes of coins to fit through. Be careful of sharp edges. Alternatively, layers of masking tape can be used to create a temporary lid. The slit can be formed by the placement of the masking tape or cut from the layers of tape after they are in place.

Encourage each family member to "pay" for each meal. (Decide as a family what each member should donate to the jar ranging from a few pennies to 50 cents.)

Additional coins could be added when a Lenten fast or resolution is accidently broken.

Help the children count up the money at the end of Holy Week. Offer the money to a charitable organization, include it in your Easter Sunday Offering or spend the money on non-perishable food and donate it to a foodbank.

Lent is the time when we repent. "Repent" does not mean "to turn one's life around": that is conversion. "Repent" in latin means "to rethink". To see the world and our lives as Jesus does: that is the beginning of repentance.

Fr. Daniel Homan, prior of St. Benedict Monastery

Lent

This Experienced Mom Idea award goes to Mary Jane C. She suggests using a larger version of one of the BLESSING EGGS, to create a piggy bank to collect money for the poor (saved from giving up sweets or other Lenten sacrifices).

Saints' Days

February 22: The Feast of the Chair of St. Peter, the Apostle

As Catholics, we believe that each Pope, by divine institution, is a direct successor of St. Peter; the rock upon which Jesus built His Church.

Say a prayer for the Pope, appreciating how he teaches and guides the flock of Christ.

Make a postcard out of a 4" x 6" piece of heavy paper or cardboard. Draw a picture or securely glue a photo of your family, on one side. Write an encouraging message to the Pope (as a family), to show your appreciation and respect for him. Address the postcard to:

Pope John Paul II
The Vatican
Rome, Italy
Europe

POPE TRIVIA
(Information from <u>Saints and Feast Days,</u> Sisters of Notre Dame of Chardon, Chicago: Loyola Press, p.120)

Pope John Paul II is the 262nd pope.

85 popes have been given the title of saint, blessed or venerable.

The most popular names chosen by popes: John (23 popes), Gregory (16 popes) and Benedict (15 popes).

This Experienced Mom Idea award goes to Shonnie Scarola (of Goldendale, WA) and the Altar Society of her Parish. They collect this money for their "Helping Hands" program which helps to buy food for the elderly.

30 Pieces of Silver

Thirty Pieces of Silver

Jesus was betrayed by Judas for 30 pieces of silver. Let's pay this ransom in reparation for this betrayal.

Make a little draw string bag out of leftover material. Make a label entitled "30 Pieces of Silver for Jesus". Use a hole punch to make a hole in the label and thread it onto the drawstring. Display the bag on the kitchen table. Collect 30 pieces of silver of as large denomination as possible (nickels, dimes, quarters and dollar coins), placing them within the bag throughout Lent.

At the end of Holy Week, remove the change and submit it with your Easter Sunday Offering or donate it to the poor.

The world took little notice of Jesus' death - I must be different.

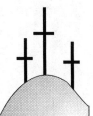

Fr. Tom Mohan

Congregation of the Priests of St. Basil

Lent

Saints' Days

1. St. Albinus, bishop *
2. Blessed Charles the Good, martyr *
3. Blessed Katharine Drexel OPTIONAL MEMORIAL
3. St. Cunegundes, empress *
4. St. Casimir MEMORIAL
5. St. John Joseph of the Cross, priest *
6. St. Colette, virgin *
7. St. Perpetua, St. Felicity, martyrs MEMORIAL
8. **St. John of God**, religious OPTIONAL MEMORIAL
9. **St. Frances of Rome**, religious OPTIONAL MEMORIAL
9. **St. Dominic Savio** *
10. St. Macarius, bishop *
11. St. Eulogius, martyr *
12. St. Theophanes the Chronicler *
13. St. Roderick, martyr *
14. St. Mathilda, queen *
15. St. Louise de Marillac, widow *
16. St. Heribert (Herbert), bishop *
17. **St. Patrick**, bishop, apostle OPTIONAL MEMORIAL
18. St. Cyril of Jerusalem, bishop, doctor OPTIONAL MEMORIAL
19. **St. Joseph**, husband of Mary SOLEMNITY
20. St. Wulfran, bishop *
21. St. Nicholas of Flue, hermit *
22. St. Lea, widow *
23. St. Turibius do Mogrovejo, bishop OPTIONAL MEMORIAL
24. St. Catherine of Sweden, virgin *
25. **The Annunciation of our Lord** SOLEMNITY
26. St. Margaret Clitherow, martyr *
27. St. Rupert of Salzburg, bishop *
28. St. Guntramnus (Gontran), king *
29. **St. Joseph of Arimathea** *
30. St. John Climacus, abbot *

The first Friday in March is the World Day of Prayer.

* Not found in the revised Roman Calendar.

Simple Suppers

During this time of Lenten Sacrifice, perhaps a simpler diet is in order. Avoid fast food restaurants. Let the children help plan the weekly menu and be involved in the grocery shopping.

Select only inexpensive food that will go a long way. Stick to rice, pasta, simple and smaller cuts of meat (or ground meat) and frozen vegetables (or in-season vegetables if there are any). Make your own bread and cook up your own homemade soup or stew with a little less variety of meat and vegetables than usual. Eliminate snack food and treats and pop from your shopping list.

Keep track of your savings, comparing your grocery bills with regular spending patterns. Set aside the amount of savings and donate this as an offering to the poor. If preferred, spend the money on non-perishable items and donate them to a food bank.

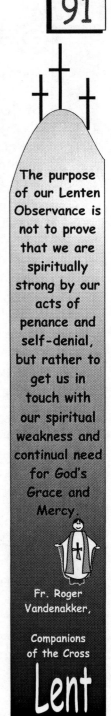

The purpose of our Lenten Observance is not to prove that we are spiritually strong by our acts of penance and self-denial, but rather to get us in touch with our spiritual weakness and continual need for God's Grace and Mercy.

Fr. Roger Vandenakker,

Companions of the Cross

Lent

**March 8: The Optional Memorial
of St. John of God**

St. John of God is the patron of hospitals, known for his humility and dedication to those in need.

Ask at your parish for a name of someone who might need a visitor...at the hospital or nursing home. Make a special visit, armed with a homemade card and perhaps flowers or a homemade gift.

**March 9: The Optional Memorial
of St. Frances of Rome**

St. Frances of Rome was also known for her dedication to those in need. She insisted on serving the poor, despite disapproval from her wealthy in-laws.

Consider volunteering in a soup kitchen or donating food to the local food bank. Make a special meal for a family who might be facing health problems or financial difficulties.

March 9: St. Dominic Savio *

St. Dominic's young life was full of poverty, work and suffering, undertaken with joy and cheerfulness. He once explained to a friend "Here we make sanctity consist in being joyful all the time and in faithfully performing our duties."

Talk about how we can imitate St. Dominic throughout our daily lives. Take on some extra chores today and carry them out with a smile!

* Does not occur in the revised Roman Calendar.

Pretzels

As part of the simpler meals and fasting days of Lent, bread pretzels are a common custom during Lent. They usually consist of only flour, water and salt and were often the main midday meal throughout Lent when fasting was observed.

These tasty treats originated as little rewards made by monks and given to children as they learned their prayers. The form of the pretzel represents two arms folded in prayer, as a reminder of the importance of prayer.

Roll out pretzel or pizza dough into a large flat piece. Cut 1/4" strips. Arrange each strip as illustrated, intertwining the ends and securing the tips to the mid-portion of the strip. Brush on an egg mixture or milk (or use vegetable oil spray) and sprinkle with course salt, sesame or flax seeds and spices, if desired.

Some recipes call for placing each formed pretzel into simmering water for 30 seconds before baking in the oven. Experiment for the taste that you prefer.

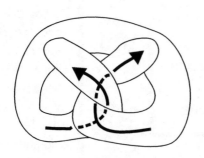

Lent

March 17: The Optional Memorial of St. Patrick

St. Patrick is the patron saint of Ireland, and credited for converting the once pagan nation to Christianity. As he evangelized, he used the shamrock to help explain the Mystery of the Trinity. The shamrock has three parts within the one leaf as the three Persons are distinct within the one Trinity.

SHAMROCK BUNS: Make some bread dough and form three small dough balls and place them close together. Roll out a smaller piece, flattening it to create the stem for the shamrock. When the pieces are placed to form the shamrock, allow the dough to rise. Beat an egg and brush it on lightly or spray with vegetable oil spray, for light browning of the bread. Mix a drop or two of green food colouring in with some coarse salt, sesame seeds and other spices and sprinkle the mixture on the top of the buns before baking.

SHAMROCK COOKIES: Make shortbread cookies with a shamrock cookie cutter, and sprinkle them with green sugar (mix a drop of green food colouring in with some sugar).

As you munch on the shamrock buns or cookies, talk about the Trinity and recite:

> God, our Father
> Jesus, His Son
> Holy Spirit
> Three in One.

As you dress in green today, recall that it is the colour of the shamrock as well as the favourite colour of the Irish, the people who were originally converted by St. Patrick.

Friend of Jesus

Jesus was disappointed by His Friends in 3 ways during this most difficult time of His Public Ministry.

We all disappoint Jesus in our daily lives, but let's try to make amends for these separate events that hurt Jesus.

1 Judas betrayed Him for 30 pieces of silver.

Collect the THIRTY PIECES OF SILVER in the linen bag as described previously. Give as much as you can truly afford, selecting the largest denomination of silver coin possible for you (nickels, dimes and dollar coins). Submit it with your Easter Sunday offering or donate it to the poor.

30 Pieces of Silver

2 None of His Friends could stay awake for the hour that He prayed in the Garden of Gethsemane.

Offer up a full hour of uninterrupted, quiet and focused prayer time. Take the phone off the hook, and agree to not answer the door (or post a note on the door).

Sit in a place within the house where you will not be distracted by things to do or see. Light a candle and focus on a picture of Jesus and pray.

3 Peter denied that he knew Jesus, 3 times.

Perhaps the most challenging: make a big banner with words that testify to your faith, such as
     WE BELIEVE IN JESUS.
Make the words clearly visible so that they can be read easily from the street when the banner is displayed in a front window. Leave the banner up for the season of Lent and Easter (or throughout the whole year!)

WE
BELIEVE
IN
JESUS!

Marilyn Rocha of Modesto, California provides her CCD class with blank plastic buttons found at a hobby store. The children create their own design, proclaiming their belief in Jesus, and are encouraged to wear them everyday.

Lent

Basket of Blessing Eggs

Eggs are a symbol of new life. Jesus' Resurrection brings us new hope and new life through Him. In preparation for this new beginning, let us serve, encourage and pray for one another.

At the beginning of Lent, create a paper mache' egg for each member of the family (or one large egg to be used as a mailbox for the whole family!)

Make a mix of watered down glue or wall paper paste for adhesive. Blow up a regular size balloon to about 6" length. Draw a 1/4" x 2" rectangle on the balloon with a marker, being careful not to burst the balloon.

Saturate one torn strip of newsprint at a time and apply to the small balloon. Do not apply the strips on top of the knot of the balloon (where it has been tied) . Work around this opening, maintaining the smooth shape of the egg.

Leave a hole where the drawn rectangle is. Strips of newspaper with one straight edge can be used to neatly frame the opening, using the rectangle as a guide. When one layer is dry, frame the opening with masking tape for reinforcement. Apply another layer of the saturated (straight-edge) newspaper strips on top of the tape, framing the opening. This opening will serve as a mail slot (for inserting messages).

Marcia Kruszewski recommends hollow plastic eggs as an alternative container for messages revealing a special sacrifice or gift of service.

When a full layer has been applied and allowed to dry, pierce the balloon through one of the openings. Apply an additional layer of paper mache', covering the hole left where the balloon knot had been.

Allow the egg to dry thoroughly. Paint each egg colourfully and include a family members' name on it, identifying it as their egg. Leave the colourfully decorated eggs in a basket on the kitchen table.

Kerry Brine of Ottawa, Ontario recommends a coat of "Podge-It" for a child-safe, shiny finish on the eggs.

Encourage everyone in the family to say special prayers and do good deeds (in secret) for each other. Let them write little messages revealing these prayers and deeds and put them in the other family member's egg.

Feel free to add other positive notes (You did a great job with your homework!, Thanks for dinner!...) into the eggs as well. Try to remember to date each message too!

As Lent goes on, these eggs will be filled with messages. On Easter Sunday, these eggs are cracked open so that everyone can read their secret messages. With the prayers and encouragement of loved ones, we celebrate our new life through Jesus, continuing to serve Him in our daily lives with renewed enthusiasm.

Alanna English of Stouffville, Ontario recommends a "Living Easter Basket". Line the basket with plastic, then fill it with soil and fast growing grass seed. Flower seeds can be added too.

Add the Blessing Eggs within the basket, once the grass has begun to grow. Eggs may be removed when the grass is regularly sprayed lightly with water.

Lent

MARCH

March 19:   The Solemnity of St. Joseph, husband of Mary, patron of the Universal Church

St. Joseph is remembered as the humble and patient, just and protective, gentle and chaste spouse of Mary, Jesus' foster father on earth. He is the head of the Holy Family; poor in worldly terms of possessions but rich in grace and virtue.

St. Joseph was the "breadwinner" of the Holy Family. Through his work as a carpenter, he provided for his family and protected them. In some Catholic Churches, the altar is decorated on this Feast Day with fancy loaves of bread.

Make some DECORATIVE BREAD TWISTS (a.k.a. "BOUNCY BREAD") in honour of St. Joseph's "bread-winning" role and the delicate work of the carpenter.

Roll out pretzel or bread dough into a flat piece. Cut 1/4"-wide strips of dough. Wind each strip of dough loosely around a wooden chopstick or wooden shish-kebob skewer. Place on a lightly greased cookie sheet and brush with a beaten egg mixture or milk (or spray with low-fat cooking oil). Sprinkle with coarse salt, sesame or flax seeds and spices. Bake according to pretzel recipes.

Gently remove the chopsticks or skewers after allowing the bread to cool slightly.
Wash the chopsticks and skewers and allow them to air-dry for the next use.

Daily Gifts to Jesus

Make a booklet with 40 pages, for each child. Each evening before bedtime, talk about the day's events and think of one special thing we did for Jesus that day. Write a few sentences or draw a picture explaining what it was. As children begin to anticipate this activity, perhaps they will make a more conscious effort to please Jesus each day.

OR Count Our Blessings Book

Make a booklet with 40 pages, for each child. Each evening before bedtime, talk about the day's events and think of something we are thankful for. It could be something we were able to do, someone who was kind to us or something else that we appreciate. Write a few sentences or draw a picture explaining what it was.

Other format variations include using 10 pages per book (dividing each page into 4) or old computer paper or banner paper of 40 connected sheets. Adding machine paper rolls can be used for miniature versions, creating decorated streamers for Easter. (White is even the right colour for the Easter season!)

If pictures are made out of construction paper or felt, they could be glued to connected pieces of durable paper towel or material, creating a long banner to be displayed. A smaller version could even be made out of toilet paper, if it is sturdy enough and care is taken to avoid ripping it! If carefully and colourfully done, these could make great banners or streamers for Easter!

These ideas were inspired by Nancy Schwerdt of Lancaster, CA.

Each year, Nancy's family pulls out the collection of "Lenten Blessing Books" during Lent.

Lent

Saints' Days

March 25: **The Solemnity of the Annunciation of our Lord.**

Exactly 9 months before Christmas, we celebrate the First Joyful Mystery of the Rosary.

We appreciate Mary's openness to the announcement from the Archangel Gabriel. He told her that she had been chosen to be the mother of the Son of God.

As a result of Mary's obedience, we celebrate the conception of Jesus within Mary's womb. This celebration of the Incarnation means that Jesus, the Second Person of God, became human on this day.

Read about the First Joyful Mystery and recite this decade of the Rosary.

Read Luke 1:26-38. Notice how the angel greets Mary with the words "Hail, favoured one! The Lord is with you!". Recognize the origin of the first few lines of the Hail Mary prayer.

This is a great opportunity to begin teaching the children the Hail Mary, if they do not know it already.

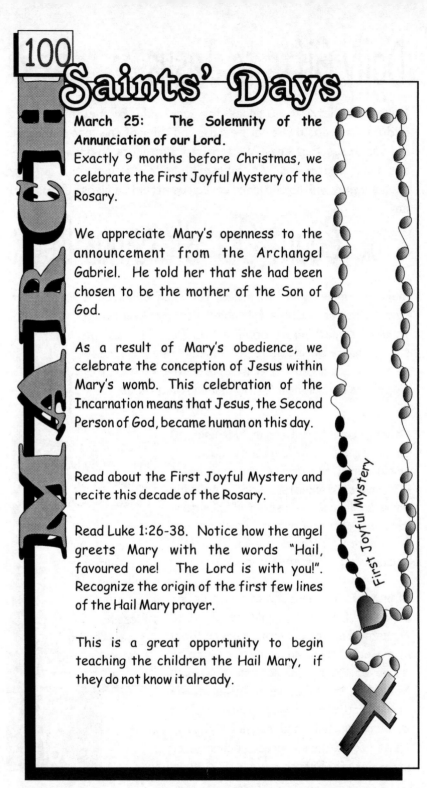

First Joyful Mystery

This EXPERIENCED MOM IDEA award goes to C.J. of Akron, Ohio! This activity is a slight variation of one used by Cathy's Children's Group. They wrote their sins on pieces of paper and placed them in medicine tubes within the box. The adults secretly placed heavier objects within the box as everyone prayed. The box was then passed around to feel the added weight.

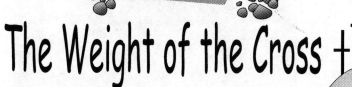

The Weight of the Cross †T†

Collect stones and rocks of different sizes, from the size of a grape to the size of an apple. Encourage everyone to regularly reflect on their sins. On each stone, record one sin either by naming the sin in pencil on the stone or taping a message to it.

Throughout Lent, these stones are regularly added to a box (with a cross drawn on it). Everyone is allowed to hold the box before and after the stones are added, to feel the increasing weight.

On Easter Sunday, the stones are removed and the box is wrapped like a present. Let everyone hold the now-empty box, feeling Jesus' gift to us as He takes away our sins through His Life, Death and Resurrection.

If the enthusiasm for adding rocks seems like incentive for the kids to sin, allow them to remove a tiny pebble each time they do a good deed. Make sure that the larger rocks remain within the box, to maintain the effect of Jesus' "weightless" Gift on Easter Sunday.

Lent

Lenten Calendar

The Lenten version of the Advent calendar holds messages of Scripture, special daily offering suggestions for the Offering Cross or pieces of the Passion Play. The contents for each day of Lent can be tucked into pockets on a felt banner or hung from pins on a bulletin board LENTEN CALENDAR.

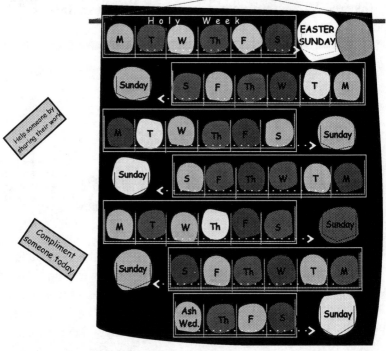

Strips of felt can be secured to a banner, sewn on the bottom and side edges, with dividers at equal intervals creating separate pockets.

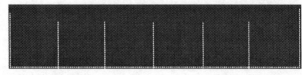

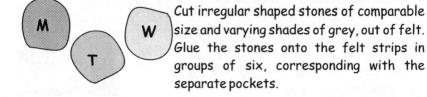

Cut irregular shaped stones of comparable size and varying shades of grey, out of felt. Glue the stones onto the felt strips in groups of six, corresponding with the separate pockets.

Glue one stone to the side of a white "EMPTY TOMB" stone for Easter Sunday. Sew in place (on three 'sides'), leaving a pocket at the top for a special Easter message (or a clue to find a basket of treats!)

EASTER SUNDAY

Sew the single Sunday stones on three 'sides", leaving the top open to access a pocket.

Sunday

The configuration becomes a path of stepping stones journeying through Lent, to the Triumph of the Empty Tomb!

The 3D LENTEN CALENDAR is made with film cannisters, positioned in the same Triumphant path of stepping stones.

Each cannister is glued or secured to a large piece of wood with a single screw through its base, leaving the lid available to open and close. (Brass fasteners can be used on a cardboard base.) The lids can be covered with the same irregular shaped stepping stones, made out of felt or paper. The special Lenten messages or activity pieces are placed within the closed containers.

Empty film cannisters may be available at a local photo store, to supplement your own collection.

Plastic pill organizers (found at a dollar store) can provide options for a mini 3D version!

Glue the stone shape on each lid. Try a combination of pill organizers and film cannisters for a bumpier path!

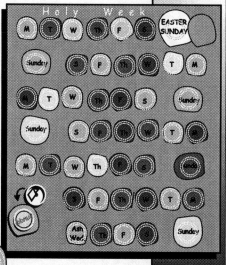

Holy Week

Lent

Crown of Thorns

Make a simple dough with 4 cups flour and 1 cup salt water. Black coffee or tea (with added salt) can be used for a dark coloured dough.

Divide dough into 3 parts and roll into long strips. Make a braid and place on a cookie sheet in the form of a ring.
Poke 6 evenly spaced holes with a thick candlestick. Try to widen the hole with your fingers (as the hole will shrink with baking).

Break at least 20 toothpicks in half. Poke the broken ends into the ring, leaving them pointing out at every angle. Leave the toothpicks in the wreath and bake at 300 degrees for at least 1 hour. Turn the oven off and allow to cool slowly.

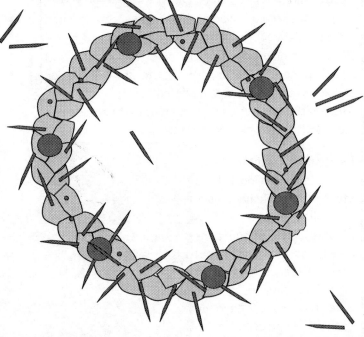

Each day, family members are encouraged to reflect on the various sacrifices and special deeds that were carried out during the day, for Jesus. Remove one toothpick half from the wreath, each day, from Monday through Saturday.

Each Sunday in Lent, light the appropriate number of candles (for the number of weeks of Lent completed).

Once all the toothpicks are removed, artificial flowers can be arranged, lightly tucked into the toothpick holes, as good deeds and sacrifices are carried out. Pieces of coloured tissue paper can be tucked into the toothpick holes to create an alternate look of flowers.

Gradually, the Crown of Thorns is transformed into the Resurrection Crown or Easter Wreath, just in time for Easter! The Easter Wreath can be further decorated with paint, glitter, plastic jewels and ribbons. A white candle lit in the centre of the wreath, completes the effect for Easter morning!

Resurrection Crown

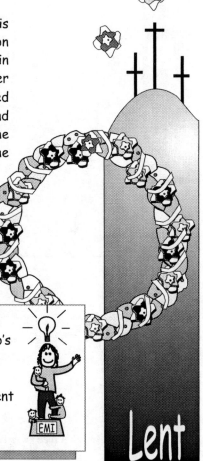

This award goes to Barbara, a contributor to Sylvia Morgado's website:
www.catholicparenting.com.
Check out the site for excellent craft ideas and Catholic material!

Lent

Saints' Days

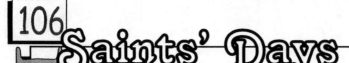

March 29: St. Joseph of Arimathea *

St. Joseph found it difficult to show his belief in Jesus, throughout Jesus' public life. However, his belief was made known as he offered his tomb for Jesus' Body after the Crucifixion.

Take this day to work on the tomb for the PASSION PLAY.

Talk about how we can make our belief in Jesus more obvious, throughout daily life.

* Not found in the revised Roman Calendar.

Offering Cross

Using a roll of brown packaging paper, cut out a cross, as big as possible. Secure the cross to a wall in a central place in the house.

Try to come up with at least 40 different "offerings". These could instruct to read a specific scriptural passage, do an extra chore, give someone a compliment today, or look up a specific teaching in the Catechism.

Cut out 40 strips of paper for each member of the family (white, purple and pink are good Lent and Easter colours). Record one "offering" on each strip of paper (some of the strips will have the same message).

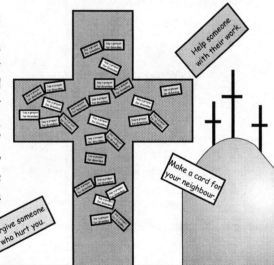

Sylvia Morgado of **www.catholicparenting.com** suggests a styrofoam cross into which artificial flowers can be poked (by their stems), as good deeds are performed. Silk flowers can be cut apart into individual flowers and stored in a basket near the cross.

Every morning of Lent, each person picks one "offering" randomly out of the bowl. At the end of the day, the strips are taped onto the cross, if the offering was carried out. At the end of Lent, we can "see" all of our offerings.

Lent

Sin Cross

Using a large bulletin board, place pins strategically to outline a cross. Wind a piece of string around the pins to create the form of the cross.

Cut small pieces of black or brown construction paper. Explain to the children that Jesus died for our sins. Talk about what we do that is sinful.

Let everyone write their sins on the small dark pieces of construction paper (one sin per piece) and pin it within the outline of the cross.

Encourage everyone to add more of these sin notes as they reflect on their sin, and when new sins are committed. If a Lenten fast or resolution is accidently broken throughout Lent, suggest another sin note be added to the cross.

Create PRAYER PETAL FLOWERS out of construction paper as extra prayers are offered throughout Lent. Concentrate on making one PRAYER PETAL FLOWER each, everyday. (See SPIRITUAL BOUQUET OF PRAYER PETAL FLOWERS in the October section of Ordinary Time.) Place the completed flowers outside of the cross (which will be littered with sin papers).

After Good Friday, the sin papers are taken off, leaving the pins in place. These pins hold the memory of our sins which Jesus died for. After the Easter Vigil, these same pins can be used to place the PRAYER PETAL FLOWERS within the Triumphant Cross. (An artificial vine of flowers can also be used if PRAYER PETAL FLOWERS were not created.)

The sin papers are saved to be burned by the Easter fire: a fire lit by the HOMEMADE PASCHAL CANDLE or other blessed candle on Easter Sunday. We are given a new beginning through Jesus!

Add a dark sky background on Good Friday, and a sun in one corner, on Easter Sunday.

Layer various sizes and shapes of colourful construction paper to create a stained glass effect, surrounding the Triumphant Cross for the Season of Easter (but maintaining the straight edge of the cross).

This idea is inspired by a mom in Tucson, Arizona.

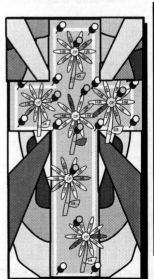

Saints' Days

1. St. Hugh, bishop *
2. St. Francis of Paola, hermit OPTIONAL MEMORIAL
3. St. Richard, bishop *
4. St. Isidore of Seville, bishop, doctor OPTIONAL MEMORIAL
5. St. Vincent Ferrer, priest OPTIONAL MEMORIAL
6. St, Marcellinus of Carthage, martyr *
7. **St. John Baptist de la Salle**, religious MEMORIAL
8. St. Julie Billiart, virgin OPTIONAL MEMORIAL
9. St. Gaucherius, abbot *
10. St. Fulbert, bishop *
11. St. Stanislaus, bishop, martyr MEMORIAL
11. St. Gemma Galgani, virgin *
12. St. Julius, pope *
13. St. Martin I, pope, martyr OPTIONAL MEMORIAL
14. St. Tiburtius, St. Valerian, St. Maximus, martyrs *
15. St. Paternus, bishop *
16. St. Benedict Joseph Labre, mendicant *
17. St. Stephen Harding, abbot *
18. St. Apollonius, martyr *
19. St. Elphege, bishop, martyr *
20. St. Marcellinus, bishop *
21. St. Anselm, bishop, doctor OPTIONAL MEMORIAL
22. St. Epipodius, St. Alexander, martyrs *
23. St. George, martyr OPTIONAL MEMORIAL
23. St. Adalbert, bishop, martyr OPTIONAL MEMORIAL
24. St. Fidelis of Sigmaringen, martyr OPTIONAL MEMORIAL
25. **St. Mark**, evangelist FEAST
26. Our Lady of Good Counsel OPTIONAL MEMORIAL
26. St. Alda (Aldobrandesca), widow *
27. **St. Zita**, virgin *
28. St. Louis Grignion de Montfort, priest OPTIONAL MEMORIAL
28. St. Peter Chanel, priest, martyr OPTIONAL MEMORIAL
29. **St. Catherine of Siena**, virgin, doctor MEMORIAL
30. St. Pius V, pope OPTIONAL MEMORIAL
30. Blessed Marie of the Incarnation, religious OPTIONAL MEMORIAL

> * Not found in the revised Roman Calendar.

Heart Cross Banner

Make a large banner out of purple material (2' x 3' or longer). Hem both ends with enough allowance for a dowel to slide in. Allow the top dowel to extend 1" beyond the fabric. Attach a piece of string, secured at both ends of the dowel. Hang the banner on the wall in a visible place. The banner can be reused Lent after Lent.

Out of brown or lavendar construction paper, cut out little crosses (3" wide x 4" high). Out of pink or white paper, cut out hearts.

Each member of the family is encouraged to reflect on their sins, throughout Lent. Teach the children to SIT, THINK and TH-A-W (see the Memorial for July 31), as well as a simple Act of Contrition Prayer. (See first Ordinary Time section.)

To respond to our sin, we record the sin on a little paper cross. We then write an act of love to counter the sin, on the heart. This act of love is an opposite action, virtue or attitude that we intend to practice.

We crucify our sin, by pinning it to the banner. We pin the heart over the cross, onto the banner to signify our intentions to overcome our sin. We reflect on Jesus' Sacrifice for our sins.

Encourage the children to continue adding their hearts and crosses throughout Lent.

> A more permanent paper and glue version can be used for young children who are unable to use pins safely. Just allow the children to glue their crosses and hearts to a felt or paper banner.

The banner becomes a record of our battle against sin, an opportunity for reflection and a decorative display of our aspirations to please Jesus.

Band-Aids for Christ

This is an exercise to acknowledge Jesus' suffering for us and to encourage earnest sacrifice for His sake.

A double sided banner is made with two large rectangular pieces of felt, sewn (or glued with fabric glue) on three sides to create a side pocket. One of the rectangular pieces is black; the other can be white or any bright Easter colour.

A brown felt cross is glued on top of the black side of the banner.

A simple Body of Christ is made with a sheet of flesh coloured craft foam. It is personalized with other pieces of foam for the facial features. A piece of white foam or felt can be used as a simple undergarment for the Body of Christ. Holes are pierced through the hands, separate feet and side of the Body. The Body is secured through holes in the cross on the front of the banner with brass fasteners, flattening the tabs on the back of the black felt.

At the beginning of each of the five weeks leading to Holy Week, a different wound of Christ's is identified (both feet, both hands, side).

Everyone is asked to reflect on a sin they wish to tackle the following week. They should plan to make every attempt to avoid or overcome it, for Jesus' sake.

At the end of the week, everyone is asked to reflect on how they did in their resolution to avoid the sin. At the end of this time of reflection (and possible discussion), the family is awarded a felt Band-Aid.

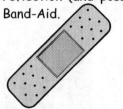

The five Band-Aids are made by the family out of felt. Within the centre third of the Band-Aid is a rectangular pad (resembling a true Band-Aid). It is a separate rectangular piece of felt, sewn on three sides, creating a pocket.

Once the felt Band-Aid is awarded, family members are encouraged to insert notes into the pocket, describing their attempts to overcome the particular sin they had chosen for the previous week.

The Band-Aid is placed over the particular Wound of Christ (discussed at the beginning of the week). Pieces of adhesive black velcro are strategically placed on the black felt (surrounding the cross), so that the Band-Aids can be positioned over the Wounds of Christ.

To ensure that the Band-Aids will be positioned correctly, push the two sides of velcro together. Cut it into small pieces. Remove the backing on one side and stick one piece on each end of the felt Band-Aid (on the backside). Remove the remaining backing while the two pieces of velcro remain stuck together, and position the Band-Aid in place. The velcro pieces can be sewn for reinforcement on both the Band-Aid and the black side of the felt banner.

Later on Good Friday, the Body of Christ is removed from the cross and placed in the inside pocket of the banner. The Band-Aids can be left in their positions, over the cross.

BAND-AID is a registered trademark of Johnson + Johnson

On Easter Sunday, the Body is no longer within the pocket of the banner! The other side of the banner is brightly coloured with a white robe sewn or attached with velcro at key points. The Body is inserted behind the white robe to show that He has Risen!!

Our "Band-Aids" and lenten observances do not take away Christ's suffering. They are our attempt to recognize Jesus' sacrifice for our sins.

Lent

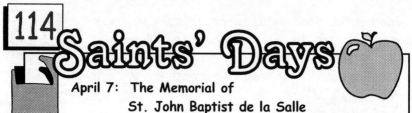

Saints' Days

**April 7: The Memorial of
St. John Baptist de la Salle**

St. John Baptist de la Salle was the founder of a religious group called Brothers of Christian Schools, dedicated to improving the standards of religious education and ensuring better access for the poor. The boys were taught catechism and prayers. They attended daily Mass. Religious training extended well beyond "religion" classes, into other subjects and well into their daily lives.

St. John Baptist de la Salle is the patron of teachers. Make a card or bake cookies for a little Teacher Appreciation Day.

Let the children take turns playing "Teacher", allowing them to quiz everyone else (including their parents!) on CATHOLIC CATEGORIES!

(See the CATHLETICS section of Ordinary Time, found in the summer months.)

April 25: The Feast of St. Mark, the evangelist

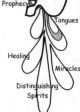

St. Mark wrote the shortest of the 4 Gospels of the New Testament. Make a commitment as a family to read his Gospel, tackling only about one half of a chapter, each evening for the next month.

Preparation!

Holy Week is an intense week of reflection on the last few days of Jesus' life on earth before the crucifixion and His ultimate Resurrection. It begins with Palm Sunday and leads us through the Holy Triduum with the Lord's Supper on Holy Thursday and Good Friday (the Passion and Death of our Lord) and concludes with the Easter Vigil (when we begin to celebrate our Lord's Resurrection).

Spring Cleaning

The custom of "spring cleaning" may be tied to the preparation for Passover. To enthuse the children to help give the house a thorough cleaning, hide pennies in places that could be overlooked in normal cleaning. Hide pennies on the tops of window frames and moldings, behind curtains, picture frames, furniture and objects on shelves. Remember to leave some pennies in more noticeable places (lower to the floor) to encourage those little ones (as long as they won't try to eat them!)

HOLY WEEK

Make a Paschal Candle

The Paschal Candle symbolizes the body of Jesus and His Return to the world through His Resurrection. He is the Light of the world. Purchase a candle or visit your local craft store to discover how to make a beeswax candle or poured wax candle from a mold. Use paint or pliable coloured wax to create the cross, the numbers and the Greek letters. Explain to the children what each symbol means, as you add it to the candle.

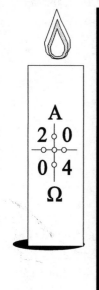

Make wax decorations by lighting a coloured candle and allowing it to drip onto a disposable foil plate or a durable counter-top. Scrape the wax off the surface while it is still warm (but not too hot to touch!). Shape into decorations while the wax is still warm and press onto the candle.

The shapes may need to be warmed by the flame to adhere to the candle. Use tweezers!

See SPECIAL INTENTIONS CANDLE in the October section of Ordinary Time for more candle decorating tips.

OR ...Make a Paschal Votive Candle

Paint all the symbols on a clean, clear glass jar. Glue the pieces of incense (or cloves) in the appropriate places **or** paint a red dot in those locations and place the incense within the jar. A tealight is placed within the jar for a PASCHAL VOTIVE CANDLE.

"**Christ yesterday and today**"   Make the vertical beam of the cross.

"**The Beginning and the End**"   Make the horizontal beam.

"**His are the times**"   Make the first number of the current year in the upper left angle of the cross.

"**And the ages**"   Make the second number of the current year in the upper right angle of the cross.

"**His are the glory and power**"   Make the third number of the current year in the lower left angle of the cross.

"**For all the ages of eternity.   Amen.**"   Make the fourth number of the current year in the lower right angle of the cross.

"**By His Holy and Glorious Wounds may Christ our Lord guard us and keep us.   Amen**"
Push 5 cloves into the candle in the cross, midway through each of the 4 stems of the cross and in the centre of the cross. (For easier insertion, push the heated end of a skewer into each location to prepare a hole for each clove.)
The cloves represent the aromatic spices brought by the women to anoint Jesus' body. Once they have been placed in position, they symbolize the 5 wounds of Christ.

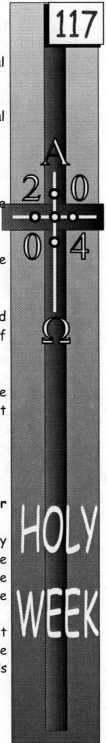

Prepare the Easter Story Eggs

Pick and choose from the following list of possible objects with their significance within the Easter Story. Use your imagination to come up with some of your own and feel free to improvise!

Egg#1: piece of a palm, toy donkey or drawing of a donkey, representing Jesus' entry into Jerusalem (Lk 19:28-38)

Egg#2: small piece of pita bread or other bread or cracker representing the Last Supper (Mt 26:26)

Egg#3: silver coins (one for each child?) representing the ransom Judas received for his betrayal of Jesus (Mt 26: 14-15)

Egg#4: toy rooster, feather or drawing of a rooster representing Peter's betrayal of Jesus (Mk 14:29-31)

Egg#5: purple cloth, picture or wire representation of crown of thorns representing how Jesus was made fun of (Mk 15:17)

Egg#6: cross, as it was carried to the place called Golgotha (Lk 23:26)

Egg #7: nail representing Jesus being crucified (Lk 23:33)

Egg#8: dice representing the fulfillment of prophecy "they cast lots for my clothes" (Jn 19:23-24)

Egg#9: material soaked in vinegar representing the drink offered to Jesus (Lk 23: 36-37)

Egg#10: material split in two, representing the temple curtain splitting at the time of Jesus' death (Lk23:44-45)

Egg#11: toothpick representing the spear that pierced Jesus' side (John 19:34)

Egg#12: white cloth representing the linen shroud used to wrap Jesus' body (Lk 23:50-54)

Egg#13: cinnamon and cloves representing the spices and ointments prepared by the women (Mk 16:1-2)

Egg#14: stone representing how the tomb was secured (Mt 27:62-65)

Egg#15: empty, reminding us of the Empty Tomb! (Mt 28:1-10)

As an alternative (or addition) to the Easter Egg hunt of candy-filled eggs, use the plastic eggs as clues to unfold the Passion Story of Jesus. Preparing these eggs is another reflective activity during Holy Week. By the time the Easter Egg hunt takes place the children will have heard several accounts of Jesus' Arrest, Death and Resurrection in the last week. This familiarity should help them easily recognize the clues, blurting out the significance of their findings and retelling the Passion Story in their own words.

Buy at least one set of 12 medium-large size plastic Easter eggs which can be opened and filled. Find small objects and toys which easily fit in the plastic eggs, representing various events of the story. Add a note of the scriptural reference in case you would like to add these readings to the event of the Easter Egg Hunt. Number the eggs with tape on the outside.

With a little more work, the eggs can be found in sequence as a treasure hunt. Add a little note to each egg, giving a clue to find the next egg in order. The final (empty) egg may have a note attached to the outside, leading the egg-hunters to a basket of treats to celebrate the victory of the Resurrection!

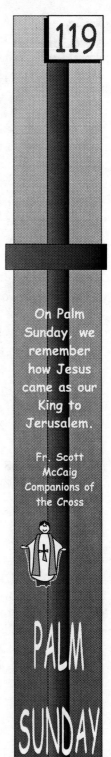

On Palm Sunday, we remember how Jesus came as our King to Jerusalem.

Fr. Scott McCaig
Companions of the Cross

PALM

SUNDAY

Simplified Seder Supper

Prepare enough place settings for each member of the family, adding an additional setting for the Prophet Elijah. Set cushions on the chairs or set up the meal at a low (coffee) table and sit on the floor with cushions.

Set the table with candles and include a small dish of water and a hand towel, as well as another bowl with salt water. Set out a plate with several pieces of pita bread, with the top 3 wrapped in a white napkin.

At each place setting, there should be a glass of wine (or white grape juice) or a glass of water.

On each plate:

A sprig of parsley
1 tsp of horseradish
1 tsp of haroset*
A small piece of lamb
A hard-boiled egg

*Haroset: mix 3 cups of applesauce, 1 tbsp cinnamon, 2 tbsp honey, 1 cup chopped walnuts, $\frac{1}{4}$ cup wine or grape juice. Chill.

Light candles and say a prayer thanking God for loving us. Ask for the Holy Spirit to give us special understanding of the Passover Feast and of our celebration of Easter.

Take 4 sips of wine (or juice or water), remembering the 4 promises that God made to Moses to save his people.

"I will bring you out of Egypt"
"I will free you from slavery"
"I will save you by My Own Hand" and
"I will be Your God"

Take another sip of your drink as the "Cup of Sanctification", remembering how Jesus offered wine saying "Take this, all of you and drink from it..."

We need clean hands and a pure heart to stand in God's Presence. Using the water bowl and hand towel, the father washes the hands of the person to his right, then the others proceed to do the same, remembering how Jesus did this for His apostles at the Last Supper.

Each person dips their parsley in the salt bowl. The parsley represents the sign of life at this time of spring. God creates life and only He can keep it alive. The salt water represents the tears of the Israelites, when they were slaves. We reflect on how we can be slaves to our sin.

We eat the pita bread (or matzah, unleavened bread) remembering the haste with which our ancestors left Egypt. They did not have the time to allow the bread to rise.

Sometimes in Scripture, leaven or yeast represents sin. Since this bread is without yeast (sin), it represents the Messiah. The three pieces wrapped in the napkin represent the Trinity.

One of the pieces is removed from the napkin. It has marks on it, just as Jesus suffered beatings and was pierced by thorns and nails and a sword. The father breaks a piece of the bread in half, representing Jesus' suffering. One half is saved for later, wrapped in the white napkin (as the shroud) and hidden as the children close their eyes.

121

HOLY

THURSDAY

Spread some horseradish on a piece of bread and eat it, remembering the bitter life of the Israelites in Egypt.

Spread some horseradish AND some haroset on a piece of bread, recognizing that sweetness can come out of bitter experiences when we have hope in God.

Notice the cushions that we sit on. We sit comfortably because now we are free!

Talk about the life of Moses, skimming through the Bible (Exodus 2-14). Moses was spared from drowning and raised by Pharaoh's daughter. He became aware of the suffering of his people and became their deliverer. Talk about the plagues which led Pharaoh to release the people (blood, frogs, lice, wild animals, cattle disease, boils, hail, locusts, darkness and death of the firstborn child in each family).

We eat the lamb, recalling the lamb's blood which served as a sign to God to protect them.

We eat the egg, a traditional offering brought to the Temple on Feast Days. The hardness of the shell reminds us of the hardness of Pharaoh's heart and of all those who don't accept God's love.

We remember again that the egg is a sign of NEW LIFE. God wants us to break down the hardness of our hearts and enjoy NEW LIFE with HIM!

We take another sip of wine (or juice or water) as the Cup of Joy, celebrating our NEW LIFE!

This is a summary of the Messianic Seder Supper developed and adapted from various sources by Cindy Halliday in PA, and celebrated by her family every year.

Children search for the hidden pita (representing the promised Messiah, Jesus). It was hidden, and now it is back, as Jesus rose from the dead.

The father breaks this piece of bread and shares it with everyone, as Jesus did at the Last Supper. We remember Jesus' words "This is my Body given for you; do this in remembrance of me". This bread is the last piece of food eaten at the Passover meal, so that its taste will stay with us. We are reminded of the significance of the bread: Jesus' Gift of the Eucharist at every Mass.

We take another sip of our drink, representing the Cup of Redemption, the blood of the Passover Lamb. "This is the cup of the new covenant of my blood, which is poured out for you...". Once again, we remember Jesus' Gift of the Eucharist.

The extra place setting is for Elijah who did not die, but was taken up to heaven riding a fiery chariot. Jewish people hoped that Elijah would come to Passover and announce the coming of the Messiah.

Someone opens the front door to welcome Elijah to the family Seder!

We pray for others still waiting for the Messiah, who do not accept Jesus.

We take another sip of our drink for the fourth and final time and give thanks and praise to our God. We thank Him for all He has created, for destroying the works of Satan both back in Egypt and through to today. We thank Him for saving us from slavery and for loving us, His Chosen.

"Lashanah haba'ah bi Yerushalayim"
"Next year, in Jerusalem!"

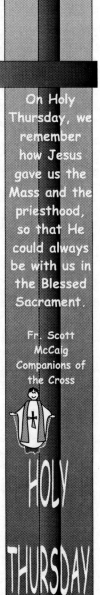

123

On Holy Thursday, we remember how Jesus gave us the Mass and the priesthood, so that He could always be with us in the Blessed Sacrament.

Fr. Scott McCaig
Companions of the Cross

HOLY

THURSDAY

Stations of the Cross

The Stations of the Cross are 14 events leading up to the placement of Jesus' body in the tomb. Reflection on the Stations is great preparation for the Feast of Jesus' Resurrection: Easter!

Although pictures of these Stations could be purchased at Catholic stores, it is a great family activity to make these pictures through drawing, or with construction paper or felt. A good set could be created throughout Lent, focusing on a few each Sunday leading up to Easter. Temporary drawn pictures could be used to be replaced by carefully made ones as they are created. This could be a project over several Lents!

Work as a family or in pairs, deciding what symbols or images might best represent the event. Give each family member a task at their capacity. Felt banners can be enhanced with glued-on objects / textures, perfect for little fingers! Drawn pictures can always use a little colouring!

When the set is complete (or stand-in Stations are available), help the children become familiar with the Stations of the Cross. Take turns putting the shuffled set in order. This will help them identify the events and retell the story. Display the set in order on a prominent wall in the house.

Or TRY THIS!

While creating a set of felt Stations, deliberately leave a key component off of each banner (leaving velcro in its place). As children retell the story, they can attach the missing piece to complete the image.

Easter Story Banner

Create a banner out of felt or use coloured paper and pin pieces to a bulletin board. Components can be added over several Holy Weeks of following years to expand the Passion Play.

The most important elements, of course, are the cross, the tomb (with the big stone hiding the interior) and the figure of Jesus. Use velcro to secure the important figures of the story, on the felt banner.

Talk about the events, reading from Scripture. Two pieces of velcro can accommodate two positions for the stone to open or close the tomb. Set the big stone aside on Easter morning to reveal the empty tomb!

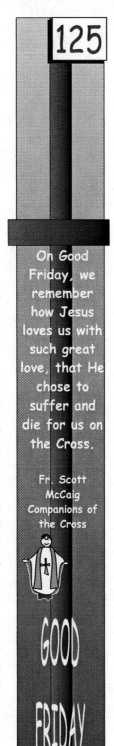

On Good Friday, we remember how Jesus loves us with such great love, that He chose to suffer and die for us on the Cross.

Fr. Scott McCaig
Companions of the Cross

GOOD

FRIDAY

Passion Play

Why not create your own little Passion Play?

Create a set with the 3 crosses and the tomb, forming the landscape and tomb structure out of paper mache'. Allow Jesus' cross to be removed, so that Jesus (and Simon) can carry the cross to Golgotha where it is repositioned with Jesus secured to it.

Make little people out of clay or make stand-up figures with cardboard. Figures can also be fashioned from clothes pegs.

This Experienced Mom Idea award goes to Grace Hadeed and her Junior Kindergarten class at Holy Spirit School in Aurora, Ontario.

She used wooden pegs and balls sold at a craft store to make the figures, and clothed them with felt. She stored them in a square ice cream container which doubled as the TOMB. Her students secured the tomb with a rock sitting on top of the lid.

CLOTHES PEG PEOPLE
Clothes pegs have ready-made forms to which clothes, a paper face, pipe cleaner arms and string hair can be added. Create the clothing out of fabric material scraps or construction paper.

Soldiers can have paper or painted shell noodle helmets and spaghetti swords. A crown of thorns can be made out of wire. The cross can be fashioned out of cardboard, popsicle sticks or scrap wood.

Sometimes household odds and ends and toy pieces can help with the accessories. Use your imagination!

PAPER ROLL PEOPLE
Similar to the CLOTHES PEG PEOPLE, little characters can be fashioned by accessorizing toilet paper rolls. Faces can be easily drawn on the cardboard surface. Pipe cleaner arms can be poked through holes made in the sides. Fabric scraps and construction paper make great clothing accessories.

Egg carton pieces can be covered with string hair to give a round shape to the top of the head while personalizing the figures. Painted egg carton pieces make great helmets for those soldiers!

See HOMEMADE NATIVITY figures in the Advent section, FELT FRIENDS from the Feast of the Holy Family, and HOLY HERO FELT FRIENDS and PUPPETS from the September section of Ordinary Time. Any of these methods can be used to create figures for a Passion Play. The FELT FRIENDS FOLDER or the PUPPET THEATRE create excellent backdrops to which various props can be added.

Choose to concentrate on one of these sets, and build it up over the various seasons of the Liturgical Calendar. Add characters as needed, with appropriate accessories and backdrops.

Begin with the key figures and gradually over many Lents, add more figures including soldiers and apostles.

Read Scripture as Jesus is arrested, condemned, ridiculed and crucified. Set Jesus in the tomb with a piece of white linen and be sure to create a boulder to close the tomb. Let the children discover Jesus missing on Sunday morning!

HOLY SATURDAY

Empty Tomb Cookies

We often take for granted the events of the original Holy Week. Those three days before the Resurrection are summed up in a few seconds when we recite the Creed, but for Jesus' friends, this was an overwhelmingly LONG time. The wait was full of sadness for their loss and confusion about what was to come.

Turn the oven to 300. Use a standard meringue shell recipe from your favourite cookbook. Single out each ingredient for it's goodness and importance to the recipe, while tying it in with the Passion Story.

For the egg whites, talk about how egg represents new life and the egg whites give the cookies a pure white appearance, reminding us of Jesus' sinless purity. Talk about the new life that Jesus made possible by giving His Life by death on the Cross.

If desired, add nuts to the recipe. Place the nuts in a plastic bag and allow the children to beat them with a wooden spoon. Talk about how Jesus was beaten after his arrest.

If $\frac{1}{4}$ tsp of cream of tartar is called for in your recipe, it may be replaced by 1 tsp of vinegar. (Use the 4:1 proportion if a different quantity of cream of tartar is listed). Talk about how Jesus was offered vinegar when He was dying on the cross.

Beat the sugar into the mix, 1 tbsp at a time, explaining how we hurt Jesus every time we sin.

If vanilla is required in your recipe, let all the children smell the sweet aroma. Talk about how Jesus' friends had prepared spices to anoint His Body after His death.

If a dash of salt is required, allow the children to taste a bit of salt and talk about the salty tears that Jesus' friends cried.

Follow your recipe closely for "beating" instructions and quantities. Shape meringue into 3" round shells on a cookie sheet. Build up the sides with the back of a spoon.

Place the cookie sheet in the oven and set the timer according to the recipe. Give each child a piece of tape to help seal the oven door, explaining how and why the tomb was sealed.

Perhaps a silent prayer time could be attempted until the timer goes off for the required heating time. Remind the children how Jesus asked His friends to wait and pray with Him for the hour before His arrest.
When the timer goes off, turn the oven OFF and GO TO BED! If the children feel sad, talk about how sad Jesus' friends must have felt when they couldn't see Him.

On Easter morning, open up the oven and show the children the ('empty') meringue shells. Explain that they represent the empty tomb and how amazed Jesus' friends were, to find it that way!

Fill each shell with Easter egg treats (chocolate or other candy eggs) and explain again that eggs represent NEW LIFE! Jesus' Resurrection as evident by the empty tomb brings us NEW LIFE in HIM!

This EXPERIENCED MOM IDEA award goes to Wanda Long. This activity is an adaptation of her recipe for "Easter Cookies" which appeared in Home Life magazine.

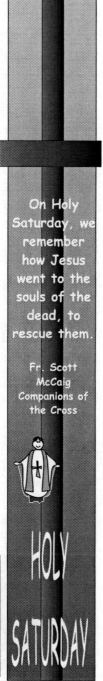

On Holy Saturday, we remember how Jesus went to the souls of the dead, to rescue them.

Fr. Scott McCaig
Companions of the Cross

HOLY

SATURDAY

 Coloured Jelly Easter Eggs

Coloured, hard boiled eggs are a traditional part of Easter Brunch, as eggs represent the new life that Jesus brings with His Death and Resurrection. How about a sweet surprise in egg cracking festivities!

Use a needle to pierce the wide end of a raw egg, piercing the egg yoke at the same time. Enlarge the hole carefully to $\frac{1}{2}$" size. Empty the contents of the egg into a bowl. The shell should remain intact. Empty 6 eggs in this way. Use the raw egg to make scrambled eggs or use in other cooking. Rinse the shells carefully with water; drain the water and allow to dry for 30 minutes. Store the shells in a clean egg carton in the fridge.

Carefully dye the empty shells along with the hard-boiled eggs coloured for Easter. Allow to dry.

Dissolve 2 envelopes of unflavoured gelatin, 1-3ounce package of fruit-flavoured gelatin in $1\frac{1}{2}$ cups (375mL) boiling water, stirring gently until dissolved completely. Allow the liquid to cool for 10 minutes.

Pour the warm liquid carefully into the empty shells and return each egg to the carton. Place the carton in the refrigerator and chill for at least 6 hours.
Serve these COLOURED JELLY EASTER EGGS, mixed in with the hard-boiled ones in a big Easter basket or platter for brunch.

If it is difficult to remove the thin white skin (from the inside of the shell) from the jelly egg, quickly dip the chilled egg into warm water before peeling.

Jell-O brand gelatin has a recipe for "Jigglers", using a reduced amount of liquid for firmer, moldable Jell-O. A few packages of Jell-O can create a bright and colourful collection of Jelly Easter Eggs, using egg shell molds.

JELL-O is a registered trademark of KRAFT

HE HAS RISEN!

Easter Sunday is a time to enjoy and appreciate any of the Lenten activities the family pursued. Encourage everyone to reflect on the family's preparation for Easter during Lent. Perhaps next year will provide the opportunity to attempt a different activity.

After Easter Brunch, have the EASTER STORY EGG hunt. Retell the Easter story and celebrate Jesus' Resurrection with a basket of treats.

While munching on Easter goodies, open up the family BLESSING EGGS. Everyone can read about all the prayers and good deeds performed on their behalf throughout Lent.

Review the DAILY GIFTS TO JESUS or the COUNT OUR BLESSINGS BOOK and marvel at the family OFFERING CROSS, SIN CROSS or HEART CROSS BANNER if they were part of your Lenten preparation.

Say some prayers around the lit FAMILY PASCHAL CANDLE today and throughout the Season of Easter (ending with Pentecost Sunday).

ALLELUIA!

WAFER CROSS COOKIES

Take two wafer cookies. Cut a portion of each cookie, the width of one cookie, to a depth of half the cookie. Make the cut to one side of the half-way point of one cookie and directly in the centre of the other cookie, so that the cookies fit together in a cross shape.

EASTER

Saints' Days

April 27: St. Zita

St. Zita is the patroness of domestic workers. She worked as a housekeeper for a wealthy family, saying her prayers while she worked, and finding time to go to daily Mass. Even with the small amount of money that she earned, she still managed to give generous gifts of food to the poor.

Legends surround St. Zita, about angels finishing her chores (as she prayed her daily devotions) and returning her coat after she had given it away to the poor.

Concentrate on developing a PRAYER HABIT like memorizing a one phrase prayer that can be said throughout the day...no matter what work we undertake.

Put notes or set alarms to establish the habit into routine. (See A FEW GOOD HABITS in the first Ordinary Time section.)

Try saying the Rosary daily, starting one decade at a time. (See October 7)

Try playing contemplative music while you do chores. Place spiritual literature in the car and the bathroom (for captive audiences!).

Decorate with holy pictures and display Crucifixes within the home, as visible signs and reminders of your Faith.

* Not found in the revised Roman Calendar.

Prayer Petal Flower Easter Baskets

If the PRAYER PETAL FLOWERS were part of your Lenten activities, transform them into a thoughtful Easter gift.

Cut one cup from an egg carton, rounding out the edges into a smooth form. Examine the cup, finding the symmetry. A strip of construction paper will be secured at both ends to opposite, symmetrical sides of the cup.

Staple one PRAYER PETAL FLOWER midway through the stem to the inside of one of the other sides of the cup. The PRAYER PETAL FLOWER should be positioned so that it easily sits upright.

Weigh down the PRAYER PETAL FLOWER EASTER BASKET with jelly beans and chocolate Easter eggs, remembering the significance of eggs as a symbol of NEW LIFE!

We rejoice that Jesus destroyed the power of death and opened the doors to heaven so that we can live with Him forever!

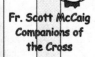

Fr. Scott McCaig
Companions of the Cross

Speaking of Easter Baskets, Marcia Kruszewski has many suggestions for a special gift idea! Fill a HOLY EASTER BASKET with: a story book about Easter, a crucifix, a colouring book about Easter, a Rosary, a SPIRITUAL BOUQUET CARD, Holy Cards, a Holy Statue, a BLESSING EGG and of course some candy or other treats!

EASTER

Saints' Days

April 27: The Memorial of St. Catherine of Siena

St. Catherine is the patroness of fire prevention. She consecrated herself to God at a very early age. She received a vision of Christ at the age of 6 years old and became a nun at the age of 16.

Prayer was always a very important element in her life. Despite being the youngest of 23 children in an overcrowded house, she insisted that she have her own room for prayer.

St. Catherine would go into trances and have conversations with Jesus, after receiving Communion. When she was tempted to believe Jesus had abandoned her, she heard Jesus say

"I am always with you in your heart, strengthening you."

Create a card saying:

"I am always with you
in your heart strengthening you."
-Love, Jesus

Send the card to someone (anonymously), who might be going through a difficult time.

Record the quote on small pieces of paper and post them throughout the house as little reminders: on the inside of kitchen cupboard doors, on mirrors, on the inside of the front door (at eye level) and on bedside tables. A little reminder from Jesus on the TV could even remind us to be discriminating about what and how much TV we sit down to watch!

Easter Mosaic

Save the coloured Easter egg shells. Crush the shells into smaller pieces with a rolling pin. Glue the coloured pieces on heavy paper or cardboard. Create an Easter symbol using the egg shell fragments, mosaic-style! Try spelling HE HAS RISEN! with the egg shells in one colour of egg shell, and fill in the surrounding space with random colours of egg shells. Display throughout the Easter season!

Other easy, colourful materials for mosaics can be found in your recycling box! Cut colourful pieces from thin cardboard packaging used for cereal, crackers, toys, etc. Cut the pieces into small, irregular shapes.

A thinner version can be made using coloured magazine pages, cut into small pieces. Glue the mosaic pieces to a piece of cardboard.

Rejoice, O Christian, for the victory has already been won! Alleluia!

Fr. Roger Vandenakker,

Companions of the Cross

EASTER

Melted Wax Stained Glass

Use a carrot peeler or vegetable shredder to create crayon shavings. Crush the shavings into small grain-size pieces. Sprinkle the coloured shavings on a piece of waxed paper.

Use coloured foil wrappers (from chocolate Easter eggs) as a new art material! Cut out little shapes or break apart into very small pieces. Other larger shapes can be cut out of construction paper for a cross or letters to spell "JOY!" or "He has RISEN!".
Sprinkle very small pieces of coloured foil wrapping on top of the crayon shavings, for a glitter effect. Finally, arrange the larger shapes on top of both the shavings and the glitter.

Place a second piece of waxed paper on top. Iron carefully (at a low temperature setting) until the crayon shavings melt. A piece of paper towel ironed on top of the waxed paper will prevent any wax from collecting on the iron. The colourful crayon shavings should blend together, surrounding the other forms.

Create a frame out of construction paper. Place the frame over the design (now encased in waxed paper). Display in a window for a stained glass effect.

Resurrection Rolls

After the big Easter Sunday celebration and after the chocolate stash begins to dwindle, we often forget that the season of Easter extends for the 50 days until Pentecost!

As a special treat and a reminder that we are still actively celebrating Jesus' Resurrection, make these RESURRECTION ROLLS.

Use a package of Pillsbury* Crescents, following the directions on the package. Before rolling up the triangles, insert one white marshmallow, representing Jesus, the Pure Lamb. Jesus is often pictured in white, representing that He is without sin. Explain how Jesus was wrapped in white linen to be buried in the tomb. Sprinkle cinnamon on the marshmallow, representing the spices that His body was anointed with.

Roll up each triangle, enclosing the marshmallow as the tomb enclosed Jesus' body.

Bake in the oven according to the directions on the package.

As each person takes a bite of their tasty treat, they are reminded of Jesus' Resurrection as they discover the crescent roll hollow and empty!

For 7 weeks of Easter, we celebrate the incredible fact that Jesus conquered our sin and even death. What else is there to be afraid of? A scared Christian is an oxymoron.

Fr. Daniel Homan
prior of
St. Benedict
Monastery

WANTED

Would the rightful Experienced Mom Idea award owner please stand up? Lots of people have heard of this idea, but no one seems to know where it came from!   Please forward info to ArmaDei@aol.com.

EMI

EASTER

Saints' Days

May 6
World Day
of Prayer
for
Vocations

1. **St. Joseph the Worker** OPTIONAL MEMORIAL
2. St. Athanasius, bishop, doctor MEMORIAL
3. **St. Philip and St. James, apostles** FEAST
4. St. Gothard, bishop *, Blessed Marie-Leonie Paradis, religious OPTIONAL MEMORIAL
5. St. Jutta (Judith), widow *
6. Blessed Edward Jones, Anthony Middleton, martyrs *
7. Blessed Gisele, widow *
8. Blessed Catherine of St. Augustine, religious *, St. Desideratus, bishop *
9. St. Pachomius, abbot *
10. St. Solange, virgin, martyr *, Blessed Damien, priest OPTIONAL MEMORIAL
11. St. Francis di Girolamo, priest *
12. St. Nereus, St. Achilleus, St. Pancras, martyrs OPTIONAL MEMORIAL
13. St. Andrew Hubert Fournet, priest *
14. **St. Matthias, apostle** FEAST
15. **St. Isidore, the Farmer *,**
15. St. Dymphna, virgin martyr *
16. St. John Nepomucene, priest, martyr *
17. St. Paschal Baylon, religious *
18. St. John I, pope, martyr OPTIONAL MEMORIAL
19. St. Dunstan, bishop*, St. Yves, priest, lawyer*
20. St. Bernardine of Siena, priest OPTIONAL MEMORIAL
21. St. Eugene de Mazenod, bishop, OPTIONAL MEMORIAL
21. St. Godric of Finchale, hermit *
22. St. Rita of Cascia, widow *
23. St. John Baptist dei Rossi, priest *
24. Blessed Louis-Zephirin Moreau, bishop *, St. Donatian, St. Rogatian, martyrs *
25. St. Bede the Venerable, priest, doctor OPTIONAL MEMORIAL
25. St. Gregory VII, pope, OPTIONAL MEMORIAL
25. St. Mary Magdalen de Pazzi, virgin OPTIONAL MEMORIAL
26. St. Philip Neri, priest MEMORIAL
27. St. Augustine of Canterbury, bishop OPTIONAL MEMORIAL
28. St. Germanus (Germain), bishop *
29. St. Maximinus of Trier, bishop *
30. St. Joan of Arc, virgin *
31. **Visitation of the Blessed Virgin Mary** FEAST

> The month of May is dedicated to Mary, our Mother. Mothers' Day appropriately occurs in this month, on the second Sunday.

> * not in revised Roman Calendar

MAY is the MONTH OF MARY.

Mary is the special focus of our celebrations this month.

MARY ALTAR

We can honour Mary by creating a family altar with a statue, holy cards and pictures of Mary. Candles enhance the altar, drawing our attention as they are lit at special times throughout the month.

The altar can serve as a reminder throughout our day to strive for the holiness and obedience to God, that Mary represents.

Statues are adorned with flowers, Mary Gardens are planted, Family Altars get special attention and processions to crown our Blessed Mother become part of May celebrations bringing honour to Mary.

MAY CROWNING

Mary's Month of May is also a time for Crowning Processions and Celebrations. May is an excellent time to introduce a statue of Mary to the family, for the MARY ALTAR or MARY GARDEN.

The crown for Mary can be made out of wild flowers woven into a delicate wreath. A more durable wreath could be fashioned out of artificial vines, flowers and greenery. For younger children, why not make a band out of a strip of white or pink paper, fastening construction paper flowers or tissue paper flowers (see December 12), for a crown to be used indoors. (The size of the flowers may need to be adjusted to fit the crown.)

> See the October section for 3D WREATHS and CROWNS which can be made carefully and prayerfully for the May Crowning!

Light the candles and have a little procession to the Mary statue, where the children can place the crown on Mary's head. Say a Rosary, or ONE decade of the Rosary or even ONE focused Hail Mary, as a family.

SATURDAY IS MARY'S DAY

Make a special effort to go to morning Mass for Mary's intentions.

Month of Mary

THE ANGELUS

Consider introducing the Angelus at special intervals throughout the day (traditionally 6am, 12 noon and 6pm, but you can improvise!). Try using a multi-alarm clock or regular events (driving, washing dishes...) throughout your daily routine to remind you to say the prayer. Strategically place reminder notes throughout the house to establish the habit.

The angel of the Lord declared unto Mary.
And she conceived of the Holy Spirit. (Hail Mary...)
Behold the handmaid of the Lord.
May it be done unto me according to Your Word. (Hail Mary...)
And the Word was made flesh.
And dwelt among us.　　　(Hail Mary...)
Pray for us, O holy Mother of God.
That we may be made worthy of the Promises of Christ.

Let us pray.
Pour forth, we beseech You, O Lord, Your grace in our hearts, that we, to whom the Incarnation of Christ, Your Son, was made known by the message of an angel, may by His Passion and Cross be brought to the glory of His Resurrection; through the same Christ our Lord. Amen　　　Assumed Public Domain

Family Mantle of Protection

In earlier centuries, artists were often commissioned to depict holy images for wealthy individuals. The client or client's family was often included in the image within the folds of Mary's mantle, representing her protection of them.

Other religious paintings depict the client (or patron) either looking on at the holy event or praying reverently off to the side of the image.

Create your own image of Mary, incorporating your family within the scene to illustrate our place in Mary's heart. This picture could become an integral part of the MARY ALTAR.

Choose a Christmas card, religious calendar or other image of Mary, as large as possible. Realistic images, close to photographic quality, work best. Look for reproductions of realistic style paintings.

Select some family photos, making sure that you have a good shot of each family member (they don't have to all be in the same photo). Keep the selected Mary image in mind as you select the family photos, choosing photos with full views of family members sitting or standing. They can be looking into the camera or off in another direction.

Take the Mary picture and the family photos to a copy centre, asking for colour copies. If possible, have the Mary picture enlarged, and reduce (or enlarge) the family photos so that family members are at a slightly smaller scale than Mary in her picture.

Carefully cut out the family members from the colour copies, keeping as much detail as possible within the silhouette. Before gluing them in place on the Mary picture, try a few layouts.

Be inventive! Let elements of the chosen Mary picture obstruct the full view of the inserted figure. Figures can be placed behind windows (looking in or out of a building) or behind furniture or building structure.

The completed collage can be taken to the copy centre for a colour copy or enlargement or reduction. It can be made into a plaque or framed.

Month of Mary

Saints' Days

May 1: The Optional Memorial of Joseph the Worker
Joseph was the husband of Mary and the adopted father of Jesus. He was the protector and provider for the Holy Family, working hard to support them.

Pray for the work of each member of the family and special friends, as well as others we rely on to carry out their work (the mailman, the bus driver, teachers, doctors, grocery store workers,...) Let us pray that we use our talents wisely to do the work that God wants us to do. Say a prayer for people who cannot find work.

✓ Take on a real WORK PROJECT today, as a family. Tackle the garage or the basement or another room of the house and work as a team to tidy and clean. Give away what you don't use, to the poor.

✓ Take some time to redecorate a room and try to get each member of the family involved.

✓ Conquer some yard work, preparing for the planting season.

✓ Put on a big family dinner. Get everyone involved with a different course of the meal. Let the little ones make decorations for the table if they cannot be involved in the food preparation.

Make the work fun for the family by playing music that everyone likes and telling family stories. Take little snack breaks and enjoy each other's company!
When the project is completed, everyone can take pride in the work that was done!

MOTHER'S DAY!
Serve breakfast in bed to Mom on her homemade
BREAKFAST TRAY!

Find a sturdy cardboard box (at least 24"x12" x12"high).
Carefully cut out the long sides, leaving a 1 1/2" border along
the sides and the top.

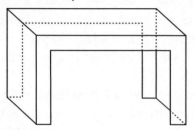

OPTIONAL!
Find a plastic or disposable cup which narrows
significantly from top to bottom.   Standard
styrofoam cups with the extra "lip" on the outside
of the cup work well.   Trace the smaller bottom
circle of the cup onto the top surface of the
TRAY. Cut out the circle only slightly larger than
the tracing (not as large as the top edge of the
cup).
Push the cup into the hole in the tray. Stack a
second cup gently on top of the cup which is set
into the TRAY. Fill with a beverage for Mom.
          OR
Fill the cup halfway with water and arrange some
cut flowers in the cup.

Month
of
Mary

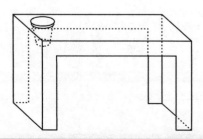

Saints' Days

May 3:   The Feast of St. Philip and St. James
May 14: The Feast of St. Matthias

With the Feast of Pentecost quickly approaching and the Feasts of 3 saints occurring this month, why not have an APOSTLE PARTY!?

Dress up in simple robes and sandals or fishermen gear, posing as different Apostles of Jesus.   Allow everyone to introduce themselves as specific Apostles, explain their costumes and continue to call each other by these names.

Learn the Apostles' names (Mark 3:16). If there are not 13 people in attendance, some guests will need to add to their attire and "play" the role of 2 (or 3) different Apostles.   Divide arbitrarily into 2 groups, standing on either side of a doorway. On the count of 3, each group sends one team member to stand in front of the open doorway, facing the opposing team member. The first one to blurt out the correct Apostle name, scores a point for their team. This activity works best if people are inventive with their costumes.

Eat bread and fish, remembering the miracle of the loaves and fish.   If fish is not a food of choice, cut cookies or sandwiches in fish shapes or munch on "Goldfish" crackers.

Remember there are actually 13 Apostles to choose from, as Matthias replaced Judas.

A P O S T L E   P A R T Y

(See other Apostle Feast Days for additional ideas for an Apostle Party!)

MARY GARDEN

The combination of Mary's month and planting season provide an excellent opportunity to get gardening!

A MARY GARDEN can be designed around a statue of Mary, offering an obvious witness to the neighbourhood.

A MARY GARDEN can also be a subtle arrangement of flowers often associated with Mary providing a meaningful sight to others who share a special devotion to Mary.

A MARY GARDEN can be woven throughout a property, creating a contemplative stage for prayer, perhaps with special markers signifying each bead of the Rosary.

Be creative, choosing the layout and flowers for your Mary Garden. Consider a cross or a heart as a layout for planting. Consider carefully chosen stones to outline the path of prayers within a Rosary or each of the 15 decades. Use your imagination to personalize your Mary Garden.

Month
of
Mary

In the middle ages, names were given to plants to give honour to Jesus, the saints, the Apostles and perhaps most often to Mary.

Morning Glory = Lady's Mantle
Pot Marigold = Mary Bud
French and African Marigolds = Mary's Gold
Pansy = St. Mary's Herb
Giant Mullein = Virgin Mary's Candle
Madonna Lily = Annunciation Lily
Lily of the Valley = Our Lady's Tears

Roses are always a great choice for their beauty and fragrance, while reminding us of the Sorrowful Mysteries with their sharp thorns. Legend has it that the rose first blossomed at Jesus' birth, closed during His Crucifixion and opened once again at His Resurrection.

Any white flowers can represent Mary's purity and holiness.

STEPPING STONES TO MARY'S HEART!

MARY GARDEN MARKERS can punctuate the MARY GARDEN offering subtle reminders of the intention of the garden to honour Mary. They can be positioned within the arrangement of flowers or used as stepping stones along a path when enjoying and maintaining the garden.

Formwork for the concrete pieces can be created out of pizza boxes or round collapsible cake tins. An octagonal shape can be made within a pizza box by adding additional pieces of cardboard set diagonally across all four corners. Experiment with other containers as well. Reusable molds are also available at most craft stores.

Keep a cookie tin, jar (or other solid container with a secure lid) for pieces of broken dishes and glass: particularly those pieces holding sentimental value. The pieces can be used for mosaic materials in projects such as these! Be careful of jagged edges!

Set a plastic garbage bag over the formwork, taping it in place. Lay some wire hangers within the form, bending them and flattening them if required so that they do not extend beyond the expected height of the MARY GARDEN MARKER.

MAY

Mix some concrete or mortar mix according to the directions on the bag, in a large bucket or garbage can. For one MARY GARDEN MARKER, scoop out approximately 2x the volume of the mold, of concrete mix powder. Add small amounts of water as needed and mix thoroughly with a small shovel, until no dry powder remains. The mix should be pliable, but not "soupy".

Scoop out or pour the mixture into the formwork. Stir the mixture within the form and gently shake the filled mold from side to side, on the ground. This will allow any air pockets to be eliminated.

Smooth out the top surface with a trowel, wooden spoon or toy shovel.

Mosaic designs can be created by placing pebbles, shells, buttons, marbles, coloured glass chips and glass pebbles, bottle caps and jar lids and other small found objects into the top concrete surface. Any sharp edges should be carefully positioned into the concrete so that only smooth surfaces remain.

Special designs can be created on the top of the MARY GARDEN MARKER, by drawing into the hardening concrete with a stick, or pressing down handprints or footprints.

Hose down the bucket (or garbage can), trowel or shovel used for mixing or smoothing the concrete, before it begins to harden.

After 24 hours, remove the dry concrete piece from the form, peeling away the plastic garbage bag. Sand any rough edges, and place strategically within the MARY GARDEN.

May 15: St. Isidore *

Plant a little herb garden or the family MARY GARDEN in honour of St. Isidore the farmer. Say a little prayer while you work, as St. Isidore worked in his devout, yet humble way.

May 20: The Feast of St. Bernardine of Siena

St. Bernardine had a great devotion to the Holy Name of Jesus. He is credited with creating the IHS symbol (representing our Lord), derived from some Greek letters in the name Jesus.

* Not found in the revised Roman Calendar.

For a little art project, make a TEXTURED SAND PLATE. Find a clean aluminum pie plate or paper or plastic dinner plate. Create the IHS by gluing string to form the outline of these letters, in the centre of the plate. Decorate the remainder of the plate with string in other patterns (irregular stained glass look or geometric patterns).

Paint the entire front of the plate (including string) with a watered down glue mixture. Pour sand to completely cover the front of the plate, while the glue is wet. Shake off the excess sand. Allow to set for at least 30 minutes.

Use bright coloured paints to fill in the shapes within the entire design. Use black paint or a black marker to colour the string. Allow to dry. Varnish, if a shiny finished look is desired.

Talk about St. Bernardine's devotion to the Holy Name of Jesus. Teach the children to bow their heads when the name Jesus is used in prayer. Teach them to say "Blessed be the name of the Lord" if they hear Jesus' name used in vain, explaining the 2nd Commandment.

MAY

MODEST MARY DOLLS

Some families find their homes filled with scantily-clad Barbies! Some talented sewing-Moms design modest robes and dresses to transform Barbie into Mother Mary! With a little extra stitching...new, modest attire can be difficult to remove! Gradually, other HOLY HEROES can be added, transforming Barbie and Ken dolls into various Saints and Bible figures!

PAPER DOLLS of MARY

A simple figure of Mary, drawn or cut from a Christmas card or calendar can be mounted onto cardboard for extra durability. Cover the figure (front and back) with clear adhesive or get it laminated at a photocopy store.

Month
of
Mary

Cut the figure out and use it to trace modest robes and dresses to change Mary's attire!. Remember to add small tabs at the shoulders and waist of the clothes, so that they can be folded to cling to the figure.

MARY COLLAGE

Saving religious Christmas cards from year to year helps to create a great selection of Marian images. Cut out the various images of Mary and make a collage!

Saints' Days

May 30: St. Joan of Arc *

St. Joan of Arc heard the voices of St. Michael the Archangel, St. Catherine of Alexandria and St. Margaret of Antioch. They told her to help the King reclaim France. She was a courageous young woman who was eventually condemned to death facing false accusations of being a heretic, sorceress and adulteress. She was burned at the stake and exonerated from all guilt, 30 years after her death.

Movies recounting the Joan of Arc story are available, but parental discretion may be advised.

May 31: The Feast of the Visitation
              of the Blessed Virgin Mary

On this day we celebrate the 2nd Joyful Mystery of the Rosary, when Mary visited Elizabeth, the mother of St. John the Baptist. Hearing the sound of Mary's voice, Elizabeth's child stirred within her womb, and Elizabeth was filled with the Holy Spirit.

Elizabeth said to Mary: "Blessed are you among women, and blessed is the fruit of your womb..." and Mary said "My soul proclaims the greatness of the Lord; my spirit rejoices in God my Saviour."

Read Luke 1:39-56.

Say the 2nd Joyful Mystery decade of the Rosary as a family.

*Not found in the revised Roman Calendar.

Prep for Pentecost!

In preparation for Pentecost (celebrating the outpouring of the Holy Spirit), let's learn more about the Gifts that are given to us by the Holy Spirit. They are intended to help us respond freely and promptly to God's Will.

Focus on one or two, each week leading to Pentecost. Define it for the family, pray to receive the gift and talk about how to strive for it, and develop and use the gift. Review the gifts as they are learned, repeatedly, throughout the weeks before Pentecost.

WISDOM
UNDERSTANDING
COUNSEL
FORTITUDE
KNOWLEDGE
PIETY
FEAR OF THE LORD

Gifts

Wisdom
Understanding
Knowledge
Fortitude
Counsel
Piety
Fear of the Lord

Ascension of the Lord

9 days before the Feast of Pentecost, Jesus ascended to heaven. Let's celebrate Ascension Thursday by flying a kite! Let's make one!

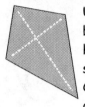

Use bamboo or thin wood dowels to create the cross bracing to fit within this shape. (Vertical = 16", horizontal = 12"). Tape or tie the cross joint securely.

Cut the kite shape from a clean garbage bag or other large plastic bag, so that it extends about 1 1/2" beyond the ends of the cross.

Centre the cross on top of the plastic shape. Fold over the 1 1/2" margin and tape it, securing the cross in place. Make an "x" with tape on the plastic shape at the location of the intersection of the cross.

Decorate the other side of the kite with tissue paper shapes. Add a 6' tail of string, tying bows of tissue paper at regular 4-6" intervals.

Find an empty liquid detergent bottle (or other small plastic bottle). Make a hole in the base of the bottle. Thread the end of the string through the hole and out the neck of the bottle and tie a knot securely. Wind about a hundred feet of string around the bottle, tying the other end around the cross joint through a hole made on the plastic shape (through the "x"). The "x" made with tape serves as reinforcement for the hole.

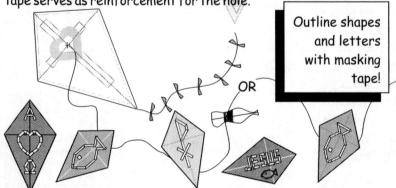

OR

Outline shapes and letters with masking tape!

From two double pages of newspaper taped together as shown (or from a large plastic bag), cut a symmetrical shape similar to the drawing shown. Add extra support to the kite by adding tape around the entire edge and along the dotted lines.

Securely tape bamboo or thin dowel along the 2 outer vertical lines.

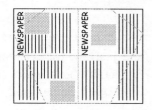

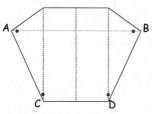

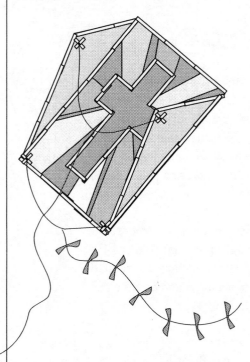

Make a small "x" at each of the points marked A, B, C and D. Make a small hole at the centre of each of the "x" marks. Securely fix 5' of string from point A to B, Securely fix a 2' piece of string from C to D.

Securely tie a 6' tail (with tissue bows) to the centre point of the 2' string linking C to D.

Decorate the kite with paint for the newspaper version or with coloured tissue paper for the plastic bag version.

Wrap about one hundred feet of string around a plastic bottle (as previously mentioned in other kite directions). Secure the other end of the fly line to the centre point of the 5' string linking A to B.

Ascension of the Lord

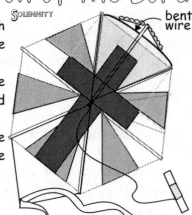

bent wire

This is a colourful kite made with tissue paper, wood, string, wire and glue (and tape for repairs!).
1/2"x1/8" bass wood pieces are intersected in the centre, secured with a small screw.
String outlines the shape of the kite, secured at the ends of the wood pieces.

bent wire

Additional string is tied between wood members and the string outline to divide the surface of the kite into sections. Each section is covered with a different piece of tissue paper. The edge of the tissue paper is wrapped and glued around the string and subsequent pieces of tissue paper are glued to each other.

2" wide pieces of tissue paper or "hummers" are folded and glued around string and tied to the back side of the kite. The long edge is scalloped. These pieces make a humming sound as they flap in the wind.

This award goes to the Brine family in Ottawa, Ontario for their kite design! Richard, Kerry, Isaiah, Evelyn and Evangeline create a different kite each year and fly it on Good Friday.

EMI

Ascension of the Lord

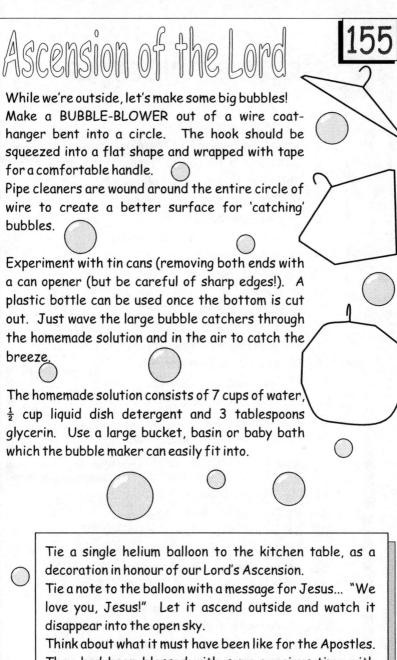

While we're outside, let's make some big bubbles! Make a BUBBLE-BLOWER out of a wire coat-hanger bent into a circle. The hook should be squeezed into a flat shape and wrapped with tape for a comfortable handle.

Pipe cleaners are wound around the entire circle of wire to create a better surface for 'catching' bubbles.

Experiment with tin cans (removing both ends with a can opener (but be careful of sharp edges!). A plastic bottle can be used once the bottom is cut out. Just wave the large bubble catchers through the homemade solution and in the air to catch the breeze.

The homemade solution consists of 7 cups of water, $\frac{1}{2}$ cup liquid dish detergent and 3 tablespoons glycerin. Use a large bucket, basin or baby bath which the bubble maker can easily fit into.

Tie a single helium balloon to the kitchen table, as a decoration in honour of our Lord's Ascension.

Tie a note to the balloon with a message for Jesus... "We love you, Jesus!" Let it ascend outside and watch it disappear into the open sky.

Think about what it must have been like for the Apostles. They had been blessed with some precious time with Jesus after His Resurrection. When the time came for Jesus to ascend into heaven, they needed to say good-bye. Once again, they found themselves alone, not yet empowered by the Holy Spirit...but wait until Pentecost!

Saints' Days

1. St. Justin, martyr MEMORIAL
2. St. Marcellinus, St. Peter, martyrs OPTIONAL MEMORIAL
3. St. Charles Lwanga and Companions, martyrs MEMORIAL
4. St. Francis Caracciolo, religious *
5. St. Boniface, bishop, martyr MEMORIAL
6. St. Norbert, bishop OPTIONAL MEMORIAL
7. St. Robert of Newminster, abbot *
8. St. Medard, bishop *
9. St. Ephrem, deacon, doctor OPTIONAL MEMORIAL
10. St. Landericus (Landry), bishop *
11. St. Barnabas, apostle MEMORIAL
12. St. Guy (Vignotelli) of Cortona, priest *
13. **St. Anthony of Padua, priest, doctor** MEMORIAL
14. St. Methodius, partriarch *
15. St. Germaine Cousin, virgin *
16. St. John Francis Regis, priest *
17. St. Harvey, abbot *
18. St. Gregory Barbarigo, bishop *
19. St. Romuald, abbot OPTIONAL MEMORIAL
20. St. Silverius, pope, martyr *
21. St. Aloysius Gonzaga, religious MEMORIAL
22. St. Paulinus of Nola, bishop OPTIONAL MEMORIAL
22. St. John Fisher, bishop, martyr OPTIONAL MEMORIAL
22. St. Thomas More, martyr OPTIONAL MEMORIAL
23. St. Ethelreda (Audry), virgin *
24. **Birth of John the Baptist** SOLEMNITY
25. St. Prosper of Reggio, bishop *
26. St. Anthelm, bishop *
27. St. Cyril of Alexandria, bishop, doctor OPTIONAL MEMORIAL
28. St. Irenaeus, bishop, martyr MEMORIAL
29. **St. Peter, St. Paul, apostles** SOLEMNITY
30. First Martyrs of the Church of Rome OPTIONAL MEMORIAL

We celebrate Father's Day within the month of June, on the 3rd Sunday.

Pentecost

The Feast of Pentecost is here! Pentecost marks the day that the Apostles were baptized with the Holy Spirit, and "clothed with power from on high" (Luke 24:49), equipped to pass on the Good News.

PRAISES PHRASES

Praise God!

The Apostles were filled with the Holy Spirit as tongues of fire came to rest on each one of them. They began to speak in different languages. (Acts 2:3-4)

Amen!

Think of some phrases which give praise to God. ("Praise God", "Alleluia", "Glory to you, Lord"...)
In honour of Pentecost, research how such phrases could be expressed in other languages. Record these phrases on little pieces of paper and scatter them around the dinner table for everyone to find. Take turns attempting to read them out loud.

ALLELUIA

ALLELUIA

German

These pieces of paper could be planted within a PENTECOST PINATA. Add dove wings, tail and head (made out of paper) to a simple round shape pinata (or uncovered balloon) to create the dove pinata. The papers could be in the shape of "tongues of fire" and inserted within the pinata form. If an "uncovered" balloon is used, the papers are tucked inside before it is blown up.

If preferable, write only the names of different languages on pieces of paper and allow each person to choose one and research a PRAISE PHRASE in that language. Add to the collection over the years.

Pentecost marks the day the Holy Spirit empowered the first Apostles to spread the Word of Jesus. The Feast may also be considered the day that the Church began! Make a birthday cake to celebrate.

DOUGH DOVES

Make doves (symbolizing the Holy Spirit), out of bread dough (or firm, white cookie dough!) Shape a handful of dough into a 1" x 3" form, loosely representing the dove's head and body. Twist at the neck to distinguish the head from the rest of the body. Insert a sunflower seed, raisin or other edible marker for the eyes.

Take another 1/2" x 3" piece of dough and flatten it, for the wings. Place the head and body piece on top of the flattened "wings" piece.

Spray with vegetable oil spray or coat lightly with milk and sprinkle with salt and spices if desired. (Red spices are great to reinforce the Holy Spirit and "Tongues of Fire" theme! Bake according to pretzel recipe (using bread dough) or cookie recipe (using cookie dough).

HOLY SPIRIT SWEETS

Make a template of the dove symbol out of paper. Carefully trace the template into rolled out sugar cookie dough, with a knife to get the required shape. Decorate with red sugar (white sugar mixed with a few drops of red food colouring) and cinnamon hearts. Those spicy cinnamon hearts will give us a physical reminder of those "Tongues of Fire"! Bake according to sugar cookie recipe.

Pentecost

Sometimes the Holy Spirit is represented by the wind. Create a wind catcher to remind us of this invisible Presence.

Find a clear plastic bag (dry cleaning bags work well). Create a wire circle or make a circle out of a strip of heavy card.

If the heavy card circle is used: tape the open end of the bag securely around the circle, (creating what looks like a fishing net). Make a small hole on two sides of the heavy card circle to fasten string.

If wire is used, make an "X" with tape on the plastic bag, where the holes will be. Pierce the centre of each "X" for each of the 2 holes. Thread an end of the string through each hole, securing the string around the wire.

Experiment by adding additional reinforced holes at the bottom of the bag, to allow a little bit of the air to escape.

Decorate the plastic bag with red tissue letters "CATCH THE SPIRIT!" or "ON FIRE WITH THE HOLY SPIRIT!", and flames, doves or fiery tongues symbolizing Pentecost and the descent of the Holy Spirit on the 12 Apostles.

Add red and white strips of (different length) paper, for added motion in the wind. Hang the wind catcher (by the attached string) outside.

Through the Gift of the Holy Spirit, Christ continues to be present among us through His Church, and He calls us to make Him present to our brothers and sisters.

Fr. Michael McGourty

Catch the Spirit

June 13: The Memorial of St. Anthony of Padua.

When the people of Rimini lost Faith and refused to listen as St. Anthony preached by the river, it is said that the fish began leaping out of the water in response to his words.

When a heretic lost Faith and stated that he would not believe in the conversion of bread and wine into the Body and Blood of Christ, until his donkey did, his donkey suddenly knelt down, when the Host was raised.

When a thief was terrified into returning a book he had stolen, as a result of an apparition, a custom arose which placed St. Anthony as the patron of lost possessions.

> **DEAR ST. ANTHONY,**
> **PLEASE COME AROUND!**
> **SOMETHING IS LOST,**
> **AND MUST BE FOUND!**
> (assumed Public Domain)

Many people will say a quick prayer to St. Anthony as they look for something that is lost. When the object is found, a Hail Mary is said for the souls in Purgatory, and a donation is often made in St. Anthony's name, to the poor.

ST. ANTHONY BOX

Fold flaps down at dotted lines.

Find or make a small gift box with a separate lid.

Create a second compartment out of cardboard (as illustrated), with the inside rectangle dimensions only slightly smaller than the dimensions within the gift box. Cut a 1/8" x 1.5" slit, centred in the main rectangle portion.

Place tier within box.

Place the cardboard piece within the gift box, folding the flaps down to act as legs for this middle tier.

The top portion of the gift box provides a safe place for any small item: the neighbour's key, the hair clip your daughter can't live without, a reply card for a Wedding (before you send it out!) and postage stamps.

When something is lost, think of how important it is to find. How much money is it worth to you, to find? Decide on a reasonable amount of money that you can part with and upon its safe return, follow through!

Collect this money for the poor (in honour of St. Anthony's great love for the poor), within the lower compartment. Gather the money regularly and add to your Sunday offering or other donations for the poor.

Some people write S.A.G. (St. Anthony Guide) on mail to be sent, asking for the Saint's protection of the parcel.

Father's Day

Ordinary Time

Talk with the children about what some of their favourite things about their Dad are. Explain how these best qualities of their father may give us a tiny glimpse of what our Heavenly Father is like. Encourage them to create Father's Day cards for both their Heavenly Father and their earthly Dads, expressing their thanks and admiration.

Thanks Dad!

...for the way you let us climb all over you when you get home from work, for the way you tell us bedtime stories, for the way you don't get mad at us when we spill something, for the...

June 24: The Solemnity of St. John the Baptist
Born 6 months before Jesus, St. John's purpose in life
was to prepare the way and announce the Messiah. He
was the last prophet of the Old Covenant.

On the eve of St. John's birth, there is a tradition of
lighting "St. John's Fires", illuminating the landscape
and lighting the way for the message:

"the Messiah has come!"

TIN LANTERNS
Find an empty tin can (at least 14 oz size). Crimp any sharp
edges of the open side using pliers. Fill the can with water
and place it in the freezer until frozen.

Plan a design for the can: a star, a symbol of Jesus or the
letters JESUS provide clear messages, but other patterns
or designs can be used as well.

Copy the design on the outside of the tin can using crayon.
Make evenly spaced holes along the lines of the design, using
a hammer and nail of different sizes.

Hammer 2 holes opposite each other at the top of the can.
The ends of a 12" wire can be inserted into these holes to
provide a handle.
The ice within the tin will provide a hard surface
for hammering and will preserve the shape of the can.

When the design is complete, remove the ice by running the can under hot water. Scrub the can to remove the crayon markings. Dry thoroughly.

Place a tea light or a candle within the can. If a candle is used, light the candle and allow some of the wax to drip into the centre of the can. Allow the wax to cool slightly before pushing the candle into the melted wax. Allow the wax to harden.

Watch the design as it is projected on to a nearby wall in a dark room.

Be careful of sharp edges at the rim and on the inside surface of the can, once the holes are hammered!

Father's Day

Father's Day is always the third Sunday in June.

Show Dad how much you appreciate him! See BREAKFAST TRAY for Mother's Day. Surprise Dad with his favourite breakfast in bed!

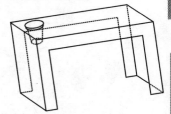

Check out the other Father's Day ideas on pages to follow!

Ordinary Time

Trinity Sunday

TRINITY BRAID PINS

Choose yarn, embroidery thread or ribbon of three different colours. Each colour represents one of the three parts of the Trinity: Father, Son and Holy Spirit.

Decide on the number of strands of each colour for the desired thickness of the braid. (If embroidery thread is used, several strands of each colour will be required.)

Tie the strands to a safety pin and braid evenly to desired length. Tie neatly with a gold ribbon or another colour of yarn, thread or ribbon.

Wear the BRAID PIN, remembering the three Persons in one God, known as the Trinity.

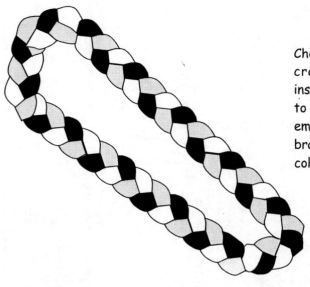

TRINITY BRACELETS

Check out your local craft store for instructions on how to make gimp or embroidery thread bracelets using 3 colours.

Immaculate Heart of Mary

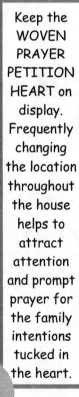

OPTIONAL MEMORIAL

On the Feast of the Immaculate Heart of Mary, we dedicate ourselves to her and ask her to help us grow closer to God. We ask for her help and protection for the world and the Church. We ask her to help us turn away from sin and please God in all that we do.

WOVEN PRAYER PETITION HEART
Select 2 different colours of 8.5"x11" construction paper (red and pink or white work well). Cut a 3"x11" strip from each paper. Fold the strip in half.

Keep the WOVEN PRAYER PETITION HEART on display. Frequently changing the location throughout the house helps to attract attention and prompt prayer for the family intentions tucked in the heart.

Round the open ends (opposite the crease) into a semi-circle. Cut straight lines in from the creased edge at equal 1" intervals.

Weave the sections through each other alternatively, maintaining a pocket inside the heart shape. Prayer petitions can be written on small pieces of paper, tucked within the woven strips.

As math tests, doctor's results and other trials come and go, replace the notes with current concerns. No longer relevant prayer petitions can be tucked inside the heart.

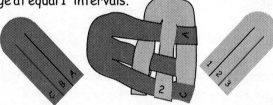

Ask Mother Mary to keep our loved ones in her heart and under her protection.

Ordinary Time

Corpus Christi

Corpus Christi is the Feast of the Body and Blood of Christ. This feast focuses on the Real Presence of Christ in the Eucharist.

Make a special point of visiting the Blessed Sacrament on this day. Remind the children of the need for reverence as we visit Jesus: genuflecting, blessing ourselves and being respectful as we walk within the Church.

A JESUS TOUR of your Church may help to promote reverence through understanding. Make it a separate event by not linking it with Mass on Sunday. Call ahead to make sure the Church is open and if a priest may be available.

Lead the children reverently around the Church, letting them look for images, statues and signs of Jesus. Explain other images of Our Lady and the Saints represented through painting, statues or stained glass. Point out the colour of linens as they reflect the Liturgical Season.

If you are able to speak to the priest, ask him to point out the vestments that he wears: the Alb, the Chasuble, the Stole.

ALB

CHASUBLE

STOLE

Remind the children of the Chalice (cup) and the Paten (plate) in which the wine and bread are offered, consecrated and consumed at the Eucharist.

Point out the Holy Water Fonts, the Sanctuary, the Altar, the Lectern, the Confessional/Reconciliation Room, the Baptistry and the Tabernacle.

Finish the tour, kneeling before the Blessed Sacrament. Point out the lit candle reminding us that "Jesus is home".

Pray for a deeper understanding of Jesus' True Presence in all the Tabernacles throughout the world.

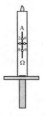

As children get restless at Mass, quietly ask them to try and remember the names of the different vestments, areas and items within the Church. Perhaps they can discreetly count the number of images and symbols of Jesus within the Church, reminding us of His Presence.

Happy Father's Day

DADDY'S CADDY

Use a clean mini Pringles cannister, a toilet paper roll and a film cannister or any combination of small containers or open boxes to make a desk organizer.

Tape a piece of cardboard to one end of the toilet paper roll, to create a container. Cover each container with a collage of small, ripped pieces of masking tape.

A few layers of masking tape wrapped around the top or bottom edge add special detail. Try to keep the layers of tape lined up precisely, to maintain a straight edge.

When the surfaces are completely covered with masking tape, apply shoe polish. Remove the excess polish with a rag and buff for a leather effect.

Staple, tape or glue the containers together, so that they sit flat on a table in an attractive configuration. If additional tape is used to secure the containers together, add shoe polish to the exposed tape and polish once again. After the polish is dry, varnish can be applied for a shiny finish, if desired.

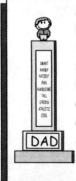

Make a trophy for Dad, using a configuration of small boxes (medicine, chocolate, film and food boxes). Wrap individual boxes with solid coloured paper such as kraft paper. Glue the boxes, one on top of the other, beginning with the largest box. Add a small rectangle of a different coloured paper, to record the name of the award, achievements, favourite qualities and characteristics of Dad. If possible, attach a small male figure on the top to represent Dad, choosing either to make one out of play dough or borrowing a toy figure.

Sacred Heart of Jesus

SOLEMNITY

The Feast of the Sacred Heart of Jesus reminds us of the depth of His love. He was willing to die on the cross for each one of us.

Create a smaller version of the WOVEN HEART as described on the Feast of the Immaculate Heart of Mary. Use strips of red and white construction paper (6"x1.5"), cutting slits at $\frac{1}{2}$ " intervals from the folded edge.

When the heart is woven together, the opening at the top will provide a pocket to hold messages. Either write directly on the inside (woven) surfaces of the heart or plant special messages on folded notepaper inside the pocket.

"JESUS LOVES YOU"
This Feast of the Sacred Heart of Jesus
is for YOU!

Sneak the special gift into a lunchbox, briefcase or book so that your " special someone" will find it today!

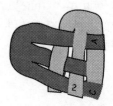

Ordinary
Time

June 29: The Solemnity of St. Peter and St. Paul

Peter and Paul are two very important characters from the Early Church. Peter was the most frequently mentioned member of the original 12 Apostles, who traveled with Jesus throughout His public ministry and could testify to the Resurrection. Paul was converted, from a strict Jew who persecuted Christians to the greatest missionary of Christianity; the Apostle of the Gentiles. He is the author of most of the Letters of the New Testament.

Peter was a fisherman when Jesus called him, and both Peter and Paul became "fishers of men".

Write messages giving scriptural references mentioning Peter or Paul, or references from Paul's Letters in the Bible.

Write other notes revealing a hiding place where a specific candy or treat is hidden. Write other messages of nice things to do ("Give someone a backrub" "Tell someone what you love about Jesus" "Give someone a compliment").

The messages can be written on construction paper, cut out into the shape of little fish. Place the messages in sealable plastic bags (or have them laminated). Use a net on a pole to fish them out of a kiddy pool (or bathtub) or attach magnets to the end of a string tied to the pole and to each message. (The magnet can become the "eye" of the fish cutout.)

Take turns fishing out the little bags (one at a time) and carrying out the messages (reading scriptural text out loud, hunting for hidden treats and carrying out nice deeds).

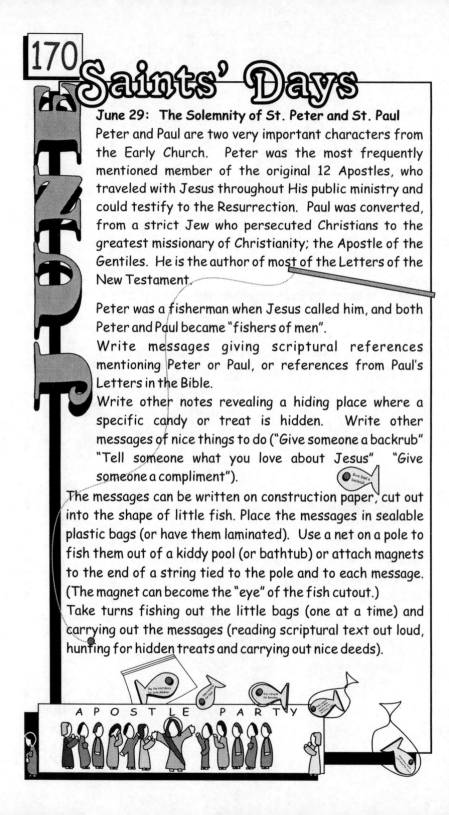

APOSTLE PARTY

A P O S T L E   P A R T Y

St. Peter is also known to be the patron saint of foot trouble. Take advantage of the warm weather with a FOOT APPRECIATION DAY.

Run around in bare feet.

With a kiddy pool or hose nearby, take turns stepping in paint (poured into old pie plates or disposable dinner plates) and walking on a few large pieces of paper or canvas, outside. Ensure that everyone's footprints are clearly visible and allow it to dry.

Use it as a table cloth for the dinner table. Save it in a safe place for a precious memento for years to come.

Layer it with older sets of feet, by repeating the exercise each year with the same piece of canvas. Use a different colour of paint each time and be sure to record the date including the year.

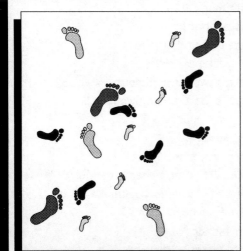

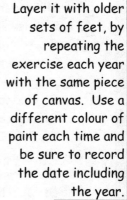

Ordinary Time

1. St. Thierry (Theodoric), abbot *
1. Blessed Junipero Serra OPTIONAL MEMORIAL
2. St. Bernardino Realino, priest *
3. **St. Thomas, apostle** FEAST
4. St. Elizabeth of Portugal OPTIONAL MEMORIAL
5. St. Anthony Zaccaria, priest OPTIONAL MEMORIAL
5. St. Athanasius the Athonite, abbot *
6. St. Maria Goretti, virgin, martyr OPTIONAL MEMORIAL
7. Blessed Ralph Milner, Roger Dickenson, martyrs *
8. St. Grimbald, abbot *
9. St. Veronica Giuliani, virgin *
10. St. Ulric, bishop *

> *Not found in the revised Roman Calendar.

11. **St. Benedict, abbot** MEMORIAL
12. St. John Gualbert, abbot *
13. St. Henry II, emperor OPTIONAL MEMORIAL
14. St. Camillus de Lellis, priest OPTIONAL MEMORIAL
14. Blessed Kateri Tekakwitha MEMORIAL
15. St. Bonaventure, bishop, doctor MEMORIAL
16. Our Lady of Mount Carmel OPTIONAL MEMORIAL
17. The Blessed Martyrs of Compiegne *
18. St. Frederick, bishop, martyr *
19. St. Arsenius, monk *
20. St. Ansegisus, abbot *
21. St. Lawrence of Brindisi, priest, doctor OPTIONAL MEMORIAL
22. St. Mary Magdalene MEMORIAL
23. St. Bridget of Sweden, religious OPTIONAL MEMORIAL
24. St. John Boste, St. George Swallowell
    St. John Ingram, martyrs *
25. **St. James, apostle** FEAST
25. **St. Christopher, martyr**
26. **St. Joachim, St. Ann, parents of Mary** MEMORIAL
27. St. Nathalia, St. Aurelius, St. Liliosa
    St. Felix, St. George, martyrs *
28. St. Samson, bishop *
29. **St. Martha, virgin** MEMORIAL
30. St. Peter Chrysologus, bishop, doctor OPTIONAL MEMORIAL
31. **St. Ignatius of Loyola, priest** MEMORIAL

School's Out!

Just because school's out, doesn't mean learning has to end! Summertime may give us a little more flexible time for art projects, outdoor adventures and traveling.

Use messy arts (like finger painting or clay sculpture) outside, protecting a picnic table or patio set with a plastic table cloth. Just hose down the area when you are finished. Invite Jesus into these activities by offering faith-filled themes for expression. Challenge your little artists to depict events in Jesus' life or other Biblical figures or events, remembering the dominance of such subjects in treasured art history.

Create scavenger hunts to add a little focus or 'purpose' to nature walks or exploring adventures. Cultivate awe in the wonders that God has made.

I believe in Jesus

Use sidewalk chalk to draw murals on driveways or sidewalks. Express your own faith-filled messages (We believe in Jesus!) to give some walking commuters something to think about.

During Ordinary Time, we learn from the stories of the Old Testament how to love God, and we listen to all the teachings, miracles, and marvelous events of the life of Jesus and His followers so that we can love Him and follow Him more closely.

Fr. Scott McCaig

Companions of the Cross

Ordinary Time

Saints' Days

July 3: The Feast of St. Thomas the Apostle
St. Thomas is the Apostle who would not believe the return of Jesus until he felt the wounds with his own hands. He is nicknamed "Doubting Thomas".
Jesus said to St. Thomas, "You believe because you see me. Happy are those who have not seen and yet believe." John 20:29

Review the Profession of Faith: our Nicene or Apostles' Creed. Pray for the Gift of Faith, to believe without having to always see proof or hear justification.

Here is another excuse to have an Apostle Party! Check out some of the other Apostle Saints' Days for ideas!

A P O S T L E   P A R T Y

CITY OF GOD
St. Thomas is the patron of Architects. Save empty juice boxes, small milk cartons, film canisters and boxes, margarine containers, Jell-O, medicine and cereal boxes, styrofoam trays and egg cartons. Once you begin collecting, you will realize how many little boxes and containers you usually discard, and will easily create a good collection.

Use these types of materials and other cardboard (intersecting forms if necessary) to make little houses for each member of the family.

Let everyone personalize their house, adding paint or paper details of windows, doors, exterior wall treatment (brick, siding...), light fixtures, mailbox and a sign with their name on it. (A few drops of liquid dish detergent mixed into the paint will help it adhere to milk cartons.)

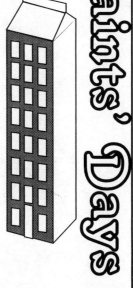

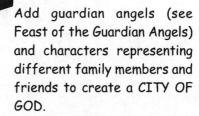

Arrange the houses on a paper mache' or large cardboard landscape. Molded cardboard fruit trays (found at grocery stores) help to create interesting landscapes. Create roads, trees, and other buildings and details to create a village or city.

Add guardian angels (see Feast of the Guardian Angels) and characters representing different family members and friends to create a CITY OF GOD.

CATHLETICS

Using different activities, games and memorization techniques ...

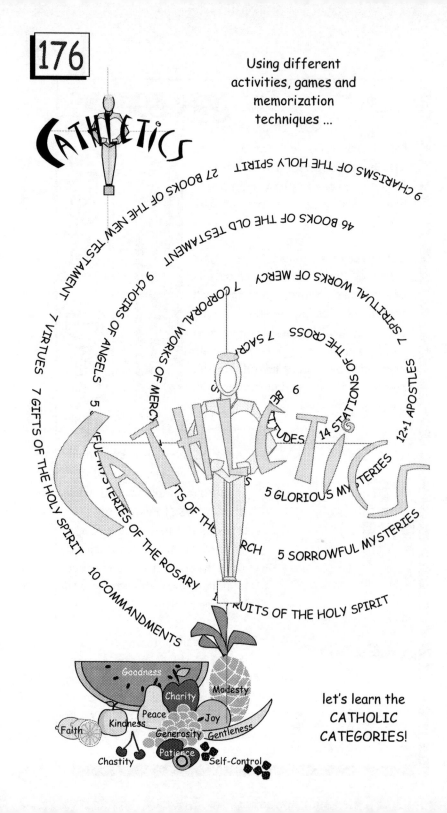

9 CHARISMS OF THE HOLY SPIRIT

27 BOOKS OF THE NEW TESTAMENT

46 BOOKS OF THE OLD TESTAMENT

7 CORPORAL WORKS OF MERCY

7 SPIRITUAL WORKS OF MERCY

7 VIRTUES

9 CHOIRS OF ANGELS

7 SACRAMENTS

7 STATIONS OF THE CROSS

12+1 APOSTLES

7 GIFTS OF THE HOLY SPIRIT

8 BEATITUDES

14 STATIONS OF THE CROSS

5 GLORIOUS MYSTERIES

5 SORROWFUL MYSTERIES

10 COMMANDMENTS

FRUITS OF THE HOLY SPIRIT

Goodness

Charity

Modesty

Peace

Joy

Faith

Kindness

Generosity

Gentleness

Chastity

Patience

Self-Control

let's learn the CATHOLIC CATEGORIES!

(ATHLETICS

Take advantage of car rides to the cottage or to visit friends, for memory games. This is a great way to feed catechism into our little ones while their memories are so eager to absorb information.

Make it a goal for everyone to be able to master some CATECHISM CATEGORIES.

Design a logo for each category. As a category is learned, create a badge with the logo and secure it to a family banner (or let each child have their own personal banner).

Badges can be made out of felt and sewn onto the banner or secured with iron-on adhesive. If badges are made out of paper, they can be pinned onto a material banner or bulletin board or glued onto poster board.

Children will take pride in their accomplishments as they collect the badges.

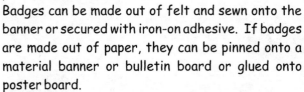

Be sure to refer to the Catechism and other reference texts to gain knowledge of the definitions of the terms of each category.

Discuss the meanings and implications and applications of these terms. If reinforced sufficiently, these memorized terms will stay with them, even if they need to "grow into" the deeper significance and meanings of the words.

(ATHLETICS

Ordinary Time

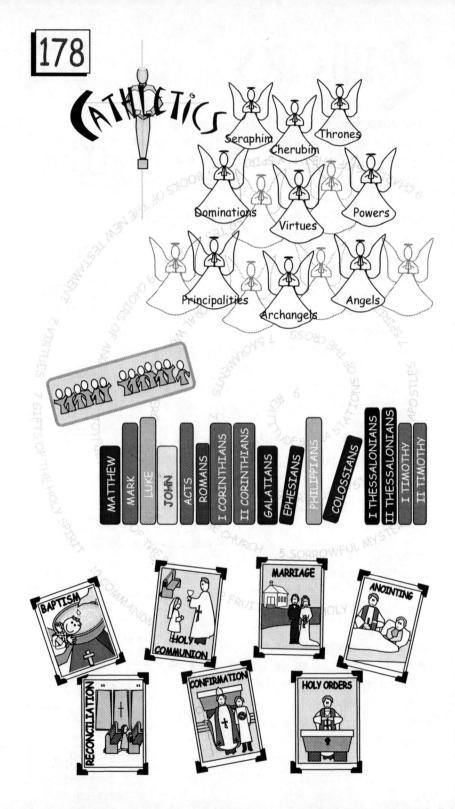

CATHLETICS

Seraphim
Cherubim
Thrones
Dominations
Virtues
Powers
Principalities
Archangels
Angels

MATTHEW · MARK · LUKE · JOHN · ACTS · ROMANS · I CORINTHIANS · II CORINTHIANS · GALATIANS · EPHESIANS · PHILIPPIANS · COLOSSIANS · I THESSALONIANS · II THESSALONIANS · I TIMOTHY · II TIMOTHY

BAPTISM
HOLY COMMUNION
MARRIAGE
ANOINTING
RECONCILIATION
CONFIRMATION
HOLY ORDERS

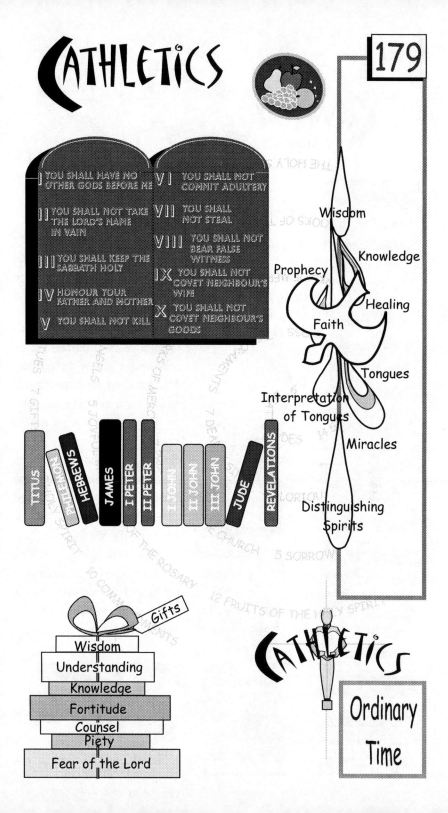

CATHLETICS

I	YOU SHALL HAVE NO OTHER GODS BEFORE ME	VI	YOU SHALL NOT COMMIT ADULTERY
II	YOU SHALL NOT TAKE THE LORD'S NAME IN VAIN	VII	YOU SHALL NOT STEAL
III	YOU SHALL KEEP THE SABBATH HOLY	VIII	YOU SHALL NOT BEAR FALSE WITNESS
IV	HONOUR YOUR FATHER AND MOTHER	IX	YOU SHALL NOT COVET NEIGHBOUR'S WIFE
V	YOU SHALL NOT KILL	X	YOU SHALL NOT COVET NEIGHBOUR'S GOODS

Wisdom
Knowledge
Prophecy
Healing
Faith
Tongues
Interpretation of Tongues
Miracles
Distinguishing Spirits

TITUS
PHILEMON
HEBREWS
JAMES
I PETER
II PETER
I JOHN
II JOHN
III JOHN
JUDE
REVELATIONS

Gifts

Wisdom
Understanding
Knowledge
Fortitude
Counsel
Piety
Fear of the Lord

CATHLETICS

Ordinary Time

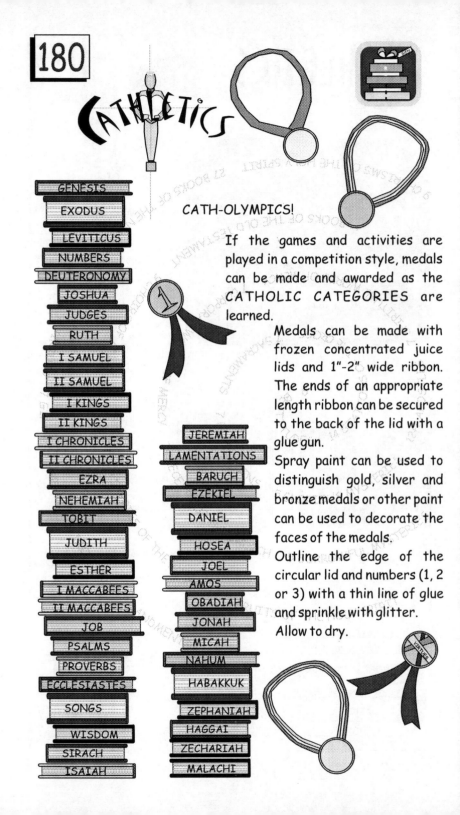

CATHLETICS

CATH-OLYMPICS!

If the games and activities are played in a competition style, medals can be made and awarded as the CATHOLIC CATEGORIES are learned.

Medals can be made with frozen concentrated juice lids and 1"-2" wide ribbon. The ends of an appropriate length ribbon can be secured to the back of the lid with a glue gun.

Spray paint can be used to distinguish gold, silver and bronze medals or other paint can be used to decorate the faces of the medals.

Outline the edge of the circular lid and numbers (1, 2 or 3) with a thin line of glue and sprinkle with glitter. Allow to dry.

GENESIS
EXODUS
LEVITICUS
NUMBERS
DEUTERONOMY
JOSHUA
JUDGES
RUTH
I SAMUEL
II SAMUEL
I KINGS
II KINGS
I CHRONICLES
II CHRONICLES
EZRA
NEHEMIAH
TOBIT
JUDITH
ESTHER
I MACCABEES
II MACCABEES
JOB
PSALMS
PROVERBS
ECCLESIASTES
SONGS
WISDOM
SIRACH
ISAIAH

JEREMIAH
LAMENTATIONS
BARUCH
EZEKIEL
DANIEL
HOSEA
JOEL
AMOS
OBADIAH
JONAH
MICAH
NAHUM
HABAKKUK
ZEPHANIAH
HAGGAI
ZECHARIAH
MALACHI

Judas · James · Simon · Andrew · James · John · Peter · Thomas · Matthew · Philip · Jude · Bartholomew · Matthias

CATHLETICS LINGO BINGO!

Make BINGO cards, placing the title of the CATHOLIC CATEGORY at the top of each column and randomly selected answers (belonging to the category) within each column. Rearrange the order of different columns or use different combinations of CATHOLIC CATEGORIES on each BINGO card, so that no 2 cards are alike.

Choose the answers randomly by selecting shuffled FLASH CARDS. Call out the CATEGORY ("Virtues"), then the individual term ("Hope"), as you would call out "B 5".

Use coins to mark the answers as they are called or place acetate over the cards and use stickers.

As children become familiar with the various CATHOLIC CATEGORIES, they may be asked to define the particular term before they place their marker.

CHARITY
FAITH
HOPE
TEMPERANCE
PRUDENCE
JUSTICE
FORTITUDE

VIRTUES

CATHLETICS

Ordinary Time

Catechism Cube

For each Catechism Cube, cut out 6 large squares out of construction paper. It works well if each square is a different colour. The squares are of equal size (4", 6" or 8").

With each square, fold all four corners into the centre, allowing a consistent 1/8" gap in between adjacent corner edges. Ensure that the folds are creased well. Fold the corners back to reveal the full square.

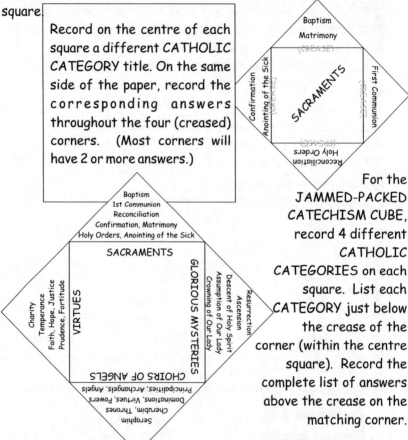

Record on the centre of each square a different CATHOLIC CATEGORY title. On the same side of the paper, record the corresponding answers throughout the four (creased) corners. (Most corners will have 2 or more answers.)

Baptism
Matrimony
Confirmation
Anointing of the Sick
SACRAMENTS
First Communion
Reconciliation
Holy Orders

Baptism
1st Communion
Reconciliation
Confirmation, Matrimony
Holy Orders, Anointing of the Sick
SACRAMENTS
Charity
Temperance
Faith, Hope, Justice
Prudence, Fortitude
VIRTUES
GLORIOUS MYSTERIES
Resurrection
Ascension
Descent of Holy Spirit
Assumption of Our Lady
Crowning of Our Lady
CHOIRS OF ANGELS
Principalities, Archangels, Angels
Dominations, Virtues, Powers
Cherubim, Thrones
Seraphim

For the JAMMED-PACKED CATECHISM CUBE, record 4 different CATHOLIC CATEGORIES on each square. List each CATEGORY just below the crease of the corner (within the centre square). Record the complete list of answers above the crease on the matching corner.

Sit in a circle and toss the cube lightly and randomly to each other. The person who catches the CUBE reads out the first CATHOLIC CATEGORY title he sees when he catches it. As the others try to call out the answers, the reader can check them with the answers written on the adjacent corner(s).

Catechism Cube

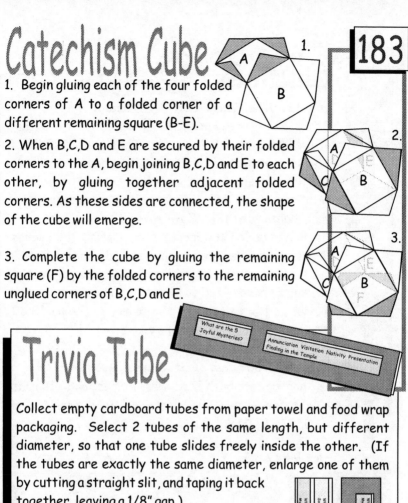

1. Begin gluing each of the four folded corners of A to a folded corner of a different remaining square (B-E).

2. When B,C,D and E are secured by their folded corners to the A, begin joining B,C,D and E to each other, by gluing together adjacent folded corners. As these sides are connected, the shape of the cube will emerge.

3. Complete the cube by gluing the remaining square (F) by the folded corners to the remaining unglued corners of B,C,D and E.

Trivia Tube

Collect empty cardboard tubes from paper towel and food wrap packaging. Select 2 tubes of the same length, but different diameter, so that one tube slides freely inside the other. (If the tubes are exactly the same diameter, enlarge one of them by cutting a straight slit, and taping it back together, leaving a 1/8" gap.)

On 1/4" strips of colored paper, record a question and answer. Ensure that the question fits within a 3" space on the left side of the strip, while the answer fits within a 4" space on the right side of the strip. Leave at least a 1" margin on both ends of the strip and in between the 2 windows. When all of the strips are secured to the smaller tube, cover with acetate for durability.

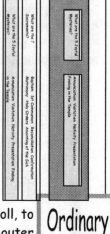

Cut 2 appropriate windows out of the larger roll, to match one set of text (one strip). Decorate the outer tube with paint or paper. Turn the smaller tube within the larger tube, to reveal the questions and answers.

Ordinary Time

July 11: The Memorial of St. Benedict
St. Benedict (the twin of St. Scholastica) is the author of the Benedictine Rule of Life. The basic principles of The Rule (including humility, prayer, obedience, silence and detachment from the world) became the basis of religious life for most religious orders and congregations of the Western world.

St. Benedict led the monks to memorize the psalms. Choose a few key lines from randomly chosen psalms and work to memorize one a day. Continue to practice previously memorized passages to build a collection of memorized prayers from the psalms. (Psalm 18:29, Psalm 43:3, Psalm 68:20...find your own!)

July 25: The Feast of St. James, Apostle
In honour of both Apostles James and Thomas, celebrated within the month of July, consider an APOSTLE PARTY!

A P O S T L E   P A R T Y

Distribute loot bags at the beginning of the party. Explain how all the Apostles left their worldly possessions and followed Jesus, giving of whatever they had to others. Insist that everyone give everything they have (from the loot bag) away to others at the party. Everyone will share, exchanging their treats and enjoying them together.

(Consider other APOSTLE PARTY ideas:
Look for the APOSTLE PARTY logo on other Apostles'
Feast Days!)

Flash Cards

Create FLASH CARDS, identifying the CATEGORY on one side of the card, and the list of answers belonging to the CATEGORY on the other side of the card.

A more extensive set of FLASH CARDS can be made with a little research. Make a set of FLASH CARDS for each CATEGORY, listing each name (within a CATEGORY) on one side and recording a definition on the back. Use the *Catechism of the Catholic Church*, as well as any other available Catholic reference books along with a dictionary to come up with a family definition for each term.

Use the numbers of the Commandments on one side and the Biblical words on the other side of the cards for the Commandment set of FLASH CARDS. The same approach can be used for the 7 Precepts, the 7 Spiritual Works of Mercy and the 7 Corporal Works of Mercy, using various Catholic References for definitions.

The first part of each Beatitude is recorded on one side; the last part is recorded on the other side. Separate the Books of the Bible into smaller subsets such as:

If these FLASH CARDS are to be used with the JELL-O BOX JEOPARDY game, please ensure that they are the correct size and orientation to fit the Jell-O boxes horizontally.

The Old Testament
The Pentateuch (Genesis - Deuteronomy)
Post-Pentateuch (Joshua - Ruth)
The Historical Books (1 Samuel - 2 Maccabees)
The Wisdom Books (Job - Sirach)
The Prophetic Books (Isaiah - Malachi)

The New Testament
The Gospels (Matthew - The Acts of the Apostles)
The New Testament Letters (Romans - Hebrews)
The Catholic Letters (James - Book of Revelation)
List the subset on one side of the card and the smaller list of books on the other side.

CATHLETICS

Ordinary Time

PROJECT: CATHLETICS DEFINITION

THE FRUIT OF CHARITY

THE FRUIT WHICH IS LOVE FOR GOD AND OTHERS

For many of the CATECHISM CATEGORIES, it would be helpful to pass more than just lists of terms, on to children. Definitions of these terms can be memorized by children at a young age, even if full understanding of the definitions evolves over time.

The exercise of researching these definitions can be made into a game, rather than just preparation for making the FLASH CARDS or JELL-O BOX games.

DEF-A-DAY

If assisting a younger child to research these definitions, aim for one definition per day. First, ask the child what he or she thinks the term might mean. Together, search for the definition by looking in the Catholic Catechism, other Catholic reference books and a general dictionary. Your own family definition may be a combination of various sources. Simpler words may be used to make the definition more "family-friendly", appealing to the younger children.

THE VIRTUE OF FAITH

THE VIRTUE BY WHICH WE BELIEVE IN GOD AND ALL THAT HE HAS REVEALED.

DEFINITION DETAIL

Although risking negative feelings toward this little research project, the task of researching a particular virtue, gift, sin, (etc.) may be assigned to children as needed. Instead of sending a child for a "time-out", set the child up with the appropriate reference materials and assign a particular term to be defined. Younger children will need more guidance and assistance.

In order to keep track of definitions as they are acquired and display the progress of PROJECT: DEFINITION, the MOMENTUM BUILDER GRID lists the key CATHOLIC CATEGORIES in need of clear definitions.

BAPTISM	SERAPHIM	CHERUBIM	THRONES	PRIDE	LUST	AVARICE	ANGER
PENANCE	DOMINATIONS	VIRTUES	POWERS	GLUTTONY	ENVY	SLOTH	CHARITY
EUCHARIST	PRINCIPALITIES	ARCHANGELS	ANGELS	WISDOM	KNOWLEDGE	FAITH	THE VIRTUE BY WHICH WE BELIEVE IN GOD AND ALL THAT HE HAS REVEALED.
CONFIRMATION	THE FRUIT WHICH IS LOVE FOR GOD AND OTHERS	JOY	PEACE	PROPHECY	TONGUES	INTERPRET TONGUES	HOPE
MATRIMONY	PATIENCE	GENEROSITY	GOODNESS	HEALING	MIRACLES	DISTINGUISH SPIRITS	TEMPERANCE
ORDERS	FAITH	KINDNESS	MODESTY	MILITANT	SUFFERING	TRIUMPHANT	PRUDENCE
ANOINTING	GENTLENESS	CHASTITY	SELF-CONTROL	AUTHORITY	INFALLIBILITY	INDEFECTABILITY	JUSTICE
WISDOM	UNDERSTANDING	KNOWLEDGE	FORTITUDE	COUNSEL	PIETY	FEAR OF THE LORD	FORTITUDE

Each square of the grid lists a particular term. Loose squares (of the same size) are cut out of coloured construction paper. A different colour may be assigned to each CATHOLIC CATEGORY or to each member or team within the family who is researching definitions.

As the definition is researched, phrased appropriately and agreed upon, it is recorded on the small coloured square. The square is then lightly taped on top of the appropriate square on the grid (listing the term). If the chart is placed on a cork board, squares may be pinned in place.

CATHLETICS

Ordinary Time

July 25: St. Christopher

St. Christopher is the patron of travelers. Legends recall St. Christopher helping people (including the Christ Child!) cross a raging stream. The name Christopher means "Christ-bearer".

Make a habit of saying a special prayer in the car before you begin to drive away (especially on long driving trips). Conclude the prayer with a special request for St. Christopher's protection, to which all family members can respond:

St. Christopher
PRAY FOR US!

July 26: The Memorial of St. Joachim and St. Ann

St. Joachim and St. Ann are the parents of Mary, and consequently the grandparents of Jesus! Celebrate a special GRANDPARENTS' DAY with a visit and maybe a picnic with grandparents (or an adopted grandparent!).

Make some homemade cards and gifts for them! (See CROWN OF ROSES FOR OUR LADY and SPECIAL INTENTIONS CANDLE within the October Rosary pages.)

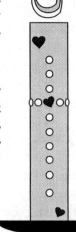

Jell-O Box JEOPARDY

This game will be a much smaller project, once the FLASH CARDS are already created.

Use a sturdy cardboard box for the frame. Push the flaps of the opened, empty box, inward.

Collect same-size Jell-O or pudding boxes. Cut a window out of the front of each box with an X-acto or other craft knife. Use the corner of a book to steady the box at the opening while making the cuts (but be careful not to cut the book!) Insert a piece of cardboard (the same width of the box), to create a divider within the box. This divider will be placed about 1/4" from the side of the box with the window.

Either thin dowels or string will be used to hold the boxes in place. If string is used, dividers will be needed to separate the boxes. Cut straws into 1/2" pieces and thread them between the boxes. The boxes are threaded through the centre of the long, narrow sides of each box. If dowels are used, holes should be made which are just smaller than the dowel diameter. The boxes should fit snugly in place on the dowel.

FLASH CARDS used for this game must be the appropriate size and orientation to be easily read through the windows of the boxes.

Place a FLASH CARD in each of the boxes, between the window and the divider of each box. Allow the definition (or answers) side of the FLASH CARD to be seen through the window of the box.

The number of points earned for the correct answer may be recorded on the back of each box. Each player selects a question box, identifying it by the column category and number of points recorded on it. The box is then turned to reveal the definition to which the player must respond with the specific term to match. The card can be removed from the box to verify the answer (by looking at the other side of the card).

VIRTUES | GIFTS | FRUITS | CHARISMS

200

400

600

The GIFT that helps us to direct our life and actions to give honour and glory to God.

CATHLETICS

Ordinary Time

300

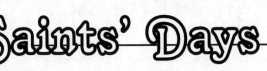

July 29: The Memorial of St. Martha

St. Martha is the patroness of cooks, likely for her choice to busily work to serve Jesus (while her sister visited with Him).

Encourage the children to give their "Busy Martha" (or regular cook) a break by planning a meal, cooking it, serving it and cleaning up after. Help the children get enthused by offering ideas of menu items within their capabilities to cook! Younger siblings can help decorate the dining room and place settings, and add creativity to a printed menu for the dinner.

St. Martha is also known for her deep Faith in Jesus. With expectant Faith, she confronted Jesus when her brother Lazarus died. She told Jesus, "I believe You are the Messiah, the Son of God" and then He raised her brother from the dead.

Continue to pray for the Gift of Faith and the Wisdom to prioritize our actions, values and concerns in ways that please Jesus.

July 31: The Memorial of St. Ignatius of Loyola

St. Ignatius is the author of *The Spiritual Exercises*. Within an intense Spiritual program of reflection, St. Ignatius encourages us to do Examinations of Conscience to help us purify ourselves and make better Confessions.

As an extremely simplified version of some of St. Ignatius' teaching, encourage the children to

SIT, THINK and TH-A-W.

Consider ways we have disappointed God by our

<u>Th</u>oughts, <u>A</u>ctions and <u>W</u>ords.

JELL-O BOXES REVISITED!

The JELL-O BOX JEOPARDY set can be used for a variety of other games.

CATHLETICS

JIG-SAW JELL-O BOXES

Instead of recording the points earned (for the correct answer) on the back of the boxes, use a different approach with lots of colour. Select a Holy picture or create one as a family. (It may need to be enlarged with a colour copier machine at your local print shop.) The image will need to be the same area (and proportion) as the array of JELL-O boxes.

Carefully mark and cut the image into segments matching the dimensions of the JELL-O boxes. Glue the segments on the back of the boxes and arrange the boxes within the frame to recreate the image. As the questions are correctly answered, the box is turned to reveal the picture segment. The whole image is gradually constructed like a jigsaw puzzle.

With little focus on who gets the correct answer, this is a less competitive game.

FOUR-IN-A-ROW

For this version, any decoration of the backs of the boxes will be fine: either the same picture technique as JIG-SAW JELL-O BOXES or covered with paint or construction paper for an abstract design.

The boxes are oriented with the windows facing outward. Behind each window is a blank coloured card, hiding a flash card placed behind it. When a specific box is chosen, the coloured card is removed to reveal a FLASHCARD answer, to which the player must respond with the proper term. If the proper term is given, the box is turned to show the pattern on the back of the box. If the answer is incorrect, a new flashcard, covered with a blank coloured card are placed within the window of the box. The first player to reveal a straight line of four boxes, wins.

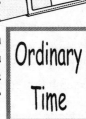

The CHARISM which gives us direction according to God's Will

Ordinary Time

Catechism Playing Cards

The more games and activities we have to introduce the CATHOLIC CATEGORIES, the more familiar they will become!

Create your own Catholic Playing Cards by recording CATHOLIC CATEGORIES on a regular set of playing cards with a ballpoint pen. Remember to press as lightly as possible so that the cards will not be indented on the back.

Use them for standard card games or add a few rules for CATHLETIC CARD GAMES, requiring players to list the CATHOLIC CATEGORIES as specific cards are played.

Allow the Jack to represent St. Joseph, the Queen to represent Mother Mary (Queen of Heaven), the King to represent Jesus (Christ the King) and the Ace to represent the Trinity (one all-powerful God). Record special titles referring to St. Joseph, Mother Mary, Jesus and the Holy Trinity on these high cards.

Theresa Johnson (of Catholic Heritage Curricula) and her family use holy cards for their Catholic Playing Cards, attaching them to regular playing cards with contact paper. They use St. Joseph, Mother Mary, Jesus and the Trinity for the high cards and family member's patron saints' for the numbered cards (for example: 3 is St. Patrick).

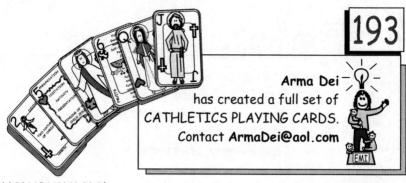

Arma Dei has created a full set of CATHLETICS PLAYING CARDS. Contact **ArmaDei@aol.com**

HOLY RUMMOLI!

Redesign the Rummoli game, using the CATHLETICS PLAYING CARDS! Decide which cards or sets of cards should be most valuable. Create a new RUMMOLI layout on a large piece of bristol board or cardboard.

The CATHLETICS PLAYING CARDS by Arma Dei use different suits: the Holy Spirit dove (Spirit instead of Spades), the Clover (representing the Trinity) instead of Clubs and the Cross instead of Diamonds. The suit of Hearts remain the same, representing the virtue of love.

These symbols create special relationships between the cards.

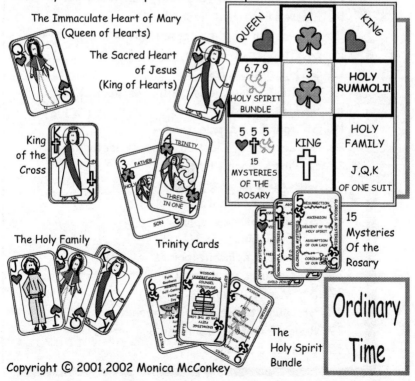

The Immaculate Heart of Mary (Queen of Hearts)

The Sacred Heart of Jesus (King of Hearts)

King of the Cross

Trinity Cards

The Holy Family

The Holy Spirit Bundle

15 Mysteries Of the Rosary

Ordinary Time

Saints' Days

1. St. Alphonsus Liguori, bishop, doctor M<small>EMORIAL</small>
2. St. Peter Julian Eymard, priest O<small>PTIONAL</small> M<small>EMORIAL</small>
2. St. Eusebius of Vercelli, bishop O<small>PTIONAL</small> M<small>EMORIAL</small>
3. St. Lydia *
4. **St. John Vianney**, priest M<small>EMORIAL</small>
5. St. Mary of the Snows *
(5. ½ **Feastday of St. Agatha**)
6. **The Transfiguration** F<small>EAST</small>
7. St. Sixtus II, pope, martyr,& Companions, martyrs
7. St. Cajetan, priest O<small>PTIONAL</small> M<small>EMORIAL</small>

> *Not found in the revised Roman Calendar.

8. St. Dominic, priest M<small>EMORIAL</small>
9. St. Romanus, martyr *
10. St. Lawrence, martyr F<small>EAST</small>
11. **St. Clare**, virgin M<small>EMORIAL</small>
12. St. Euplius, martyr *
13. St. Pontian, pope, & St. Hippolytus, priest, martyrs O<small>PTIONAL</small> M<small>EMORIAL</small>
14. St. Maximilian Kolbe, priest, martyr M<small>EMORIAL</small>
14. Blessed Eberhard, abbot *
15. **Assumption of the Blessed Virgin Mary** S<small>OLEMNITY</small>
16. St. Stephen of Hungary, king O<small>PTIONAL</small> M<small>EMORIAL</small>
17. St. Hyacinth, priest *
18. St. Jane Frances de Chantal, religious O<small>PTIONAL</small> M<small>EMORIAL</small>
18. St. Helena, widow *
19. St. John Eudes, priest O<small>PTIONAL</small> M<small>EMORIAL</small>
20. St. Bernard of Clairvaux, abbot, doctor M<small>EMORIAL</small>
21. St. Pius X, pope M<small>EMORIAL</small>
22. **Queenship of Mary** M<small>EMORIAL</small>
23. St. Rose of Lima, virgin O<small>PTIONAL</small> M<small>EMORIAL</small>
24. **St. Bartholomew**, apostle F<small>EAST</small>
25. St. Louis, king O<small>PTIONAL</small> M<small>EMORIAL</small>
25. St. Joseph Calasanz, priest O<small>PTIONAL</small> M<small>EMORIAL</small>
26. St. Caesarius of Arles, bishop *
27. **St. Monica**, widow M<small>EMORIAL</small>
28. **St. Augustine**, bishop, doctor M<small>EMORIAL</small>
29. Beheading of St. John the Baptist M<small>EMORIAL</small>
30. St. Fiacre, hermit *

LISTS AND LEVELS

LISTS AND LEVELS is a program within CATHLETICS which organizes key lists of terms into tiers. Each tier or level provides a challenge for memorizing; each one slightly more demanding than the last.

LISTS AND LEVELS provides a program structure and incentives for learning. Ceremonies can take place where badges are given and CATHLETIC contestants graduate to the next level.

Use your imagination and keep it fun!

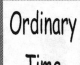

Ordinary Time

LEVEL IV

CATHLETICS

Let kids earn extra badges! Let them look through Catholic reference books and the Bible for additional lists. They can be given the first chance to learn them and earn a special badge!

LEVEL III

3 Kings:
GASPAR
MELCHIOR
BALTHASAR

3 Persons in the One God:
FATHER
SON
HOLY SPIRIT

3 Theological Virtues:
FAITH
HOPE
CHARITY (LOVE)

3 Conditions for a Mortal Sin:
GRAVE MATTER
FULL KNOWLEDGE
DELIBERATE CONSENT

2 Natures of Christ's One Person:

DIVINE
HUMAN

2 Parts of the Bible:
OLD TESTAMENT
NEW TESTAMENT

1 ONE God

4 FOUR Cardinal Virtues:
JUSTICE PRUDENCE
FORTITUDE TEMPERANCE

4 FOUR Marks of the True Church:
ONE HOLY CATHOLIC APOSTOLIC

4 FOUR Gospels:
MATTHEW MARK LUKE JOHN

IV

3 States
of the Church:
PILGRIMS
(on Earth)
DISCIPLES BEING PURIFIED
(in Purgatory)
THE BLESSED
(in Heaven)

3 Duties
of the Bishop
(with the help of priests):
To TEACH
To GOVERN
To SANCTIFY

3 Evangelical
Counsels:
POVERTY
CHASTITY
OBEDIENCE

3 Attributes
of the Church:
AUTHORITY
INFALLIBILITY
INDEFECTIBILITY

III

2 Truths
Revealed by God:

SACRED SCRIPTURE
SACRED TRADITION

II

LEVEL II

CATHLETICS

LEVEL I

I

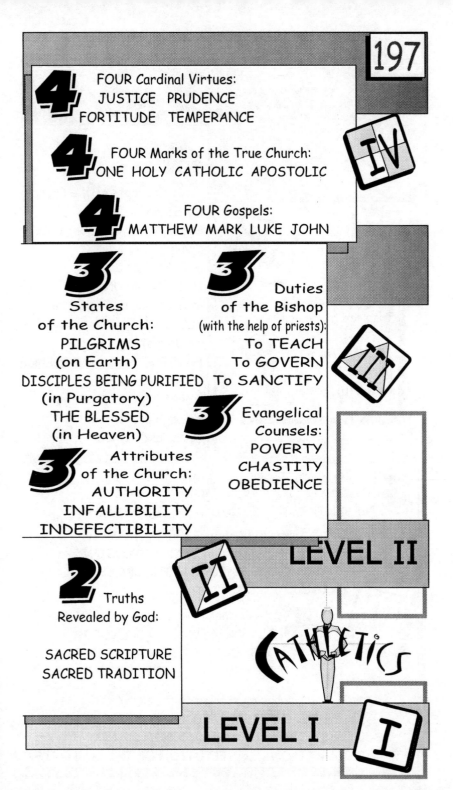

CATHLETICS

LEVEL VI

Inspired by James Tucker's *List of Christian Things* posted on www.catholic.net.

6 Precepts of the Church:
MASS on all Sundays
and Holy Days of Obligation
CONFESSION
at least once a year
HOLY COMMUNION
at least during Easter time
KEEP HOLY the Holy Days
of Obligation
FASTING AND ABSTINENCE
on prescribed days
SUPPORT THE CHURCH
through prayer and
financial donations

5 Joyful Mysteries of the ROSARY:
ANNUNCIATION   VISITATION   NATIVITY
PRESENTATION   FINDING IN THE TEMPLE

5 Sorrowful Mysteries of the ROSARY:
AGONY IN THE GARDEN   SCOURGING
CROWNING   CARRYING THE CROSS
CRUCIFIXION

5 Glorious Mysteries of the ROSARY:
RESURRECTION   ASCENSION
DESCENT OF THE HOLY SPIRIT
ASSUMPTION   CORONATION

5 Luminous Mysteries of the ROSARY:
JESUS' BAPTISM   WEDDING AT CANA
PREACHING OF THE KINGDOM OF GOD
TRANSFIGURATION   INSTITUTION OF THE EUCHARIST

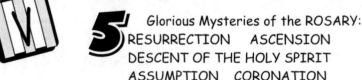

6 Days of Creation:
GOD created LIGHT,
and separated light from darkness

GOD created the SKY, separating the water

GOD created dry LAND (earth),
separated from water (sea) and VEGETATION

GOD created the SUN, the MOON and the STARS

GOD created the BIRDS and the FISH

GOD created ANIMALS to roam the land
and GOD created MAN

LEVEL V

5 Sacred Wounds of Christ:
4 NAIL WOUNDS
in hands and feet
1 SPEAR WOUND
in side

5 (First) Books of the Bible
(The Pentateuch):
GENESIS
EXODUS
LEVITICUS
NUMBERS
DEUTERONOMY

Ordinary Time

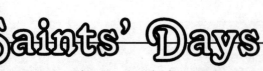

Saints' Days

August 4: The Memorial of St. John Vianney

St. John Vianney is the patron of priests. He spent 10-15 hours a day hearing confessions, stopping only to celebrate Mass, pray (and eat and sleep a little). This priest had a special gift, enabling people to make very earnest confessions: he could tell them of past sins they had not confessed in the past.

Take this opportunity to go to confession, making a resolution to receive this sacrament more frequently throughout the year.

August 5: ½ Feast of St. Agatha

Remember the February 5th Feast of St. Agatha when we celebrate this saint who is invoked against fires? Occurring 6 months after this feast, August 5 provides another excellent opportunity to check fire alarms and carbon monoxide detectors! Appreciate the summer warmth as you host your SEMI-ANNUAL FAMILY FIRE DRILL!

Celebrate a successful FAMILY FIRE DRILL with plenty of cold drinks and a BAR-B-Q ... roasting marshmallows on a BON FIRE (if it is safe to do so in your area).

Create a MINIATURE BON FIRE in a large coffee can (1kg size). Before building the fire, stabilize the can by pushing it into sand or dig a small pit (the size of the can). Arrange rocks around the can perimeter. Use small pieces of dry wood and scrunched up paper pushed between branches.

Drench the can with water when you are finished enjoying the MINIATURE BON FIRE (and all the marshmallows are gone!)

CATHLETICS
LEVEL VII

7 SACRAMENTS:
BAPTISM
CONFIRMATION
EUCHARIST
RECONCILIATION
ANOINTING OF THE
 SICK
HOLY ORDERS
MATRIMONY

7 GIFTS of the HOLY SPIRIT:
WISDOM
UNDERSTANDING
COUNSEL
FORTITUDE
KNOWLEDGE
PIETY
FEAR of the LORD

7 VIRTUES:
CHARITY FAITH
HOPE TEMPERANCE
PRUDENCE JUSTICE
FORTITUDE

7 CAPITAL (DEADLY) SINS:
PRIDE LUST
AVARICE ANGER
GLUTTONY ENVY
SLOTH

7 SPIRITUAL WORKS OF MERCY:
ADMONISH the sinner   INSTRUCT the ignorant
COUNSEL the doubtful   COMFORT the sorrowing
BEAR wrongs patiently   FORGIVE all injuries
PRAY for the living and the dead

7 CORPORAL WORKS OF MERCY:
FEED the hungry   GIVE DRINK to the thirsty
CLOTHE the naked   VISIT the imprisoned
SHELTER the homeless
VISIT the sick   BURY the dead

7 SORROWS OF THE VIRGIN MARY:
PROPHECY of Simeon   FLIGHT into Egypt
LOSS of Jesus in the Temple
MEETING JESUS on His way to Calvary   CRUCIFIXION
TAKING Jesus' Body from the cross   BURIAL of Jesus

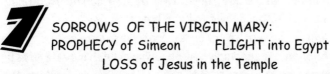

August 6: The Feast of the Transfiguration

On this day we remember what happened when Jesus took 3 of His Apostles (Peter, James and John) to the top of a high mountain. The Apostles watched Jesus as His Appearance changed, reflecting His Divinity through His Humanity. They watched as Jesus spoke with Moses and Elijah, two heroes from their Jewish history.

Let us create something we can wear to represent our good human qualities shining forth!

Encourage everyone to reflect on the Fruits of the Holy Spirit. They are: charity, joy, peace, patience, kindness, goodness, generosity, gentleness, faithfulness, modesty, self-control, chastity.   These 12 human qualities are activated within us, by the Holy Spirit. Let's remember to use them!

Let each person choose one and consider how to practice this quality more fully.   Create a mask, hat or other accessory to express this quality and call each other by their chosen Fruit name, while they wear their creations!

August 11: The Memorial of St. Clare

While St. Clare is the patroness of sore eyes, she has also become the patroness of television. She miraculously saw and heard Mass, even when she was too sick to attend!

Make a resolution to prevent sore eyes caused by too much television! Pick shows selectively. Some families create a token system, rationing viewing by requiring viewers to "PAY-PER-VIEW". Buttons, poker chips or other sets of small game pieces can be used as tokens (handed out weekly), or a TIME SHEET can be used to log in or out TV programs to keep track.

Help children to choose programs carefully.   Help children to recognize how programs which may be cute or funny, do not necessarily reflect family values. Keep the dialogue going and talk about the differences!

LEVEL IX

9 CHOIRS OF ANGELS:
SERAPHIM CHERUBIM THRONES
DOMINATIONS VIRTUES POWERS
PRINCIPALITIES ARCHANGELS ANGELS

9 CHARISMS OF THE HOLY SPIRIT:
WISDOM   KNOWLEDGE
FAITH PROPHECY TONGUES
INTERPRETATION OF TONGUES
HEALING MIRACLES
DISTINGUISHING SPIRITS

LEVEL VIII

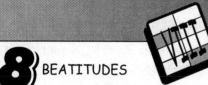

8 BEATITUDES

BLESSED are the poor in spirit; for theirs is the Kingdom of God.

BLESSED are those who mourn, for they shall be comforted.

BLESSED are the meek, for they shall inherit the earth.

BLESSED are those who hunger and thirst for righteousness (or holiness), for they shall be satisfied.

BLESSED are those who show mercy, mercy shall be theirs.

BLESSED are the pure of heart, they shall see God.

BLESSED are the peacemakers, for they shall be called sons of God.

BLESSED are those who are persecuted for holiness' sake, for theirs is the Kingdom of God.

Saints' Days

August 15: The Solemnity of the Assumption of the Blessed Virgin Mary

This feast celebrates the 4th Glorious Mystery of the Rosary when Mary's body was taken up into heaven.

Mary's body was the first tabernacle of Jesus. Talk about the precious Presence of Jesus.

Say the 4th Glorious Decade of the Rosary as a family.

August 22: The Memorial of the Queenship of Mary

We celebrate Mary's crowning as Queen of Heaven:

by God the Father as His beloved Daughter,
by God the Son as His dearest Mother
and by God the Holy Spirit as His chosen Spouse

By these three most important roles, Mary is the most perfect adorer of the Trinity.

Say the 5th Glorious Decade of the Rosary as a family.

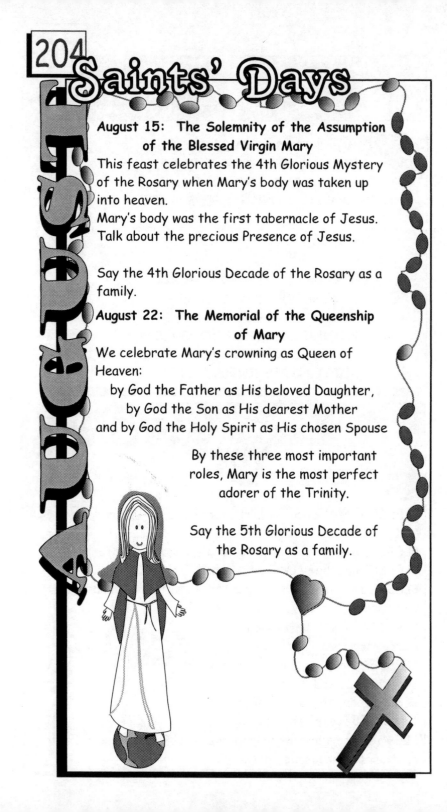

LEVEL XII

12 APOSTLES:
SIMON PETER   ANDREW   JAMES the Greater
JOHN PHILIP BARTHOLOMEW THOMAS
MATTHEW   JAMES the Lesser JUDE THADDEUS
SIMON the Zealot
JUDAS the Traitor or MATTHIAS (Judas' replacement)

12 FRUITS of the HOLY SPIRIT:
CHARITY JOY PEACE PATIENCE GENEROSITY
GOODNESS FAITH KINDNESS MODESTY
GENTLENESS CHASTITY SELF-CONTROL

12 SONS OF JACOB
(FOUNDERS OF THE TRIBES OF ISRAEL)
REUBEN SIMEON LEVI JUDAH ZEBULUN
ISSACHAR DAN GAD ASHER NAPHTALI
JOSEPH BENJAMIN

LEVEL X

10 COMMANDMENTS
You shall have NO OTHER GODS BEFORE ME
You shall NOT TAKE THE LORD'S NAME IN VAIN
You shall KEEP THE SABBATH HOLY
HONOUR your FATHER and MOTHER
You shall NOT KILL
You shall NOT COMMIT ADULTERY
You shall NOT STEAL
You shall NOT BEAR FALSE WITNESS
You shall NOT COVET NEIGHBOUR'S WIFE
You shall NOT COVET NEIGHBOUR'S GOODS

 LEVEL XII

BELIEFS of the APOSTLES CREED:

I believe in GOD, the Father Almighty, Creator of Heaven and Earth

I believe in JESUS CHRIST, His only Son, our Lord

He was CONCEIVED BY THE POWER OF THE HOLY SPIRIT and born of the VIRGIN MARY

He suffered under Pontius Pilate, was CRUCIFIED, DIED and was BURIED

He DESCENDED into HELL. On the third day HE ROSE AGAIN

He ASCENDED into Heaven and is seated at the right hand of the Father

He will COME AGAIN to JUDGE the living and the dead

I believe in the HOLY SPIRIT

I believe in the HOLY CATHOLIC CHURCH, the COMMUNION OF SAINTS

I believe in the FORGIVENESS of SINS

I believe in the RESURRECTION of the BODY

I believe in LIFE EVERLASTING

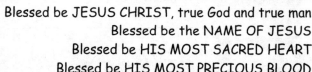

DIVINE PRAISES:
Blessed be GOD
Blessed be HIS HOLY NAME
Blessed be JESUS CHRIST, true God and true man
Blessed be the NAME OF JESUS
Blessed be HIS MOST SACRED HEART
Blessed be HIS MOST PRECIOUS BLOOD
Blessed be JESUS in the most HOLY SACRAMENT of the ALTAR
Blessed be the HOLY SPIRIT, the PARACLETE
Blessed be the great MOTHER OF GOD, MARY most HOLY
Blessed be her HOLY and IMMACULATE CONCEPTION
Blessed be her GLORIOUS ASSUMPTION
Blessed be the name of MARY, Virgin and Mother
Blessed be SAINT JOSEPH, her most chaste spouse
Blessed be GOD in His ANGELS and in His SAINTS

STATIONS OF THE CROSS:
Jesus is CONDEMNED to DEATH
Jesus CARRIES the CROSS
Jesus FALLS for the FIRST TIME
Jesus MEETS His MOTHER
SIMON helps CARRY the CROSS
VERONICA WIPES the FACE of JESUS
Jesus FALLS for the SECOND TIME
The WOMEN WEEP for Jesus
Jesus FALLS for the THIRD TIME
Jesus is STRIPPED of His Garments
Jesus is NAILED to the CROSS
Jesus DIES on the CROSS
Jesus is TAKEN DOWN from the CROSS
Jesus is BURIED in the TOMB

Ordinary Time

August 24: The Feast of St. Bartholomew
Look for the APOSTLE PARTY logo for ideas to celebrate this Feast!

With the Feasts of St. Monica and her son, St. Augustine so close together, a Mom-and-Son event is definitely in order. Go on a special little outing together and enjoy each other's company!

August 27: The Memorial of St. Monica
St. Monica is remembered as having a stressful life, between her ill-tempered husband and rebellious son! Through persistent prayer and sacrifice, and her patience and gentleness, St. Monica's husband converted before he died and her rebellious son was also converted and became a bishop and doctor of the Church, and eventually a saint as well!
With patience and gentleness, St. Monica reminds us to pray for others, even when they are difficult to get along with. She offers us hope in our prayer for those who stray from Jesus.

This day may also be considered another "Mother's Day". Offer prayers for all mothers including pregnant first time moms!

AUGUST

August 28:   The Memorial of St. Augustine

The son of St. Monica, St. Augustine was a rebellious teen experimenting in various immoral behaviour and questionable philosophies. With his mother quietly praying for him in the background and his career drawing him to Milan where he encountered the sermons of St. Ambrose, St. Augustine was led to conversion.

St. Augustine recognized that through his rebellious lifestyle he had been searching for the meaning of real love in all the wrong places. Within his extensive writings, he wrote:

"You were within me, but I was outside, and it was there that I searched for you. You were with me, but I was not with You."

Consider how God is within us even when we stray from Him. Pray for constant reminders of His Presence and the strength and courage to please Him in all that we do.

Consider placing religious artwork around the house in an effort to provide reminders of God's Presence.   Frequently circulate the pieces throughout the house to draw attention to them and prompt reflection. Consider introducing A FEW GOOD HABITS (found in the first section of Ordinary Time).

Extraordinary Events in Ordinary Time

First-time experiences can be so exciting, but a little scary sometimes too. There are so many of these FUSS-WORTHY FIRSTS within the early lives of our children.

There is the FIRST day of school,
the FIRST practice,
the FIRST lesson,
the FIRST goal or homerun,
The FIRST "A" or "B" in a tough subject
the FIRST Communion,
the FIRST Reconciliation,
the FIRST medical appointment or procedure.

Build survival skills for these FIRSTS, respecting the gravity of the event and recording them for years to come!

Along the ideas of these FUSS-WORTHY FIRSTS are other events of monumental impact...births, deaths and moving (or friends' moving...), to name a few.

Create a FAMILY JOURNAL OF FIRSTS & FAMILY EVENTS. Let children record their personal FIRSTS and their feelings about them within the journal in words or drawings. Welcome other entries reflecting on FAMILY EVENTS such as births and deaths of relatives and close friends.

Extraordinary Events in Ordinary Time

Create MEMORY CATCHER CARDS using postcards or create your own out of similar size cards, mounting favourite photos on one side.

Record details of FIRSTS & FAMILY EVENTS. Multiple MEMORY CATCHER CARDS could be used to recount the same event, each written by a different family member. Store the MEMORY CATCHER CARDS in the FAMILY TREASURE CHEST.

Today was Joey's First Communion. He was all dressed up. We had a nice dinner with Joey's favourite food and Grandma and Grandpa came.

Our neighbour Mrs. Davis died today. I will miss her. She always let me smell the flowers in her garden and shared her homemade cookies with me.

Have a family SPECIAL INTENTIONS CANDLE within the home to remain lit (when someone is home) during the approximate time of FUSS-WORTHY FIRSTS, to remind the rookie that family thoughts and prayers are with him. Decorations may be embedded in the wax of the candle as a remembrance of certain FUSS-WORTHY FIRSTS as they are prayed for and completed! Use a hair dryer to smooth the wax surrounding the embedded symbolic pieces.

Actually, there is no "ordinary time" for a Christian. Every day is filled with burning bushes; it's just that some are more obvious than others.

Fr. Daniel Homan, prior of St. Benedict Monastery

co-author of *Benedict's Way* and *Here I Am, Lord*

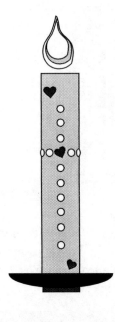

Ordinary Time

Extraordinary Events

The BIRTHDAY JOURNAL is a journal written by the parents (and possibly siblings) about a particular child. The entries are only positive messages reflecting the qualities most loved about the child, the child's accomplishments and special memories created. Entries are written at least once a year (if not more at certain milestones or at random). The journal becomes a collection of love letters to the child. It is a beautiful gift for the child to appreciate, given to them as they become an adult.

Be sure to throw in special birthday or holiday cards and postcards addressed to the child. Try to date all entries.

Caroline McLaren of Markham Ontario writes a letter to each child for each birthday and Sacrament, saving the letters in a shoebox for a thoughtful gift to be given at a later adult milestone (18th or 21st birthday, marriage, first baby...).

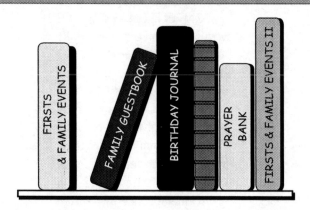

The FAMILY GUESTBOOK is a collection of contributions from special family and friends. The entries are thoughtful and meaningful and cherished for years to come. Family events (surprise birthday parties and anniversary celebrations) may be deserving of a few pages woven throughout the book as well!

Extraordinary Events

The CALENDAR SCROLL is used to record important dates: FUSS-WORTHY FIRSTS and other FAMILY EVENTS like births, Sacraments, deaths and moving.

Use a roll of parchment paper, blank cupboard liner, or trace paper: any roll of paper that can easily be written on. Computer (banner) paper (with pages still connected) can be used as well. If a roll of paper is not available, 12 pages of paper can be taped together at the seams in a long banner.

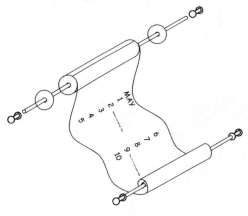

Find 2 cardboard (paper towel/food wrap) rolls.

Find 2 dowels (2" longer than each cardboard roll).

Cut out 4 circles of cardboard, the size of the end of the paper roll. Make centered holes (the same width as the dowel) on all 4 of these circles of cardboard.

For both rolls, glue the small circles at the ends and thread the dowel through the holes. Secure one paper roll at each end of the paper.

Glue empty thread spools or other wood pieces or ornaments to the ends of the dowels.

Store carefully (rolled up), preferably within a box (which can be decorated).

Record the FUSS-WORTHY FIRSTS, SACRAMENTS and other important FAMILY EVENT dates within the calendar dates on the scroll.

If you ever need an excuse to have a special dinner or activity, take out the CALENDAR SCROLL to look up the closest FAMILY EVENT ANNIVERSARY!

Ordinary Time

Extraordinary Events

Make a FAMILY TREE by cutting out a tree shape (as illustrated), extra branches out of brown construction paper and leaves out of green construction paper. The larger the tree, the easier it will be to record the details with a sharp white pencil crayon..

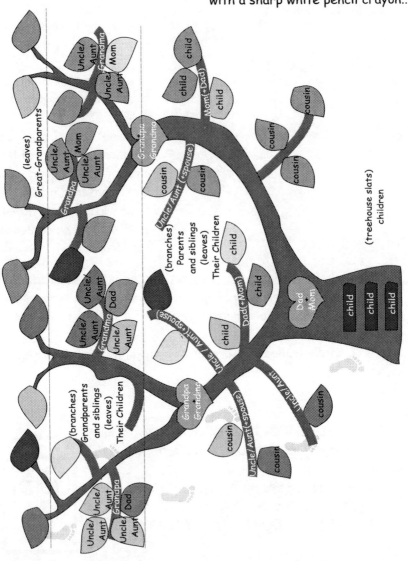

Beginning at the ground and working up, the climbing slats on the trunk are used to record each child's name. The heart at the top of the trunk is used to record the parents' names.

The left limb represents the father's side of the family.

Each branch off this limb is used to record either Dad's name or one of his siblings' names. The names are recorded in order of birth, with the older siblings on the higher branches, working down to the youngest on the lowest branch of this limb. Names of spouses can be added on these branches as well.

On each of these branches, leaves are attached with the names of the children in order of birth from the main limb out to the tip of the branch (oldest to youngest).

At the top of this left limb there is a heart with the Dad's parents (child's grandparents) recorded. If there is enough information (and room on the tree!), the siblings of these grandparents can be recorded (in the same fashion as the child's aunts and uncles).

The very top tips of the tree represent the paternal great-grandparents and the maternal great-grandparents.

The same exercise is carried out with the mother's side of the tree.

Birthdays can be recorded on the leaves and branches, as well as dates of marriage and/or death, where appropriate.

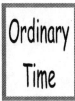

Ordinary Time

Make a FAMILY TREASURE CHEST. Save a short (3.5L) laundry detergent box. Fold a few sheets of newspaper so that one length matches the long dimension of the box. Roll the newspaper loosely and tape in place at the top of the lid portion of the box. Fold a few more sheets into a rectangle to fit in the underside of the lid, and tape it in place.

Cut or carefully rip a 3" wide strip of newspaper, the full length of the open newspaper. Fold into a 1" long strip. Wrap the strip around the top outer edge of the main portion of the box, and tape in place.

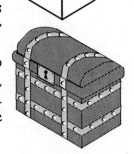

Paper mache' with newspaper strips saturated in watered-down glue or wallpaper paste. Paint. The more detail, the better.

To paint bolts on top of the chest straps, dip a flat end of a pen or pen cap into black paint, and push at equal intervals along the straps. When sufficiently dry, add the same imprints in yellow, on top of the black dots.

A perfect impression is not necessary. Irregular impressions add character and realistic 3D effects.

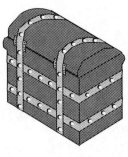

Fill the TREASURE CHEST with favourite photos, newspaper articles and other articles of public recognition of interest or achievements involving family members. Add certificates and awards from extracurricular and academic activities. Add birth announcements for new members and add MEMORY CATCHER CARDS recounting special events and capturing memories of loved ones, both on earth and in heaven!

The BIRTH of a SIBLING

Whether it's decorating, buying supplies or creating a gift for the new baby, try to get the other siblings involved.

Here is an idea for a gift for the new baby which all can take part in. The BABY SURVIVAL KIT can include an introduction to the Faith as well as a Time Capsule to capture the climate of the world on the day of birth.

Include:

Crucifix / Holy images

DREAM TEAM OF SAINTS Info Pack (Holy Cards and biographies of the child's Patron Saint(s) and favourite family saints)

Guardian Angel (see Feast of Guardian Angels)

Newpaper: front page of each section (or whole newspaper), local food flyer, TV Guide,

Special cards, notes and emails welcoming the baby

Welcoming drawings / letters from siblings

The DEATH of a LOVED ONE

Losing a loved one will affect everyone in the family differently and sensitivity reigns over this activity. Let those who want to take part in this activity do so at their own pace, leaving others the option to make their contribution in the years to come.

Encourage everyone to reflect on favourite memories with the deceased loved one, (as they feel ready to do so).

Record special memories or favourite qualities about the person in writing (or drawing) on MEMORY CATCHER CARDS. Collect favourite photos of the loved one.

Quietly collect these precious contributions in the FAMILY TREASURE CHEST, alongside other treasured mementos reminding us of happier times.

Ordinary Time

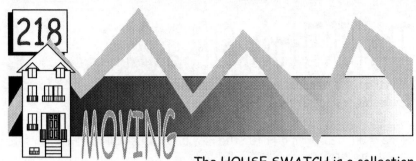

MOVING

The HOUSE SWATCH is a collection of photos and samples to keep memories of past houses alive. It could include:

Photos of the neighbourhood, interior spaces (with furniture, holy pictures and other belongings in place), exterior spaces and views (Make sure you photograph the garden, special trees, memorable 'imprints' or 'scars' on house...before they are repaired!)

Casual family portraits in key rooms in the house (especially where special occasions were celebrated)

Pressed flowers (from the garden)

Rocks (kids are always collecting these anyway...)

Tracings of height chart (if measurements were recorded on the wall)

Wallpaper samples, carpet samples, paint samples (a brush stroke of remaining paint)

Say a prayer for the new inhabitants of the house and all those who will enter the home.

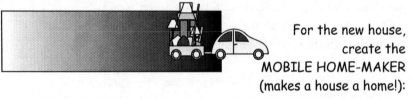

For the new house, create the MOBILE HOME-MAKER (makes a house a home!):

St. Joseph statue
A crucifix for each room
Lots of Christian artwork

A special prayer to read
and Holy water to sprinkle before moving in

Invite your new parish priest over for dinner and a house blessing!

CELEBRATING SACRAMENTS

Celebrate the actual events with a special family dinner, honouring the newly initiated. Invite special guests, select religious items if gifts are given and take pictures on the day of the event for years to come.

Mark all dates of Sacraments on the CALENDAR SCROLL. Refer to this record regularly to keep these dates remembered throughout the years, and celebrate the anniversaries with candle-lighting, special dinners and guests.

Certain sacraments like First Communion, First Confession and Confirmation often take place in the Church around the same time of year (dependent on the Liturgical Calendar). When these dates are close together, celebrate with a SACRAMENT ANNIVERSARY PARTY. Decorate the table with special souvenirs from the different events (certificates, religious gifts and family photos) to keep the memories alive. Special prayers and toasts can remind everyone of the independent events being celebrated. Mention the original dates so that the appropriate family members can be remembered in a special way on their specific SACRAMENT ANNIVERSARIES.

Each Sunday (throughout the whole year) is celebrated as a "mini-Easter", the highlight of each week, marveling at Jesus' Resurrection!

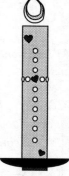

We have the assurance that we will rise too!

Fr. Leslie Tamas

Ordinary Time

As September approaches we confront the beginning of a new school year as well as other extra-curricular activities. As the journey becomes even more hectic, build FAITH-BUILDING ACTIVITIES into your weekly routine. Insist on as many FAMILY DINNERS as possible, and incorporate into these precious moments the fruits of on-going FAITH-BUILDING ACTIVITIES, such as the FAMILY BLESSINGS MAILBOX and THE GOD BOX.

Prayer Time and Mass Prep

Try to establish prayer habits and prayer rituals. (See first section of Ordinary Time).

At least once a day, pray with your children. Introduce traditional prayers alongside spontaneous ones.

> Caroline McLaren of Markham Ontario recommends introducing young children to include prayers of Thanksgiving ("Thank-you Jesus for.....today") and remind them to reflect on what they should or should not have done today (Sorry Jesus for....today").

Encourage children to continue saying these prayers as they get older (silently, if they feel more comfortable).

Select one night per week to prepare (as a family) for Mass by reading and reflecting on the gospel and /or readings for the following Sunday. Read the readings out loud and pause for 10 minutes for everyone to reflect on them. Encourage everyone to record their thoughts in writing (or drawings by the younger ones). Keep these READING REFLECTIONS together for a precious FAMILY FAITH JOURNAL.

After Mass, ask everyone to find the STRONGEST LINK! Was there a common theme within some or all of today's Readings, Psalm, Gospel, Homily and Hymns?

Use the backs of outdated business cards or cut your own set of cards from heavy stock or construction paper.

TABERNACLE

Create one set of cards for each young child who will be using them so that there won't be any fighting during Mass!

HOLY WATER FONT

To simplify things, give only 3 cards to each child for each Mass. They will take pride in their growing collection over many Sunday Masses.

PRIEST

Draw a simple picture on each card of something found inside your Church. Clearly print the name of the item on the card. Colour the picture, decorate the card and laminate it for extra durability.

CROSS

Let the child quietly select one (face down) card at a time. When the child locates the item within the Church (matching the picture on the card), the child can slip the card into an accompanying pocket photo album or envelope. Strategically placed slits in construction paper can hold business cards by their corners.

WATER & WINE

ALB

For Little Kids During Mass!

CHALICE

If drawing is difficult, consider taking close-up snapshots of "things found in Churches", with permission of the priest! Collect from different parishes!

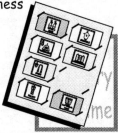

JESUS	LECTIONARY	PRIEST'S CHAIR	PEWS
NATIVITY	SANCTUARY LIGHT	CONFESSIONAL	MARY
STOLE	PATEN	ROSARY	THURIBLE
BAPTISMAL FONT	ORGAN	ALTAR	CHASUBLE
GENUFLECT	ALTAR SERVERS	CHURCH BELL	PULPIT
CHOIR	PASCHAL CANDLE	HOLY SPIRIT	STATIONS OF THE CROSS

PROCESSION

READINGS

GOSPEL

OFFERTORY

CONSECRATION

COMMUNION

BLESSING

RECESSION

Mass Parts + Prayers

For Big Kids!

Use the backs of outdated business cards or cut your own set from heavy stock or construction paper.

Select one-phrase segments out of regular Mass prayers and responses, using a Sunday Missal. Carefully print one phrase on each card (by hand or computer). Decorate the card colourfully with hand-drawn pictures and symbols and religious stickers. Take care making these cards so that the children will enjoy playing with them! Laminate them for extra durability.

"Lord have mercy"
"Father, you are holy indeed"
"For you alone are the Holy One"
"And also with you"
"Blessed are you, Lord, God of all creation"
"Take this, all of you, and eat it"
"Lord, hear our prayer"
"The Word of the Lord"
"Hosanna in the highest"

Shuffle the cards and set a time limit for each child to put them in order. Check with a Missal for correct sequence.

This game is suitable for older children who can read. Playing this game regularly (perhaps in the car on the way to or from Church) may help children to become more aware of the words spoken at Mass.

Ordinary Time

Family Blessings Mailbox

Regularly write thank-you notes to God or to other members of the family and place them in the box. Thank God for answering a prayer; thank a family member for helping with a chore. Words of encouragement and positive messages affirming good deeds or accomplishments are also included in the notes.

Every Sunday after a family meal is shared, read the notes out loud.

The God Box

The God Box is a prayer box. It can be a box kept for the whole family, or each person may have their own. Any small box will work, as long as it closes. It is nice to have a decorated one...decorate it personally or as a family!

The idea of prayer petitions can be discussed with examples of the power of prayer. Everyone is encouraged to write down a single petition on a small piece of paper, as often as the need arises...weekly, daily, hourly(!) and date the requests. The small paper is folded and placed in the box in an attempt to hand it over to the Lord! The box is locked or closed with a rubber band, as we surrender it, out of our hands.

The neat thing about the private God box for each person is that everyone can decorate their box personally and periodically weed through the little pieces of paper. Prayers that have been answered can be discarded. Some people may choose to mark (and date) the answered prayer notes and leave them in the box as a reminder of the Lord's Hand in our lives, as He answers our prayers.

This EXPERIENCED MOM IDEA award goes to M.S. of Tewksbury, Massachusetts. She uses this prayer box with her 7th grade CCD students throughout the whole year.

She secures the box with a rubber band and takes the box home with her each week, assuring them that none of the contents will be read! The box is frequently blessed by the visiting parish priest or brought up with the Gifts at Mass.

EMI

If the God Box is shared by the whole family, everyone is encouraged (only if they feel comfortable doing so) to share out loud what their petitions are and when a prayer has been answered.

If privacy is an issue, assign each member of the family a colour of note paper or insist that notes are signed on the outside after they are folded. Notes can then be sifted through as a family, returning the notes to their rightful owners and allowing each member to reflect on their answered or outstanding prayers. Encourage sharing, but do not insist on it or the box will not be used! Have a good family discussion about respect for privacy and prevent sneak peeks!

Make sure that everyone knows that ANY prayer request can go into the God Box. God wants to be with us for every math test or sickness and every worry throughout our daily lives.

Ordinary
Time

Family Fridge Calendar

SPECIAL PHONE NUMBERS				4	5	6	7
	8	9	10	11	12	13	14
	15	16	17	18	19	20	21
	22	23	24	25	26	27	28
	29	30	31				SPECIAL INTENTIONS

CUT-AND-PASTE FRIDGE CALENDAR

This version uses the free wall calendars which are often given away by your bank, real estate office or other local business.

Select the calendar for the size of the individual day boxes: the larger, the better. Month-by-month calendars will work better than the year-in-a-view type.

Use an X-Acto knife (or other craft knife) to make a clean, straight cut through the pages, trimming the binding and any advertising strip at the bottom of each page.

Tape or lightly glue-stick each month on coloured paper or poster board, leaving a generous border all the way around.

SPECIAL EVENT MARKERS

Design special logos for doctor's appointments, school tests/exams, school trips, special intentions, birthdays and other occasions. These logos can be created on small pieces of cardboard or poster board. A small magnet can be glued to the back of each piece. A small magnetic strip roll with adhesive backing can be used, cutting each piece to the appropriate size.

If desired, a system of colour coded frames could be used behind the SPECIAL EVENT MARKERS to identify whose special event is to take place. These frames can be simple coloured shapes, held in place by the slightly smaller SPECIAL EVENT MARKERS. Special phone numbers and special intentions can be listed and held in place with magnets.

BUILD-YOUR-OWN FRIDGE CALENDAR
Use a large piece of poster board cut to a width just slightly narrower than the fridge. Draw a grid of boxes: 7 boxes wide, 6 boxes high.

Collect at least 40 frozen concentrated juice lids. Use paint, glitter glue, stickers or glued-on paper to number each of 31 lids.

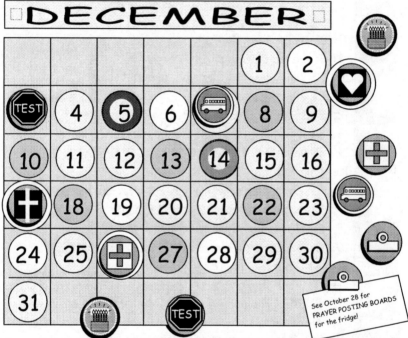

Some juice lids have a slight lip all the way around the rim. If construction paper is cut to the exact size of the circular lid, it can be pushed in place and held by the rim. (Numbers or messages can be recorded on this paper.) Attach a generous piece of adhesive magnetic strip to the back of each lid.

Decorate the remaining 9+ lids with the SPECIAL EVENT MARKER logos. A construction paper circle, (cut larger than the lid) can serve to colour code the event, identifying which family member is involved. It will be held in place by the magnetic SPECIAL EVENT MARKER lid (placed on top of it).

Other lids can be adorned with heavy duty clips to hold appointment cards, permission slips or other small pieces of paper often collected on the fridge.

SEPTEMBER

1. St. Giles, abbot *
2. St. Ingrid of Sweden, virgin *
3. **St. Gregory the Great**, pope, doctor MEMORIAL
4. Blessed Dina Bélanger, religious OPTIONAL MEMORIAL
4. St. Rosalia, virgin *
5. St. Bertin, religious *
6. Blessed Bertrand of Garrigues, priest *
7. St. Regina, virgin, martyr *
8. **Birth of Mary** FEAST
9. St. Peter Claver, priest MEMORIAL
10. St. Nicholas of Tolentine, priest *
11. St. Adelphus, bishop *
12. Blessed Apollinaris & Companions, martyrs *
13. St. John Chrysostom, bishop, doctor MEMORIAL
14. **Triumph of the Cross** FEAST
15. **Our Lady of Sorrows** MEMORIAL
16. St. Cornelius, pope, martyr, MEMORIAL St. Cyprian, bishop, martyr MEMORIAL
17. St. Robert Bellarmine, bishop, doctor OPTIONAL MEMORIAL
18. St. Joseph of Cupertino, priest *
19. St. Januarius (Gennaro), bishop, martyr OPTIONAL MEMORIAL
20. St. Andrew Kim Taegon, priest MEMORIAL
20. St. Paul Chong Hasang, lay apostle & Companions, martyrs MEMORIAL
20. Blessed Thomas Johnson, John Davy & Companions, martyrs *
21. **St. Matthew**, apostle, evangelist FEAST
22. St. Thomas of Villanova, bishop *
23. St. Constantius, layman *
24. St. Pacific of San Severino, priest *
25. St. Finbar (Barry), bishop *
25. Blessed Herman the Cripple, religious *
26. St. John de Brebeuf & St. Isaac Jogues, priests, martyrs FEAST
26. St. Cosmas, St. Damian, martyrs OPTIONAL MEMORIAL
27. **St. Vincent de Paul**, priest MEMORIAL
28. St, Wenceslaus, martyr, OPTIONAL MEMORIAL St. Lawrence Ruiz & Companions OPTIONAL MEMORIAL
29. **St. Michael, St. Gabriel, St. Raphael**, Archangels FEAST
30. St. Jerome, priest, doctor MEMORIAL

*Not found in the revised Roman Calendar.

This is an exercise to consider what burdens and worries weigh most heavily on loved ones and how we can share each other's concerns and lessen the load.

Fill flat bottom ice cream cones with cake batter (to half-full). Bake according to cupcake instructions, checking with a toothpick for proper baking.

Allow to cool.

Gather together as a family to decorate the "torches" with icing, chocolate chips, chocolate bar squares and other cake decoration candies. Encourage everyone to add certain decorations to represent their various worries (size in proportion to the "weight" of the worry). Hershey kisses propped in thick gooey icing make great TORCH flames, representing any main concerns or worries.

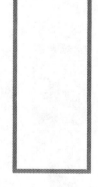

Encourage one another to express their worries, represented on their TORCH, if they are comfortable doing so.

PASS THE TORCH to the person on your left and give them permission to pray for your intentions (expressed or not), while you take on the TORCH and worries of the person on your right.

Ordinary Time

Saints' Days

September 3: The Memorial of St. Gregory the Great
St. Gregory is often accredited with "Gregorian Chant".

Play some Gregorian Chant during dinner or have a family game of GREGORIAN CHANT CHAIRS: musical chairs set to Gregorian Chant! See LITURGICAL CHAIRS in the All Saints' Day Party section.

September 8: The Feast of the Birth of Mary
Have a special birthday celebration for Mary! Decorate in white and light blue. Make a birthday cake for Mary; a simple white one with decorative flowers or a cake from a ring mold, in the shape of a crown and decorated with candy 'jewels'! Encourage the children to make birthday cards for Mary and sing Happy Birthday before the cake is cut!

Genesis 6,7,8

Choose a favourite reading or chapter from the Bible or select one of the readings which will be heard at the next Sunday Mass. Select words from the passage which are important to the story. Create bingo cards out of cardboard, craft foam, construction paper or felt. The card can take on the shape of a key element of the Bible passage.

ox	honor	land	cloud
steal	Moses	sin	Sinai
work	kill	peace	mercy
God	wife	vain	covet

Exodus 19,20:1-21

Jonah1,2

Hebrew	rise	sea
ship	pray	men
holy	fish	son
sister	happy	cloud

Luke2:1-20

sign	Moses	God
Mary	star	fear
Jesus	birth	people

Arrange the selected words on a grid of 3x3, 4x4 or 5x5 spaces. Select enough words so that a random selection can be printed neatly on each card within the spaces. Some words may appear on more than one card, in different positions. Be careful not to duplicate words on the same card. Add a few words not found in the passage to add a little challenge.

Genesis3:1-24

Markers can be used on felt or craft foam, while pencils, markers or crayons can be used on cardboard or construction paper.

Give each person a card with a handful of buttons, macaroni noodles or other place markers. Use larger cards and markers when little ones are playing the game.

If the cards are made out of paper, staple a piece of clear acetate (tranparency) to cover the face of the card. Stickers can be used to mark each space when it is called. At the end of the game, the stickers are removed. (Non-permanent markers can be used to "X" each space on these transparencies and then wiped clean for a new game.)

Ordinary Time

Saints' Days

September 14: The Feast of the Triumph of the Cross
When Jesus' body was removed, the Cross was hidden so that followers would not find it. About 300 years later the True Cross was found.
Constantine the Great had a vision of the Cross which led him to victory. In response, Constantine had the image of the Cross placed on the shields of his soldiers.
Although stolen in 614 by the King of Persia, the Cross was restored in its proper place in the Church of the Holy Sepulcher in 629.

The Sign of the Cross remains as an important symbol uniting Christians in our Faith in Jesus. The symbol of the Cross reminds us of Jesus' sacrifice and encourages us on in our daily struggles.

Teach the children to bless themselves reverently with the Sign of the Cross. Trace a large cross with an outstretched (right) hand to the head, heart and left then right shoulders reciting: "In the Name of the Father, the Son and the Holy Spirit."
This represents the dedication of our head/intellect, heart and whole being to God.

When we bless ourselves before the Gospel at Mass, tracing a small cross with the thumb on the forehead, lips and heart, we ask God to bless our thoughts, words and desires.

Check out WAFER CROSS COOKIES in the Easter section.

SEPTEMBER

September 15: The Memorial of Our Lady of Sorrows
On this Feast we recall
the 7 Sorrows of our Mother Mary:
The Prophecy of Simeon,
the Flight into Egypt,
the 3 Days Looking for Jesus,
meeting Jesus on the Way to Calvary,
Mary at the foot of the Cross,
Jesus taken down from the Cross and the
Burial of Jesus.

Make little booklets, stapling 3 folded blank pieces of
paper together. Encourage the children to illustrate one
of the 7 Sorrows on each of the inside pages. Decorate
the cover with "The 7 Sorrows of Mary".

September 21: The Feast of St. Matthew, Apostle, Evangelist
If the children are old enough to be careful...
Hide coins in a loaf/fish shaped cake, in honour of Matthew the
Tax Collector. Decide as a group (of Apostles) where the money
should go.

APOSTLE PARTY

Make some APOSTLE FELT FRIENDS! See next pages for details!
Check out more APOSTLE PARTY ideas on the other Apostles'
Feast Days.

Retell the Lives of the Saints and favourite Bible stories with a growing collection of FELT FRIENDS. (See the Feast of the Holy Family.)

Concentrate on one Bible story at a time, recreating the most important characters, accessories and backdrop. OR

Take care in creating a particular Saint as part of their Feast Day celebration. Children will take ownership over the Saints they are named after and take pride in their collection.

APOSTLE PARTY

Create a collection of APOSTLE FELT FRIENDS as each Apostle Feast Day occurs.

Felt Friends' Folder

Extra cardboard panels can be covered with flannel or felt for additional backdrops!

A mesh bag can be made to store the collection of felt pieces.

Create a FELT FRIENDS' FOLDER out of a cardboard box. Carefully cut a straight line down each of the corner edges of the box. Decide how many panels are desired. Decide how the folder should collapse, scoring the outer surface of the cardboard (1/4" away from the crease) if needed, for an easy fold. Two of the panels may fold inward, while the other two panels may fold outward (if not removed altogether).

Cut a piece of flannel to the shape of the cardboard, with an added 1" border all the way around. Make short diagonal cuts at the inside angles of the flannel shape.

Place pieces of double sided tape (in the shape of an "x") in the centre of each panel on the side to be covered with flannel (the "inside" surface, when folded).

With the cardboard laying flat, centre the flannel over the surface, pressing it into the tape "x" marks and securing it on the back with tape. Make sure that the fabric is not too tight and that the cardboard can still be folded as designed.

Turn the cardboard shape over. Apply black tape in a straight line along the entire edge of the flannel.

Poke holes at the centre points of the creases. Insert brass fasteners to keep the flannel in place.

CARDBOARD OUTSIDE
FELT INSIDE

(BACK)

(FRONT)

Elastic ribbing can be used to hold the folded panels shut.

Alternatively, separate panels can be covered (on both sides) with flannel. Cut two pieces of flannel, 1" larger than the cardboard panel, in both dimensions. Create a sleeve for each panel: sew the 2 pieces of flannel together on 3 sides (with a 1/4" hem). Turn inside out, slide the panel in and sew shut. A hem sewn around the entire shape can ensure a snug fit. Sew the two flannel-covered panels together, along one long side.

Homemade puppets offer another venue for Bible and Saint stories!

Figures can be traced from catalogues, newspapers and storybooks. Once coloured, personalized and cut out, they are mounted to the ends of popsicle sticks. Felt versions can also be glued to popsicle sticks.

Other figures can be personalized from "single" socks who have lost their mate to the washing machine. Personalize with string, buttons, sequins, embroidery or fabric paint and clothe with fabric scraps.

Laura Owens of Louisville, KY has lots of ideas for making puppets! She recommends a contact lens case (for disposable or soft contacts)with lids removed and marbles glued in the wells, for sock puppet eyes.

For extra stuffing for sock puppets, she suggests fiber fill or dryer lint!

Be inventive! Look for other materials to recycle for puppets: paper bags, pill bottles, single gloves and mittens!

Simple felt (or other fabric) puppets can be made from a general pattern and personalized for easy identification, using fabric scraps, buttons and other small found objects! The seam can be sewn or secured with fabric glue!

Laura Owens also suggests other "found" objects for puppet-making: oval Advantrix film cannisters (just cut a slit in one end and push the popsicle stick in and decorate!) or an acorn used as a head, glued onto a thread spool!

Holy Heroes Puppets

Cut-out puppets can be made with paper, cardboard, craft foam or stiff felt. Holes are strategically cut to allow the fingers to protrude as legs while anchoring the figure to sit upright. An added "skirt" is taped or glued at the stomach to cover the knees for a more modest outfit!

Similar to the other paper and felt puppets, the outline of the puppet can be quite simple, derived from a simple pattern or traced from animated or real-life characters in storybooks or catalogues. The puppet's personality will evolve as hair, facial features, clothes and accessories are added.

More labour-intensive puppets can be made with paper mache' built up over a small balloon and attached to fabric clothes. Just leave a hole at the base of the balloon for at least one finger to maneuver the head!

Cut out fingers from old gloves for easy finger puppets. Sew a small hem on the cut edge to keep it from unraveling! Add felt, buttons, pipe cleaners and other odds and ends to personalize!

Build up the paper mache', overlaying scrunched-up pieces of newspaper with the saturated strips, for the nose, eyebrows, lips, ears and cheekbones. Paint and add string hair and fabric-scrap clothes for evolving personality!

The form of the body takes the shape of the clothes, made out of material. The bottom half of the body is stuffed and closed, while the top half of the body remains open (and empty) for the hand to manipulate the head and arms.

The HOLY HEROES PUPPET THEATRE is made out of a sturdy cardboard box.

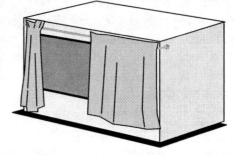

Cut a window from the bottom of the box, leaving generous borders, including a relatively thick one along one length (to serve as the "stage"). Set the box on its side, with the thickest border resting on the floor.

Reinforce the cut edges with black or coloured tape. Paint or cover the box with decorative paper or fabric.

Use thick elastic thread or ribbon, secured at the top corners of the sides of the box, adjacent to the large window to hold a 2 piece curtain. The ends of the elastic thread are pushed through the cardboard with a needle and knotted inside the box. The curtain can be open and shut by sliding the fabric across the window, along the elastic thread.

CURTAIN
(BACK)

A SHADOW-BOX PUPPET THEATRE can be used with simple outline puppets. These puppets do not require any detail other than a silhouette! They are secured to thin dowels or wood skewers, horizontally at their midpoint.

A desk lamp is set up at the rear opening of the theatre. The front window is covered with light fabric or tissue paper.

The puppets enter the theatre and are manipulated through vertical slits on both sides of the box.

Holy Cards

Holy cards help to pass on our rich Tradition and intercession with the Saints, prompting imaginations with these familiar images. Encourage your children to collect Holy Cards as you add to their collection on birthdays, NAMEDAYS, BAPDAYS and other Saints' days and Feast days. Holy cards can be protected in photo albums for easy access or hung in picture frames.

Make a HOLY HERO ALBUM for Mass. Collect Holy Cards in a mini album. Point at the various Holy Heroes throughout the album, as children get restless. Over time, ask them to identify the different Saints.

Holy Card Memory Game

Duplicates of Holy Cards can be used in this special way. Secure the cards to thicker paper or cardboard with photo corner mounts or tuck the corners of the Holy cards into diagonal slits made in the corners of the cardboard or paper cards. Alternatively, tape or glue can be used if you are not worried about damaging the cards.

Turn them over randomly with the Holy Card image side down and try to choose matching pairs, identifying the pairs by the name of the Saint or image.

Little medals are available in honour of many Saints. Encourage a collection of HOLY MEDALS by building a HOLY MEDAL BRACELET, adding medals to a chain bracelet (much like a "charm bracelet").

Ordinary Time

Saints' Days

September 27: The Memorial of St. Vincent de Paul
Schedule an annual clothes drive in your home! Sort through closets, encouraging everyone to get rid of as many articles of clothing as possible. Select a reasonable time frame within which if it hasn't been worn, give it away!

Roll coins from all the piggy banks and loose coins throughout the house. Convert to cash and donate some or all to the St. Vincent de Paul box at Church!

September 29: The Feast of the Archangels:
St. Michael, St. Gabriel, St. Raphael
The original SUPER HEROES! The Transcendent Trio:

St. Michael, whose name means "Who is like God?", brings justice and strength as he guards God's people in the Book of Daniel. He is credited with winning the battle against Satan.

St. Gabriel, whose name means "strength of God" seems to be the key messenger, explaining visions (to Daniel) and announcing future events to Zechariah (regarding the birth of John the Baptist) and to Mary regarding the birth of Jesus.

St. Raphael's name means "God's healing". He is credited with the healing of Tobit and the success of Tobit's journey.

We are encouraged to pray to the Archangels for their guidance and assistance.

Pray to St. Michael in times of temptation.
Pray to St. Gabriel when discerning God's Will.
Pray to St. Raphael in times of sickness.

Add these SAINTLY SUPER HEROES to your FAMILY DREAM TEAM OF SAINTS and your FELT FRIENDS collection!

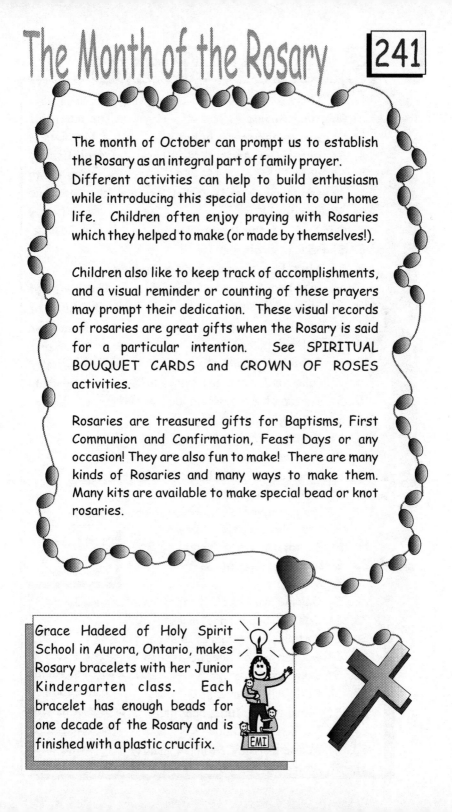

The month of October can prompt us to establish the Rosary as an integral part of family prayer. Different activities can help to build enthusiasm while introducing this special devotion to our home life. Children often enjoy praying with Rosaries which they helped to make (or made by themselves!).

Children also like to keep track of accomplishments, and a visual reminder or counting of these prayers may prompt their dedication. These visual records of rosaries are great gifts when the Rosary is said for a particular intention. See SPIRITUAL BOUQUET CARDS and CROWN OF ROSES activities.

Rosaries are treasured gifts for Baptisms, First Communion and Confirmation, Feast Days or any occasion! They are also fun to make! There are many kinds of Rosaries and many ways to make them. Many kits are available to make special bead or knot rosaries.

Grace Hadeed of Holy Spirit School in Aurora, Ontario, makes Rosary bracelets with her Junior Kindergarten class. Each bracelet has enough beads for one decade of the Rosary and is finished with a plastic crucifix.

Saints' Days

1. **St. Theresa of the Child Jesus**, virgin, doctor MEMORIAL
2. **Guardian Angels** MEMORIAL
3. St. Gerard of Brogne, abbot *
4. **St. Francis of Assisi** MEMORIAL
5. St. Flora *
6. Blessed Marie-Rose Durocher OPTIONAL MEMORIAL
6. St. Bruno OPTIONAL MEMORIAL
7. **Our Lady of the Rosary** MEMORIAL
8. St. Pelagia, virgin, martyr *
9. St. Denis, bishop and Companions, martyrs OPTIONAL MEMORIAL
9. St. John Leonardi, priest OPTIONAL MEMORIAL
10. St. Ghislain (Gislenus), abbot *
11. St. Firminus, bishop *
12. St. Wilfrid, bishop *
13. St. Gerald of Aurillac *
14. St. Callistus I, pope, martyr OPTIONAL MEMORIAL
15. St. Teresa of Avila, virgin, doctor MEMORIAL
16. St. Hedwig, religious OPTIONAL MEMORIAL
16. St. Margaret Mary Alacoque, virgin OPTIONAL MEMORIAL
16. **St. Gerard Majella**, religious *
17. St. Ignatius of Antioch, bishop, martyr MEMORIAL
18. **St. Luke**, evangelist FEAST
19. St. Isaac Jogues, St. John de Brebeuf, priests and Companions, martyrs MEMORIAL
19. St. Paul of the Cross, priest OPTIONAL MEMORIAL
20. Blessed Adeline, abbess *
21. St. Celine *
22. St. Salome, mother of the Apostles James and John *
23. St. John of Capistrano, priest OPTIONAL MEMORIAL
24. St. Anthony Mary Claret, bishop OPTIONAL MEMORIAL
25. St. Gaudentius of Brescia, bishop *
26. St. Demetrius, martyr *
27. Blessed Emilina, lay sister *
28. **St. Simon, St. Jude**, apostles FEAST
29. St. Narcissus, bishop *
30. St. Marcellus the Centurion, martyr *
31. St. Wolfgang, bishop *

The month of October is traditionally devoted to our Lady and specifically the Rosary.

The Feast of Our Lady of the Rosary on October 7 reinforces this monthly theme.

*Not found in the revised Roman Calendar.

The Feast of Guardian Angels on October 2 provides us with the excuse for some angel crafts!

HOMEMADE ROSARIES

Personalized Rosaries can be made with a variety of store-bought beads.

With large varieties of colour and bead shapes available, it is easy to make specialized Rosaries with easily distinguished decades. Substantial knots on both sides of each Our Father bead help to separate the decades and keep the sets of beads in place.

Unfinished wood beads can be purchased, brightly painted and varnished. 3/4"-1" size beads work well. Large wood beads are particularly attractive to little fingers when they are big, colourful and shiny! String the beads randomly or in sets of 10 same coloured beads. Our Father beads could be larger or painted in a special colour, separated by adequate knots in the durable string.

Wooden crosses and heart shapes can also be purchased and personalized with paint for the cross and the Marian bead (beginning the 1st decade).

Personalized Rosaries can also be made with handmade beads, made of clay or rolled paper. There are many types of modelling clay available at your local craft store. Check out their ideas for special jewellery beads.

ROSE BEAD ROSARIES
This special dough made out of rose petals works well for making rosary beads. Mix 1/3 cup wheat flour, 1 Tbsp. salt and 2 Tbsp. Water. Cut 3 cups of rose petals into tiny pieces, place them in a small plastic bag and continue to crush them. Combine as much of the rose petals as possible, before the dough becomes crumbly. Form the beads. Push a toothpick through the centre of the beads. Allow to dry, removing the toothpicks before they become too hard. Continue drying several days or bake in a very low oven, watching carefully.
Store the assembled ROSE BEAD ROSARIES in a clear glass jar with a cotton ball soaked in rose scent, taped or glued to the inside of the lid.

PAPER BEADS are made with cut or torn strips of construction paper, wrapping paper or wallpaper. Generally, a 24" strip will make a 1/4" diameter bead, depending on the thickness of the paper.

Cover knitting needle or skewer with vaseline. Coat paper strip with wallpaper paste or glue and roll the strip tightly on the knitting needle (wider end of strip first).

Remove to dry.
Re-thread on knitting needle to paint or varnish and dry. Experiment with tapered strips, different lengths and widths of strips, different thickness, texture and colour of paper. Special paper can be created with spray, splatter and marble paint effects.

Spiritual Bouquet

SPIRITUAL BOUQUET OF PRAYER PETAL FLOWERS

This activity may help to initiate the process of saying the prayers within the Rosary while offering a more concrete way of keeping track of the prayers.

A Spiritual Bouquet of Prayer Petal Flowers makes a great gift... especially if the decade or Rosary has been said for a special intention of the receiver.

Begin by introducing the concept of the Rosary, one decade at a time. Each day, focus on only one decade of the Rosary: one Joyful, Sorrowful, Glorious or Luminous Mystery of the 20.

Before you begin to pray together, cut out a series of flower petals, stems and leaves for each person who will be taking part. There should be 1 stem (representing the Mystery), 10 petals (representing the Hail Marys), 1 little circle or centre for each flower (representing the Our Father) and 1 leaf (representing the Glory be...). Either you or the children can carefully print the corresponding prayer (or Mystery) on the appropriate pieces.

As the Mystery is announced and described, everyone holds a stem. As the Our Father is said, the circle is glued to the end of the stem. As each Hail Mary is said, a petal is glued to the circle. As the decade is concluded with the Glory be..., glue the leaf onto the stem.

As the days go by and the decades are said, a great collection of flowers will reflect the achievement!

Saints' Days

October 1: The Memorial of St. Theresa of the Child Jesus

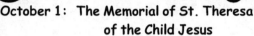

St. Theresa said YES to God through everything that she did. She carried out every menial task with love for God, refusing to complain and offering up any suffering or boredom for Him.

Consider establishing some PRAYER HABITS. (See the first Ordinary Time section.) As chores are performed, pray for those who will benefit from your work. Pray for others when you are suddenly reminded of them throughout each day.

In *The Story of a Soul*, St. Theresa writes about her spiritual journey. Consider beginning a SPIRITUAL JOURNEY JOURNAL. Each day record your thoughts, reflections and concerns. Follow this writing with a period of scripture reading and prayer, followed by silence. Record what Jesus might be saying to you.

OCTOBER

Saints' Days

Nicknamed "The Little Flower", St. Theresa is often associated with flowers. She was true to her word that after her death she would send a shower of roses. To this day, many people report the scent or unexpected receipt of roses corresponding with a special answer to prayer, when they pray for St. Theresa's intercession.

Laura Owens of Louisville, KY gives FOIL KISS ROSES as inexpensive give-aways!

Loosely roll a 12" square piece of foil. Start at one end, crunching the foil into a stem (about 6" long). Insert leaf-shaped foil pieces into the loose part of the stem before crunching it tightly (or glue gun them on later).

Continue crunching the foil stem until 2-3" from the loose end. Separate the layers of loose foil until there is enough room to place a Hershey's Kiss in the centre. Shape the individual layers of foil around the Kiss to look like petals in various stages of opening. Group 3 foil roses and tie with a bow or pipe cleaner.

EMI

October 2: The Memorial of the Guardian Angels
STRING OF GUARDIAN ANGELS

Cut a 8 1/2"x11" piece of white paper lengthwise into 2 equal pieces (of 4 1/4"x11").

Fold one of the pieces of paper accordion style, at about 2 1/4" intervals along the 11" length.

Carefully cut the silhouette of an angel (complete with halo!) out of the folded piece of paper, allowing the arms to extend past the wings to the folds of the accordion.

When the cutting is complete, unfold the accordion to reveal a set of angels holding hands.

Angels...

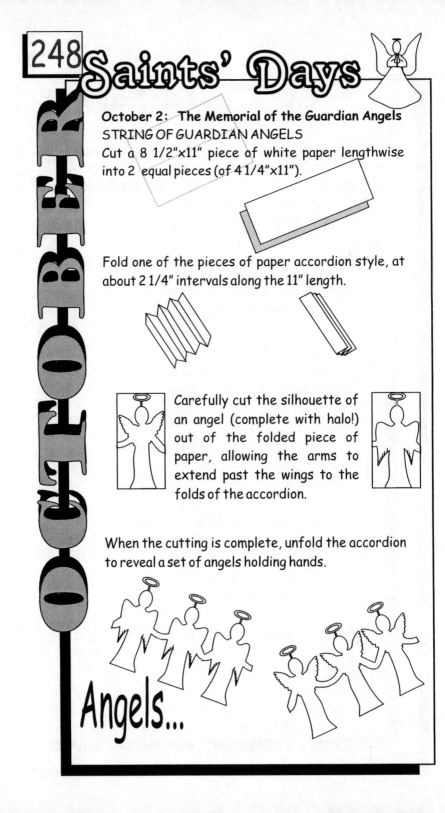

Attach a small note with the words of the GUARDIAN ANGEL PRAYER.

249

OCTOBER

Saints' Days

Create SPOON ANGELS with plastic spoons and some white material, tulle or lace.

Paint a simple face or glue googly eyes and a paper or string mouth in place, on the inside bowl of the spoon.

Make the halo out of a white pipe cleaner. Form a loop at one end and wrap the other end around the neck of the spoon. Alternatively, a 1/4"x2 1/2" strip of paper could be glued or taped in a ring and secured to the back of the bowl of the spoon to "hover" above the "face".

Gather a 3"x5" piece of the white material, tulle or tissue paper, positioning the 5" length along a 2" piece of tape. Leave $\frac{1}{4}$" to $\frac{1}{2}$" of each end of the tape untouched and position the material on the lower half of the length of the tape. Use the remaining sticky part of the tape to secure the material around the neck of the spoon.

Fold a 4"x12" (or larger) piece of white material (tulle or tissue paper...) into a rectangle (4"x6"). Twist at the centre to create bow tie wings. Secure the centre with string or ribbon, tying the wings around the neck of the spoon.

Tape pieces of thin gift-wrapping ribbon to the top of the spoon to create hair. Carefully pull the ribbon firmly across a ruler or scissors' edge to create curly ringlets, guiding the ribbon with your thumb.

Tie some fishing line or several strands of white, clear or metallic thread around the neck of the spoon, to suspend the angel.

Customize your angel by using different materials! Use a 2" wide decorative ribbon tied into a bow as an alternate style of wings.

OCTOBER

Laura Owens of Louisville, KY makes special little guardian angels.

She collects pictures of angels, either hand-drawn, on old Christmas cards or found on the web. She cuts them out and traces over some of the outlines with a thin line of glue (the outline of the wings or one side of the angel's gown for a 3D effect). She sprinkles glitter over the picture, shaking the excess off.

Laura glues the finished angel to a craft stick...but these could also be suspended from the ANGEL MOBILE!

JELLY BEAN ANGEL

This angel is mentioned as a potential prize at the ALL SAINTS' DAY PARTY.

Fill a 2L clear, plastic pop bottle with colourful jelly beans.

Carve a circle out of a styrofoam ball, the size of the bottle cap. When hollowed out to a 1/2" depth, this sphere fits on top of the lid and becomes the head of the angel. Add string hair and facial features out of paper, string, coloured push pins, material or paint.

Add tissue paper or material wings and garments, partially covering the enticing contents!

The feet can be cut out of construction paper or cardboard and glued in place.

A pipe cleaner halo can be secured into the styrofoam head.

Angels...

Saints' Days

SWEET ANGEL TREATS

Laura Owens of Louisville, KY makes little candy packets to give away to the homeless men at a centre where she volunteers. She fills empty film canisters with hard candies, red hots, lemon drops or jelly beans, reasoning that these are something that those who are short on funds do not buy. She and her daughters decorated the canisters and wrote special messages like "You are loved" and "Peace".

To make SWEET ANGEL TREATS, Laura and her daughters place the hard candies in the centre of a coffee filter, and close it with a rubber band. They wrap one end of a gold pipe cleaner around the gathered part and extend the other end up and bend it into a circle for a halo. The wings can be made out of a tissue or another coffee filter, gathered and twisted in the centre into a bow-tie. They can either be glued in place or secured to the back of the neck with the existing rubber band and pipe cleaner. Facial features are added with fabric paint or permanent markers.

These SWEET ANGEL TREATS (with a special Christian message attached) are a great way to continue taking part in neighbourhood shell-out fun at Halloween while reintroducing themes of holiness. Just use wrapped candies!

Collect gold or silver chocolate bar wrappers for another handy craft material! This shiny foil is great for wings and halos!

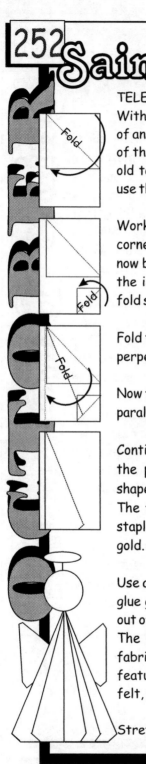

TELEPHONE BOOK ANGEL

With a sharp utility knife, cut through the spine of an old telephone book, cutting away a 1" section of the thick book. (If you would like to recycle an old telephone directory of 1/2" -1" size, you can use the entire book.)

Working with one page at a time, fold the top corner inward. The top edge of the page should now be parallel to the spine, comfortably close to the inner crease of the book. Smooth the new fold so that the folded corner lays flat.

Fold the bottom corner up, this time only about 2" perpendicular to the outer edge of the book.

Now fold once again, bringing the top diagonal fold parallel and comfortably close to the spine.

Continue folding each page in this manner, until the pages make a uniform, 3-dimensional cone shape. This will become the bodice of the angel. The first and last folded pages will need to be stapled or glued together. Spray paint white or gold.

Use a styrofoam ball for the head. Secure with a glue gun. For firmer contact, carve a small cone out of the ball to fit the peak of the body.
The ball can be spray painted or covered with fabric to create a smoother texture. Add facial features with paint or other materials such as felt, paper or string.

Stretch nylon over wire to create the angel wings.

PAPER MACHE ANGEL

Create a paper mache angel with white tissue paper or paper towel, using a wine bottle (coated with vaseline or a clear plastic bag) for the form of the body.

Carve a hole out of a styrofoam ball so that it fits the top of the bottle snugly like a lid. Apply paper mache to the ball for the head.

Arrange paper mache in the form of joined wings, on saran wrap or wax paper. Ripples and creases and seams of paper mache' strips will provide interesting texture to the surface of the wings.

Wings can also be made by stretching white nylon on wire frames (fashioned into wing shapes).

Apply white string to the styrofoam ball (for hair), liberally coating the strands with the watered down glue mixture used for paper mache'.

Create the halo with wire or a thin strip of white paper.

Glue the components together, using thin strips of paper mache to strengthen the bond.

Apply lace material to create a flowing dress with generous flowing sleeves, coated (and hardened) in place by the paper mache mixture.

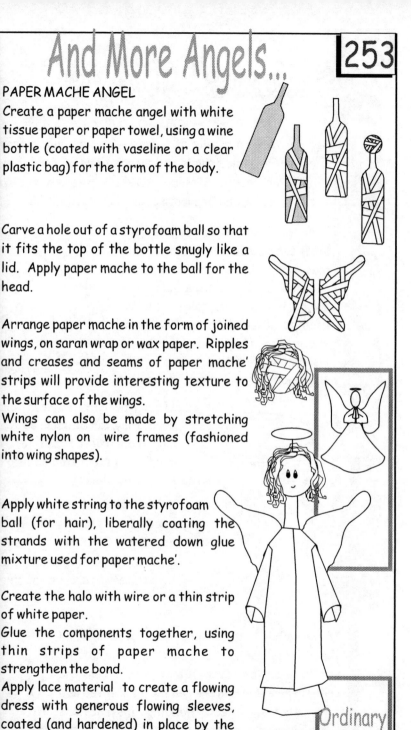

Ordinary Time

Saints' Days

GUARDIAN ANGEL MOBILE

Make a mobile of angels. Cut the angels from Christmas cards and mount them on cardboard or create SIMPLE ANGELS (see Alternative Halloween Decorating) or SPOON ANGELS.

Two wood sticks or dowels (12" long) can be secured together in a plus sign, winding string or tape securely at the centre joint. A string tied at this centre can be used to suspend the mobile from the ceiling, while the objects can also be tied to this centre as well as the ends of the sticks, balancing the mobile.

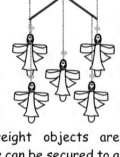

If lightweight objects are used, they can be secured to a ring constructed out of a cardboard strip stapled into a circle (a big halo!).

An embroidery hoop can be used for slightly heavier objects. If a ring is used, ensure the objects are tied at equal intervals around the ring.

If the mobile is to be hung in a baby's room and the objects are not baby safe, ensure that the mobile is secured well out of reach from the crib, suspended from the ceiling. If created as a gift, enclose these hanging instructions together with a hand-printed note of the GUARDIAN ANGEL PRAYER.

OCTOBER

OCTOBER

October 4: The Memorial of St. Francis of Assisi

St. Francis is known for his love of all creatures. He was always aware of everything as God's creation and treated all with dignity.

Create a treasure hunt, making a list of things to find at a particular park or even in your own backyard! Combined with poems or riddles, the treasure hunt can be carried out in a certain sequence, leading all participants on a Nature Walk!. Appreciate the finest details of God's creation as you examine your findings!

Keep an adventure record, saving the findings in a decorated container or in a scrap book. Flowers and leaves can be dried within a thick phone book.

Leaves can also be preserved and protected by ironing them between two sheets of waxed paper while they are fresh. Add some crayon shavings (made using a carrot peeler or vegetable grater) for some extra colour! Crush the shavings into speckles and sprinkle them around the leaves on top of the wax paper. Add the second piece of waxed paper on top and iron. Make a frame out of construction paper to mount on top of the waxed paper and display in a window for a stained glass effect.

St. Francis was often asked by others to pray for them. He always made a point of praying immediately for them before he could be distracted. Let prayer interrupt and augment your day, woven throughout your daily routine.

Saints' Days

October 7: The Memorial of Our Lady of the Rosary
ROSARY REFRESHER!
Here's how to pray the Rosary!

1. Holding the Cross of the Rosary, we make the SIGN OF THE CROSS (see September 14)
2. Recite the "I believe in God..." (APOSTLE'S CREED see p. 206 of this book)
3. Holding the first bead, recite the "Our Father..." in honour of the Pope.

4. Recite the "Hail Mary..." for each of the following 3 beads, praying for the virtues of Faith, Hope and Charity.
5. Recite the "Glory be to the Father..." prayer.
6. Recite the "O my Jesus..." prayer.

See p. 68 for Our Father, Hail Mary, Glory Be and O My Jesus prayers!

7. For each of the 5 decades of the Rosary, announce the Joyful, Sorrowful, Glorious or Luminous Mystery to be meditated on.
8. Recite the "Our Father" with the first bead.

9. For each of the following 10 beads, recite the "Hail Mary".
10. Recite the "Glory be to the Father..." prayer.
11. Recite the "O my Jesus..." prayer.

Without a Rosary, just keep track of the prayers by counting them with your fingers! Don't be afraid to scatter decades throughout your day. It may be easier to focus on one decade at a time.

OCTOBER

OCTOBER

Recount the events of the Mysteries and meditate on one for each decade. Look up the scriptural passages for more detail.

THE JOYFUL MYSTERIES

The Annunciation: The angel Gabriel appeared to Mary, informing her that she was chosen to conceive the Son of God.

Ask Mary for the virtue of humility.

The Visitation:

Mary's cousin Elizabeth confirmed God's message saying "Blessed are you among women and blessed is the fruit of your womb!"

Ask Mary for the virtue of love of our brothers and sisters (charity).

The Birth of Our Lord:

Jesus is born in a manger.

Ask Mary for the spirit of poverty (detachment from the world).

The Presentation of Jesus:

In accordance with Jewish Law, Jesus is presented in the Temple.

Ask Mary for the virtue of purity.

The Finding of Jesus:

After having looked for Him for 3 days, Mary and Joseph found Jesus in the Temple speaking to the doctors.

Ask Mary for the virtue of obedience to the Will of God.

Rozann Huiras of Sleepy Eye, MN has a great idea for busy moms trying to fit the Rosary throughout their day! She uses articles of clothing as counters as she folds laundry (in stacks of 10) or dishes (washed and dried in groups of 10!)

OCTOBER

Jesus' Baptism in the Jordan
(pray for understanding)
Wedding at Cana (pray for kindness)
Preaching on the Kingdom of God
(pray for peace)
Jesus' Transfiguration
(pray for wisdom)
Institution of the Eucharist
(pray for generosity)

THE SORROWFUL
MYSTERIES

The Agony in the Garden:
Jesus prays before He is arrested.
Ask Mary for the virtue of resignation to the Will of God.

The Scourging at the Pillar:
Jesus is beaten.
Ask Mary for purity of body and spirit.

The Crowning with Thorns:
Jesus is mocked and adorned with a painful
crown of thorns.
Ask Mary to help us avoid sins of pride (humility).

The Carrying of the Cross:
Jesus was forced to carry His cross to Calvary.
Ask Mary to help us accept our trials with patience
(patience in adversity).

The Crucifixion and Death:
Jesus dies on the Cross.
Ask Mary for the conversion of sinners and for the virtue of
love of our enemies.

The ONE DECADE ROSARY: to introduce
little ones to the Rosary with a better
chance of keeping their attentions!

Pray each of the 5 Mysteries,
saying only 1 Our Father and 2 Hail
Mary's for each one. Introduce
the "Glory be..." and the "O my
Jesus..." prayers too! This idea
was passed on by Mary, a mom
from The Catholic Mothers Email
Discussion List.

EMI

OCTOBER

THE GLORIOUS MYSTERIES:

The Resurrection:
Jesus arose from the dead, 3 days after His death.
Ask Mary for a greater Faith.

The Ascension:
Forty days after the Resurrection, Jesus ascended into heaven as the Apostles watched.
Ask Mary for the virtue of Hope in God.

The Descent of the Holy Spirit:
The Holy Spirit descended on the Apostles and empowered them with special Gifts.
Ask Mary for the Gifts of the Holy Spirit.

The Assumption of Mary:
Mary dies and her body which was Jesus' first Tabernacle, is taken up to heaven and reinfused with her soul.
Ask Mary for the grace of a happy death and union with Christ.

The Coronation of Mary:
Mary is crowned as the Queen of Heaven by God the Father as His Daughter, by God the Son as His beloved Mother and by God the Holy Spirit as His chosen Spouse.
Pray that we may imitate Mary in all that we do and be united with her.

The FINGER ROSARY is a ring with a decade's worth of beads! The beads can be strung together on a piece of string or wire. It fits on a finger (or a child's thumb!) and easily spins around the finger, one bead at a time, as prayers are said.

If the Spiritual Bouquet Prayer Card is given blank, include a description of the significance of the card and suggestions for prayers to be said. If the person shares their name with a Saint, try to find a prayer card or novena to that Saint and include it with the card.

Spiritual Bouquet Prayer Cards make excellent gifts. They can be given blank to encourage prayer or can be filled with stickers representing prayers already said for a particular intention. Look through Catholic Prayer books for particular prayers that you would like the children to learn or novenas of special significance to the family. Decide how many days the prayer will be said, to complete the card: a week or month's worth of days, a countdown to a particular birthday or event, or the age of the person who will receive the card as a gift.

Save religious images from Christmas cards and calendars or create a simple design with a cross or heart shape. Lightly print the numbers (representing days that the prayer is said) randomly throughout the picture.

As the chosen prayers are said, stickers are placed on the appropriate number. This exercise may entice children to "make up" missed prayers.

If the card is given as a gift, be sure to explain the significance of the stickers. Explain what prayers were said for their special intention.

OCTOBER

ROSARY GIFT CARDS

Draw a rosary: draw the chord of the rosary either in an irregular closed shape or a circle or heart. Add the stem, leading to the cross. Make a light pencil mark, dividing the outline into 5 equal sections. Draw a bead on each pencil mark. Draw 10 beads within each section (roughly equally spaced).

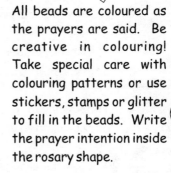

All beads are coloured as the prayers are said. Be creative in colouring! Take special care with colouring patterns or use stickers, stamps or glitter to fill in the beads. Write the prayer intention inside the rosary shape.

These ideas were inspired by Marcy Marklin of St. Louis, Missouri. She has designed and created a whole variety of **Marvelous Scripts Catholic Cards**, ready to be given as gifts, blank or filled with specially designed stickers. Perfect as special intention cards, sympathy cards, All Soul's Day cards (honouring deceased loved ones) and thoughtful gifts for birthdays, Easter, Christmas and every occasion!

Email her at MMARKLIN@aol.com

Represent the new LUMINOUS MYSTERIES as radiant roses or use other sparkling imagery!

Crown of Roses

In *Rosary Novenas to Our Lady* by Charles V. Lacey, the prayers of the Rosary are imagined as roses, bound together in decades as bouquets and offered to Our Lady in the imagery of a crown.

Create a thoughtful gift to show this imagery as prayers are said for a particular person or intention.

THE SINGLE-ROSARY CROWN
Each of the three special Rosaries can make a distinct crown! Consider:
The Rosary of the Joyful Mysteries: prayers can be represented as snow-white buds!

The Rosary of the Sorrowful Mysteries: prayers can be represented as blood-red roses!

The Rosary of the Glorious Mysteries: prayers can be represented as full-blown white roses!

The special crowns can be given as thoughtful cards either separately or in sets!

 Ideally, stickers could be found to represent the different types of roses for the least amount of work.

However, individual rose symbols can be created in a variety of ways. They could be drawn or cut out of construction paper and detailed with a black or gold marker to create the different flowers.
Either approach could be quite time-consuming, considering the numbers of symbols needed in a single rosary.
Check out POTATO STAMPING!

OCTOBER

Potato Stamping

Let's try potato-stamping! Make a sketch of the symbols you would like to use, on paper. Place the paper over the flat surface of the potato half and retrace the template, making imprints on the potato surface to transfer the pattern.

Carve the appropriate symbols out of the potato halves, so that the symbol sticks out at least 1/8". Carefully cut detail by removing thin slits from the raised surface.

Flower buds and full flowers,

leaves and thorns

Keep it simple! Minimal detail is required as the colours used to stamp will help to further articulate the symbol.

The stamps will likely be rather large for individual beads, so the end result may require bristol board!

The Three-Rosary Crown

The Three-Rosary-Crown includes all three sets of Mysteries in one crown. After creating the shape of the crown, use stickers, construction paper or HOMEMADE POTATO STAMPS to create **leaves** for the Joyful Mysteries, **thorns** for the Sorrowful Mysteries and **roses** for the Glorious Mysteries.

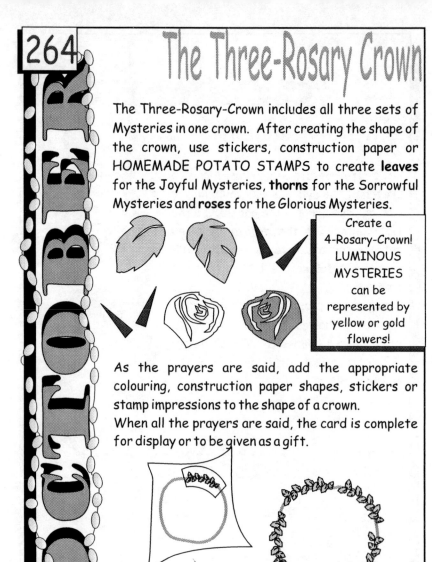

Create a 4-Rosary-Crown! LUMINOUS MYSTERIES can be represented by yellow or gold flowers!

As the prayers are said, add the appropriate colouring, construction paper shapes, stickers or stamp impressions to the shape of a crown.

When all the prayers are said, the card is complete for display or to be given as a gift.

If one decade is said, per day, work on the appropriate additions on just one section of the rosary or wreath shape at a time so that it will not look complete, until all the prayers are said.

A mask may be made out of paper or clear acetate. Just cut a window (the size of a 1/5th section) to keep the children focused on this one area. It will also serve to protect the rest of the card.

OCTOBER
Crowns and Wreaths

3-D ROSARY WREATH

A 3-D version of the wreath or crown could be made out of dough, adding flowers and buds (or flowers, leaves and thorns) as prayers are said.

Begin with a ring of dough. Add flowers and tear-drop shaped pieces for the buds throughout the wreath. Alternatively, leaves and flowers could be made out of dough. Toothpicks (broken in half) can be used for the thorns.

For a colourful wreath, dye portions of the dough different colours: bright colours for the buds and flowers, and green for the leaves and the ring. Pre-dyed dough may be much easier (for children) than painting small detailed pieces after the wreath has dried.

The prayers of the Rosary can also be depicted as different jewels on a crown for our Queen of Heaven.

CROWN OF JEWELS

Make a 3D crown out of construction paper or craft foam, or cut a pattern into a clean margarine or sour cream container. (See the Epiphany Party PARADE OF KINGS or the Feast of Christ the King for crown instructions).

Use sequins, jewel stickers, coloured glass stones or buttons to mark the different prayers. Distinguish each new decade with a very special-looking "jewel".

This crown would be a great addition to the MAY CROWNING. (See Month of May activities.)

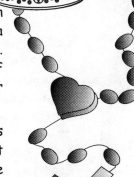

Saints' Days

October 16: The Feast of St. Gerard Majella *

St. Gerard is the patron of pregnant mothers as a result of a miracle that occurred when he prayed for a woman in labour.

Pregnant Mother's Day!
Offer an hour of your time to a pregnant Mom for cleaning or errands. Make some nursery decorations!

Cook some full dinners for the pregnant Mom's family, either for now or for the first weeks with the new baby. Label with the contents and date.

*Not found in the revised Roman Calendar.

October 18: The Feast of St. Luke the Evangelist

St. Luke is the author of the 3rd Gospel, as well as the Acts of the Apostles. He is the patron of doctors and painters, as he was both in his lifetime.

St. Luke's detailed Gospel portrays the human qualities of Jesus, showing His compassion and gentleness. St. Luke includes the Good Samaritan story and The Prodigal Son. He presents the disciples very favourably, as they give their lives generously for Jesus.

OCTOBER

Special Intentions Candle

Buy a candle and decorate it. Add a decoration for every Rosary, special prayer or Mass offered, or every prayer intention. The person receiving the candle as a gift can light the candle every time they have a special need or prayer.

Holy medals, decorative metal buttons or charms, shells or rocks can be used as decorations. Just dig out the approximate shape from the side of a finished candle, push the object in and blow a hot hair dryer over the area a few times to smooth the wax.

Other objects can be added by dipping them in melted clear paraffin wax and pressing them into the candle sides (with tweezers). Clear craft glue can also be used to attach certain decorations.

Other wax decorations can be made by hand. Try hole punching tools and craft knives to cut shapes from smooth sheets of coloured wax (available at most craft stores). OR

Light coloured candles and allow sufficient wax to melt. Carefully allow the candle to drip onto a disposable foil pie plate or durable countertop. Scrape the wax off the surface while it is still warm (but not too hot to touch!). Fashion the warm wax into 3D shapes and stick to the side of the candle. Once again, a hair dryer might be useful to help the wax adhere.

A meaningful gift in the form of a candle, to continue prayers for special intentions.

Try decorating a homemade picture frame with stickers or homemade modelled flowers representing each special prayer said, and include the picture of the child (who said the prayers) within the frame.

Saints' Days

October 18: The Feast of St. Luke the Evangelist

PROFILE of JESUS

St. Luke emphasizes the good human qualities of Jesus while recognizing His Divinity. God gave us a precious gift when He sent His Son to us. Jesus is human, like us, in all things but sin. We can relate to Him through His humanity as we try to grasp some understanding of Divinity.

Try to recreate the PROFILE of JESUS, compiling the most treasured qualities of people you know for a deeper understanding of Jesus' perfect humanity.

What human qualities are most important and admirable to you?

What people in your life exhibit such qualities most perfectly?

Consider each one of these qualities. In its most perfect form, each one can give us a tiny glimpse of one aspect of Jesus. If we could compile a comprehensive set of these close-to-perfect examples, we could almost imagine what He was like as He walked the earth.

Think of someone who always invites you to talk to them, with compassion and warmth. Think of someone who loves you unconditionally. Think of someone who is always willing to give their time, offering help or a listening ear. Think of someone who is a great speaker, easily sustaining your interest and passing on their enthusiasm. Think of someone who teaches with patience and understanding, translating big ideas into words you can understand.

Write a thank-you note to some of these people in your life, thanking them for their gift of _____ which offers you a tiny glimpse of what Jesus must have been like on earth.

OCTOBER

Saints' Days

In honour of St. Luke as the patron of painters, create a painting to express your gratitude to these important people in your life.

PAINTING is always fun. Make patterns out of handprints and use an assortment of brushes, string, sponges and other utensils.

BUBBLE PAINTING Pour ¼ cup of dishwashing liquid into a container. Add liquid paint in small amounts until desired colour is achieved. Powder paints (mixed with water) work well.

Blow with a straw into the container until the bubbles begin to overflow. Gently roll the paper on top of the bubbles without bursting the bubbles. Try different colours on the same page for different effects and allow to dry.

ETCHED PAINTING   Draw with a variety of coloured crayons. Brush on a coat of thin powder paint, preferably in a dark colour to show the contrast of light and bright coloured crayons. Dark crayons can be contrasted with a coat of a light coloured thin powder paint.

SQUEEZED PAINT PAINTINGS. Mix equal amounts of flour and salt, adding paint to form a paste. Pour the mixture into plastic squeeze bottles, squeezing the thick paint onto heavy paper or cardboard.

Laura Owens of Louisville, KY makes a PAINT PALETTE out of old contact lens cases or film canisters secured to a frozen pizza cardboard circle.

The caps keep the paint from drying up!

In honour of St. Luke as patron of doctors, write your family doctor/ favourite medical specialist a thank-you note or paint a picture on a Happy St. Luke's Day card (adding "patron of doctors" for a little reminder of the day's significance).

optional cut for handle

Saints' Days

October 28: The Feast of St. Simon and St. Jude
Celebrating the lives of these two apostles, we return to the APOSTLE PARTY theme, offering a few more activities.

APOSTLE PARTY

SIN PIN BOWLING

Remember that Jesus chose ordinary people for His Apostles; people who struggled with the same sin that we do!

The sin pins are made out of empty plastic bottles. The more variety of bottles, the more fun to decorate and play! Look for water, liquid detergent, pop, ketchup, shampoo and other household plastic bottles.

Fill one third of the bottle with sand. Close the bottle with the cap or tape thoroughly with layers of masking tape. A 'head' can be created at the top by adding a crumpled ball of paper with paper mache'. Decorate with paint, glitter, buttons, string and other found objects to express either the 7 CAPITAL SINS (pride, gluttony, envy, lust, avarice, sloth and anger) or the 6 SINS AGAINST THE HOLY SPIRIT (despair, presumption, envy, obstinacy in sin, final impenitence and deliberate resistance to known truth). Use a clear varnish or "Podge-It" for a clear durable finish.

Try to conquer the sins by knocking them over, rolling (or "bowling") a ball at them.

FISHERS OF MEN COIN TOSS

Create the 12 Apostles out of bottles, as described for the SIN PINS.

Add crumpled paper and paper mache' to create a head on each bottle.

Create a flap out of the front of the bottle, cutting 2 sides and the top so that it opens folding down. Paint the flap with crossed lines representing a net. Prop the flap open, gluing cardboard in place to prevent it from closing.

FRONT   SIDE

Add paper arms and hands (as if holding onto the net). Paint a face, and feet with sandals. Paint or add string or fabric for the hair and clothing.

Stand the Apostles side by side and take turns trying to throw coins into the "nets" of the Apostles, without pushing them over. The coins represent the followers who the Apostles "caught" for Jesus.

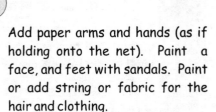

A P O S T L E   P A R T Y

Saints' Days

OCTOBER

October 28: The Feast of St. Jude

> Saint Jude, glorious Apostle, faithful servant
> and friend of Jesus
> The name of the traitor
> has caused you to be forgotten by many,
> but the True Church invokes you universally
> as the patron of things despaired of.
> Pray for me, who am so miserable;
> Pray for me,
> that finally I may receive
> the consolations and the aid of heaven
> in all my troubles, tribulations
> and sufferings,
> particularly____(request)_____,
> and that I may bless God
> with the elect
> throughout Eternity.
> Amen.
> (assumed public domain)

St. Jude is the patron of hopeless cases. We are encouraged to pray for his intercession for our biggest, most stressful concerns.

ST. JUDE FILES

Families often have a number of special intentions to keep praying for throughout family prayers. Sometimes people ask others to pray for them. Sometimes we are made aware of a tragedy or critical health scare concerning people we don't even know. This family activity is very helpful for both "desperate cases" for St. Jude's attention and the everyday concerns to be included in family prayer petitions.

Perhaps two different PRAYER POSTING BOARDS could be made for these different petitions.

> Use chalkboard paint to make personalized chalkboards for writing special prayer petitions!

OCTOBER

FRIDGE FRAME of PRAYER POSTINGS

Create a frame out of cardboard, decorated with paint or construction paper. Cut rectangles out of the frame so that prayer notes can be inserted behind and seen through the openings.

Perhaps the words of the St. Jude prayer could be used to decorate the frame. Glue small magnets to the back of the frame or use adhesive magnetic tape. When there is a particular intention for St. Jude, it can be recorded on a piece of paper and held to the fridge with the St. Jude frame. This can serve as a reminder for the family to pray for St. Jude's intercession.

MOBILE PRAYER POSTING BOARDS

Other versions are more mobile and can be circulated throughout the house to keep getting our attention.

A PRAYER POSTING BOARD can be made with foil-covered cardboard, securing rectangular prayer posts with elastics stretched around the board.

A PRAYER POSTING BOARD can be made with decorated cardboard (covered with wallpaper for example), with prayer posts secured with brass fasteners. Prayer posts should be hole-punched before-hand to match pre-made holes poked into the cardboard with a hammer and nail.

Alternative Halloween Decorating

Hallowe'en originates from All Hallow's Eve, celebrating the night before All Saints' Day. Take this opportunity to re-introduce themes of holiness in place of scary and disturbing costumes and decorating.

Check out the Guardian Angel crafts (earlier in the October section). These provide the perfect alternative to ghost and goblin decorations, conveying themes of holiness in preparation for All Saints' Day.

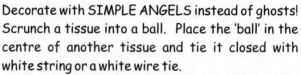

Decorate with SIMPLE ANGELS instead of ghosts! Scrunch a tissue into a ball. Place the 'ball' in the centre of another tissue and tie it closed with white string or a white wire tie.

Make butterfly wings out of white paper. Cut or punch a small hole near the top centre of the wings.

Form a white, silver or gold pipe cleaner (or white wire tie) into a small circle with a stem. Poke the stem through the hole in the wings and wrap the stem around the 'neck' (where the tissue was previously tied).

Carefully draw a happy face with a pen or thin marker. Draw or add string for hair. Suspend a series of these angels from trees or around your doorway.

Adapt these SIMPLE ANGELS into SWEET ANGEL TREATS (see the Guardian Angel crafts). Attach a little note such as "Happy All Hallow's Eve!" or "Happy All Saints' Day!" or a brief explanation of the origin of Halloween:

"Halloween was once called All Hallow's Eve: the night before All Saints' Day! We remember the holy heroes of our Church...all the Saints who served Jesus so diligently and are with Him in heaven."

This is one way to join in the neighbourhood festivities while witnessing to our Faith!

Alternative Halloween Decorating

Make ANGEL PUMPKINS. Cut out a round piece out of the top or bottom of the pumpkin and remove the insides. Braid a few gold or silver pipe cleaners into a halo and allow it to "hover" over the pumpkin by securing it with a thin wire.

Create a happy face on the side of the pumpkin. Tie a bow around the stem, as if it is a lock of hair on a cherub. Brush on a light coat of watered down glue and lightly sprinkle glitter on the pumpkin.

Make sure there are adequate holes for venting (adding a hole at the top and to the back of the pumpkin if necessary).
Insert a small votive candle within the carved pumpkin.
Set the pumpkin down on white material or tulle to suggest the wings of the angel, sprinkling additional glitter if desired.

When in doubt, just carve a really happy face! It might be a welcomed departure from all the scary sights on your street!

Remember a face is not the only way to carve a pumpkin! Uplifting written messages can be carved conveying our enthusiasm for All Saints' Day or our faith in God (Happy All Hallow's Eve! or God bless you!)

Ordinary Time

Alternative Halloween Costumes

Celebrate All Saints' Day while joining in on the neighbourhood Halloween fun! Introduce costumes of Biblical figures or symbols (star of Bethlehem, 10 Commandments) or choose from the huge collection of Saints (appropriately celebrating the eve of All Saints' Day).

Noah's Ark: Make a boat out of a cardboard box. Ensure that there is a hole in the bottom of the box, large enough for the child to fit their legs and waist through. Extra cardboard can be used to make smooth sides, joined together at one end to form the bow and attached to the sides of the box.

Extra cardboard can be used to square off the chest and shoulders into the "cabin" of the boat. String, ribbon or twine secured through holes in the box help to hang the boat in place, supported by the child's shoulders and "floating" at the child's waist. Fill the remaining space of the box with stuffed animals. The child can be dressed up as Noah, sporting a cotton or yarn beard and a robe.

Mother Mary, Angel, St. Joseph, St. Nicholas, St. Peter, an Apostle (fisherman)...

(Most saint costumes can begin with this simple sleeveless gown...just try and find a shirt or sweater of matching colour to wear underneath, and accessorize appropriately: white gown with light blue cape or hood, aluminum foil crown, etc. for Mary)

Make a plain robe or dress by cutting two appropriately sized rectangles. Sew 3 sides of the rectangles together, leaving a generous centred opening at the top (shorter side) and at the top of both long sides. Turn inside out to hide seams.

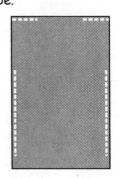

Nancy Federico uses fabric glue to hem costumes. She says that the glue withstands washing!

Mary: white gown with light blue cape or hood, crown, baby Jesus, rosary bead belt,...

Angel: white gown, cardboard wings or fabric stretched on wire wings, halo,...

St. Joseph: brown robe, rope belt with tools attached (or neutral coloured toolbelt)...

St. Nicholas: red robe, cardboard Bishop's miter covered with white or gold material or paint, staff (broom handle with curled end formed out of foil)...

St. Peter: either a robe and large cardboard keys wrapped with foil OR a large cardboard or stuffed material ROCK and possibly keys attached

An Apostle: fisherman attire or robe, large nets, sandals, basket with material or paper mache' loaves and fish (basket used also to collect candy)

Kerry and Richard Brine of Ottawa, Ontario made a St. Francis costume for their son Isaiah, to go to their parish All Saints' Day Party. The brown monk's robe was cut from a large square piece of material, folded diagonally. A slit was cut out of the centre of the fold to fit the head.

Two small triangles were cut from the middle of the 2 other sides of the triangle and the material was sewn inside out, leaving the openings for the head and arms.

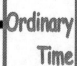

Two of the 4 small triangles left by these cuts were pieced together to form a pointed hood, attached to the opening for the head (cut from the fold). Unfortunately, the directions are just too complicated to pass on!

A rope, thick cord or belt is used to tighten the robe around the waist.

This is a very versatile costume which can be adapted for many different Saints belonging to religious orders!

Ordinary Time

Kerry and Richard Brine of Ottawa, Ontario made a St. Theresa costume for their daughter, Evelyn, to go to their parish All Saints' Day Party.

They made a "T" shaped garment, across the fold of the gray material. A piece of white material was sewn across the fold of gray material.

(fold)

A slit was cut along the middle section of the fold as well as enlarged with a joining perpendicular slit at the centre on the front of the garment. The slits were hemmed for a finished look.

A rectangular piece of gray material was hemmed with a 1" border of white along one length. It was pinned in place as a veil, but could likely be secured with velcro, buttons or snaps.

This is a versatile costume for a nun. It could be adapted and personalized to fit many Saints who were nuns. Just add accessories!

Alternative Halloween Costumes

Warrior Saints (St. Joan of Arc, St. George....) or St. Michael, the Archangel may be popular costumes.

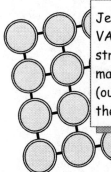

Jeanette Menas of Richmond, VA uses old plastic onion bags or string potato sacks for chain mail. Just spray-paint gold (outside on newspaper) and allow them to dry on the clothes line!

Alternate chain mail can be made stringing frozen juice lids together. Juice lids can be attached in different ways. Ribbons or string can be glued to tie the lids together or holes can be punched (carefully!) with a hammer and nail and the lids can be strung together with fishing line or other strong string.

Sharon Mehl, the Craft Editor at the Craft Exchange (www.kidsdomain.com) creates a helmet out of a plastic gallon milk jug. Before cutting, turn the jug upside down and sketch the helmet shape onto the jug (making sure that the handle will be part of the form to be discarded).

The helmet should fit loosely, across the forehead, covering both ears and extending toward the base of the neck. Trim any jagged edges. The helmet can be spray painted.

A visor can be attached with a brass fastener. Just tape over the flaps of the brass fastener on the inside of the helmet to avoid any scratches!

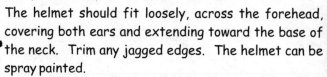

Ordinary Time

Saints' Days

1. **All Saints** SOLEMNITY
2. **All Souls**
3. St. Martin de Porres, religious OPTIONAL MEMORIAL
4. St. Charles Borromeo, bishop MEMORIAL
5. St. Sylvia, mother of St. Gregory the Great *
6. St. Bertille, religious *
7. St. Carina and Companions, martyrs *
8. St. Godfrey (Geoffrey), bishop *
9. Dedication of St. John Lateran FEAST
10. St. Leo the Great, pope and doctor MEMORIAL
11. St. Martin of Tours, bishop MEMORIAL
12. St. Josaphat, bishop and martyr MEMORIAL
13. St. Frances Xavier Cabrini, virgin MEMORIAL
14. St. Sidonius, abbot *
15. St. Albert the Great, bishop and doctor OPTIONAL MEMORIAL
16. St. Margaret of Scotland OPTIONAL MEMORIAL
16. St. Gertrude, virgin OPTIONAL MEMORIAL
17. St. Elizabeth of Hungary, religious MEMORIAL
18. **Dedication of the Churches of St. Peter and St. Paul, apostles** OPTIONAL MEMORIAL
18. St. Rose Philippine Duchesne, virgin OPTIONAL MEMORIAL
19. St. Mathilda *
20. St. Bernward, bishop *
21. **Presentation of Mary** MEMORIAL
22. **St. Cecilia**, virgin and martyr MEMORIAL
23. St. Clement I, pope and martyr OPTIONAL MEMORIAL
23. St. Columban, abbot OPTIONAL MEMORIAL
23. Blessed Miguel Agustin Pro OPTIONAL MEMORIAL
24. St. Flora and St. Mary, virgins, martyrs *
24. St. Andrew Dung-Lac, priest & Companions, martyrs MEMORIAL
25. St. Catherine Laboure, virgin *
26. St. John Berchmans, religious *
27. St. Maximus, bishop *
28. St. James of the March, priest *
29. St. Saturninus, bishop, martyr *
30. **St. Andrew**, apostle FEAST

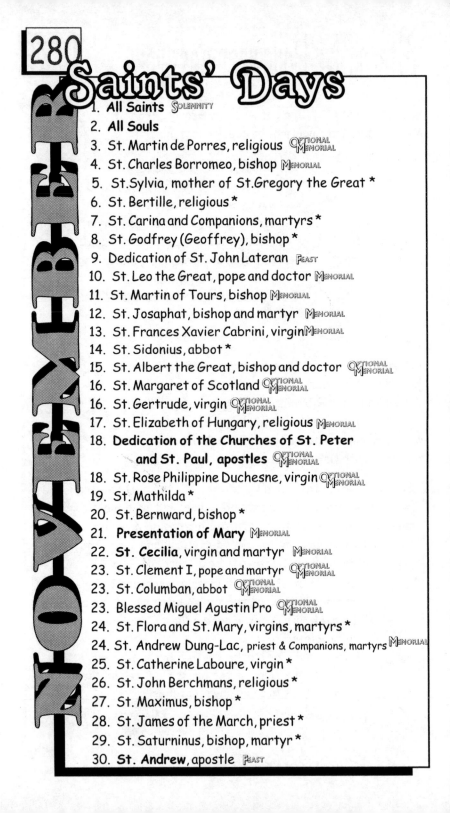

NOVEMBER

Saints' Days

November 1: The Solemnity of All Saints

Dream Team of Saints

Naming choices and special circumstances bring a special group of patron saints together. These holy heroes all have their own different backgrounds and significance, but are meshed together into a family of guardians, patrons and models of our Faith, unique to each family.

Make a list of the DREAM TEAM of SAINTS sharing names with members of the family. Add saints of special devotions or significance to the family.

Create your own FAMILY LITANY OF THE SAINTS. During family prayer, one person announces the name of a certain saint, to which everyone else responds "Pray for us".

Collect holy cards and information about each member of the family's DREAM TEAM of SAINTS.

Everyone in Gwen's family pulls a Saint's name out of a jar on All Saints Day, to select their SPECIAL SAINT for the next year. This offers a great opportunity to learn about a new saint, possibly expanding the FAMILY DREAM TEAM OF SAINTS as more associations with new saints are made!

See HOLY HEROES and FELT FRIENDS and build your collections by adding your DREAM TEAM of SAINTS! See Feast of the Holy Family and September activities.

Saints' Days
Dream Team of Saints

Make your own DREAM TEAM PHOTO. Create a collage from holy cards of members of your DREAM TEAM.

OR

A pre-cut matting with enough openings for each saint can be used within a frame. Label and display within the home.

OUR FAMILY DREAM TEAM OF SAINTS!

Create a DREAM TEAM MOBILE. Create a ring structure out of heavy card or a balanced mobile with straws and string. (See GUARDIAN ANGEL MOBILE.) Attach a holy card for each saint and hang over the kitchen table or other highly visible place.

Think of the DREAM TEAM of SAINTS as a crew of cheerleaders, cheering your family to holiness. These saints comprise a twin family, offering models of virtue to which we should aspire.

NOVEMBER

Saints' Days

This EXPERIENCED MOM IDEA award goes to Lori Nettles and the Respect Life Committee, with thanks! They have been hosting the ALL SAINTS' DAY PARTY for years with many of these ideas. Thanks for permission to offer these ideas, Lori!

All Saints' Day Party

The ALL SAINT'S DAY PARTY is an excellent alternative to Halloween trick-or-treating, if friends want to opt out of traditional Halloween festivities.

Let the children dress up in ALTERNATIVE HALLOWEEN COSTUMES of BIBLE STARS and HOLY HEROES (Saints)! and have a parade! Take lots of pictures!

Decorate with ALTERNATIVE HALLOWEEN DECORATING, using a theme of SAINTS and ANGELS.

Play liturgical music, especially uplifting songs that the kids will recognize from children's liturgies. The ALL SAINTS' DAY PARTY provides a great opportunity to replay those special hymns learned for First Communion, Confirmation and other school Masses. Just a subtle reminder of our journey to holiness!

Check out LITURGICAL CHAIRS!

Saints' Days

All Saints' Day Party

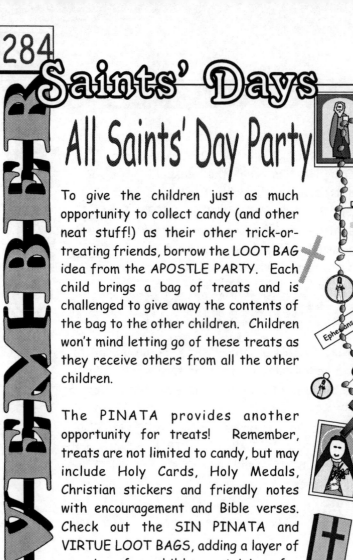

To give the children just as much opportunity to collect candy (and other neat stuff!) as their other trick-or-treating friends, borrow the LOOT BAG idea from the APOSTLE PARTY. Each child brings a bag of treats and is challenged to give away the contents of the bag to the other children. Children won't mind letting go of these treats as they receive others from all the other children.

The PINATA provides another opportunity for treats! Remember, treats are not limited to candy, but may include Holy Cards, Holy Medals, Christian stickers and friendly notes with encouragement and Bible verses. Check out the SIN PINATA and VIRTUE LOOT BAGS, adding a layer of meaning for children striving for SAINTLY holiness.

Additional prizes and treats could include: goldfish (in bags of water or in bowls), religious books, Holy Cards or Holy medals, JELLY BEAN ANGELS (see activities for the Feast of the Guardian Angels) and little HOLY WATER BOTTLES.

HOLY WATER BOTTLES Decorate little bottles with paint, stickers and ribbons and fill with holy water.

NOVEMBER

NOVEMBER

All Saints' Day Party

LITURGICAL CHAIRS

This is a little variation of "Musical Chairs", obviously with liturgical music guiding the activity. Place chairs back to back in a row (one less chair then there are children). As the music is played, children walk or dance (and sing) around the chairs. When the music stops, children scramble to sit on the chairs. The one child without a chair leaves the game and the music continues with one less chair...

ARMOUR OF GOD

This game, modeled after Ephesians 6:14-17, is a race to get suited up for God's team! Create the armour of God, recording the key words of TRUTH, RIGHTEOUSNESS, READINESS, FAITH, SALVATION AND THE WORD OF GOD on the appropriate pieces. Consider stuffing the pieces to make them bulky and give the appearance that there is plenty of "room to grow into". This will add to the skill required to get dressed in the armour and add to the humour and fun.

Children are timed as they don the attire as fast as possible, completing their task by shouting a Word of God (Bible quote). Make sure you take a picture of each child dressed in the armour. It will be a neat souvenir from the party, showing the oversized armour on top of the child's costume.

Saints' Days

WORKS OF MERCY RELAY RACE

Children take turns bringing food to a parent (FEED THE HUNGRY), serving a drink to a parent (FEED THE THIRSTY), dressing a doll (CLOTHE THE NAKED), building a fort out of blankets and chairs and helping someone to get inside (SHELTER THE HOMELESS), making a get well card and delivering it to the parent with a thermometer in his/her mouth (TEND TO THE SICK), find the parent 'imprisoned' behind some chairs (VISIT THE IMPRISONED) and wrap a parent in a sheet (BURY THE DEAD).

CATHLETICS COMPETITION

The children are divided into 2 teams. Two adults hold a sheet blocking the view for opposing teams, lined up on either side.

One member from each team approaches the sheet. As one of the adults names a CATHOLIC CATEGORY, they drop the sheet so that the competing members face each other. The first one to give an answer for that category wins a point for their team.

To stir things up, the adult can call out a term, to which the competing members need to respond with the CATEGORY.

If the ages of the children range quite a bit, it is recommended that several matches occur between similar age groups.

SAINT NAME GAME

In a similar style to the CATHLETICS COMPETITION, 2 teams (of children and adults in HOLY HEROES' costumes) line up on either side of a sheet.

As the sheet is dropped, 2 players from opposite teams face each other. The winner of the match is the first one to name the BIBLE STAR or Saint represented by the other player's costume. The fastest correct answer wins a point for the team.

All Saints' Day Party

Saints' Days

LIST AND TWIST

Use the FLASH CARDS from the CATHLETICS section of the book.

Make a LIST AND TWIST playing field out of an old blanket or sheet. Paint, quilt or use iron-on adhesive to secure rows of evenly-spaced coloured circles: each row has a set of circles of one colour (red, blue, green, yellow, purple...).

Select a CATHLETICS category for each colour used.

FLASH CARDS (belonging only to the chosen categories) are shuffled and selected, one at a time.

If the CATEGORY is called, the player must name one of the answers for that CATEGORY. If the term is named, the player must identify to which CATEGORY the answer belongs.

The person calling out the CATEGORIES (or terms), randomly assigns which foot or hand must be used to touch the appropriate colour BEFORE he selects a FLASH CARD and names the CATEGORY or ANSWER.

The player then proceeds to touch a circle of the appropriate colour with the assigned hand or foot.

Saints' Days
All Saints' Day Party

DAVID AND GOLIATH BEAN BAG TOSS
A poster is created of the large giant, Goliath. Small bean bag "stones" are made out of panty hose. 1 or 2 strips of velcro are attached to the giant's head. Children take turns throwing the "stones" at Goliath's head.

SACRAMENTAL MEMORY GAME
A tray of Catholic items (Holy Card, Rosary, Holy Medal, Crucifix, Catechism...) is revealed to each child for a few seconds and then hidden from view. The child tries to remember all of the items.

COUNT THE ROSARIES IN THE JAR
A jar is filled with many rosaries. The child to most accurately guess how many rosaries are in the jar, wins...a rosary of his choice?

ROSARY BEE
Beads and string are provided for children to create their own Rosaries. Contests for the fastest creations and/or the most attractive Rosaries could become part of the activity.

HALO TOSS
Take turns tossing a large styrofoam ring HALO over sitting parents' heads. A donut-shaped pillow could be made for a softer, safer version of the game!

See SIN PIN BOWLING and FISHERS OF MEN COIN TOSS on the Feast of St. Jude and St. Simon, October 28.

HOLY HEROES' HALO GAME

Prepare a large poster or mural with a few figures on it (from the waist up). Some of the figures should be recognizable saints, others could be celebrities or guests of the ALL SAINTS' DAY PARTY. If recognizable artwork is a problem, use a photocopier to make enlargements of selected pictures.

The completed artwork can be secured to a sheet of cork (for the "pin" version) or laminated for durability (for the "tape" version). Rolls of clear adhesive can be found with other cupboard liners, and can be used to 'laminate' large surfaces.

Create a halo out of cardboard. It can be decorated with glitter or gold or white paint and pinned or taped in place, by the children.

Children take turns being blindfolded, turned around and slightly disoriented, and allowed to pin the HALO on the HOLY HERO, attempting to pick a real saint on the mural.

All Saints' Day Party

Saints' Days

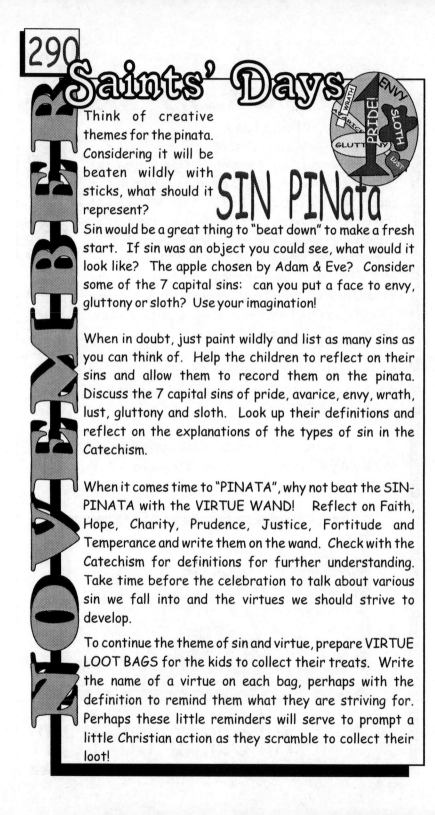

Think of creative themes for the pinata. Considering it will be beaten wildly with sticks, what should it represent?

SIN PINata

Sin would be a great thing to "beat down" to make a fresh start. If sin was an object you could see, what would it look like? The apple chosen by Adam & Eve? Consider some of the 7 capital sins: can you put a face to envy, gluttony or sloth? Use your imagination!

When in doubt, just paint wildly and list as many sins as you can think of. Help the children to reflect on their sins and allow them to record them on the pinata. Discuss the 7 capital sins of pride, avarice, envy, wrath, lust, gluttony and sloth. Look up their definitions and reflect on the explanations of the types of sin in the Catechism.

When it comes time to "PINATA", why not beat the SIN-PINATA with the VIRTUE WAND! Reflect on Faith, Hope, Charity, Prudence, Justice, Fortitude and Temperance and write them on the wand. Check with the Catechism for definitions for further understanding. Take time before the celebration to talk about various sin we fall into and the virtues we should strive to develop.

To continue the theme of sin and virtue, prepare VIRTUE LOOT BAGS for the kids to collect their treats. Write the name of a virtue on each bag, perhaps with the definition to remind them what they are striving for. Perhaps these little reminders will serve to prompt a little Christian action as they scramble to collect their loot!

NOVEMBER

NOVEMBER

A PINATA can be made by covering a balloon with paper mache' (strips of torn newspaper or scrap paper coated with watered down glue or wallpaper paste). By adding various other size balloons or scrunched up newspaper, covering it and connecting it to the balloon, other shapes can be applied to create other animals or objects. Use your imagination (or your children's!) to come up with fun shaped pinatas to continue the theme of the celebration!

Allow layers to dry before beginning another. The more layers, the stronger the pinata will be. Try winding a little string or yarn around the entire shape in all directions within one of the layers of paper mache'. This will add strength to the pinata.

Don't forget to leave a hole in the paper mache' so that the balloon can be poked (when the paper mache' has dried sufficiently) and treats can be added. Cover the hole with more paper mache' and allow to dry. Paint away!

In a pinch, a paper bag can be used as a pinata. Just fill the bag with the loot, tie a string around the top of the bag to close it, and string it up! It may not be as appealing or elaborate as the homemade paper mache' pinata, but with a little paint and decoration...and a lot of fun stuff inside, it will still be a great event.

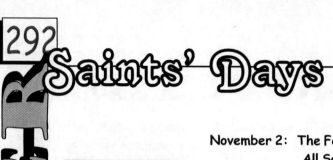

Saints' Days

November 2: The Feast of All Souls

Capture memories of deceased loved ones by recalling happy events and memories. Record stories as they are told on video camera or tape recorder.

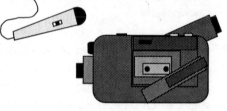

Stories can also be expressed through writing or drawing on MEMORY CATCHER CARDS and placed in the FAMILY TREASURE CHEST.

Keep photos of deceased loved ones visible not only in the month of November but all through the year.

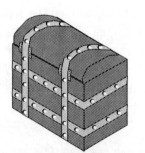

All Souls

NOVEMBER

NOVEMBER

November 18: **The Optional Memorial of the** ✝
Dedication of Churches of St. Peter and St. Paul
Do a little research project on different styles of
Churches. Make a model of a Church out of boxes
(of different sizes) and pieces of cardboard.

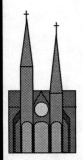

OR
Explain how many Cathedrals were
decorated with paintings along the walls
and ceiling. Artists spent long hours laying
on their backs on scaffolding painting
these elaborate religious scenes.
Tape some paper on the underside of a
table and let everyone pretend to paint
the ceiling of the Sistine Chapel.

OR
Go on a JESUS TOUR at your parish. See
the Feast of Corpus Christi.

November 21: **The Memorial of the**
Presentation of Mary
Mary is referred to as the Temple of the Holy
Spirit because she was full of grace from the
moment of her Immaculate Conception. Jesus was
conceived within her womb by the Holy Spirit.

Although we are not sinless (as Mary was from the moment of her
Conception), we must strive for holiness. Jesus resides in us also,
particularly when we receive the Holy Eucharist.

Perhaps this is a good opportunity to have open family discussions
regarding chastity, purity and the pursuit of holiness.

See PURE WHITE DINNER (December 8).

November 22: The Memorial of St. Cecilia,
patron of musicians

Make some homemade musical instruments for your budding musicians.

WATER XYLOPHONE: Fill glasses with different levels of water and tap with a spoon or wood dowel.

Fill glass bottles with varying amounts of water and blow across the opening until a note is heard.

GUITAR: Stretch elastic bands of varying thickness around an open cookie tin or shoe box.

DRUM: Find an open tin can (or small cookie tin) and ensure there are no jagged edges. Stretch a piece of a balloon over the opening and secure it in place with an elastic.

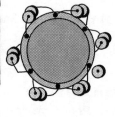

TAMBOURINE: Glue two tin pie plates together around the edge. Use a hole punch to make holes at 1" or 2" intervals around the perimeter. Use a hammer and nail to punch a hole in the centre of some bottle caps. Thread 2 bottle caps within each interval, weaving the string in and out of the hole-punched pie plates.

RATTLE: Use containers with matching lids and fill (1/4 to $\frac{1}{2}$ full) with beans or popcorn kernels.

November 30: The Feast of St. Andrew the Apostle
See APOSTLE PARTY on various Apostle Feast Days.

A P O S T L E   P A R T Y

Christt the King!

Create a ROYAL KING'S CROWN for the table centrepiece with 1"
strips of white or gold or other royal coloured paper.
Cut one long strip and staple, glue or tape it to form a circular
band to fit snug around a head.
Cut 4 shorter, equal length strips. Stack two strips together and
staple one end. Do the same with the other two.
Mark 4 "x" marks at equal intervals around the circular band.

Staple, glue or tape the 2
ends of one of the pairs of
strips at 2 of the "x" marks
(across from each other) on
the circular band. Staple,
glue or tape the ends of the
other connected strips,
across from each other at
the other "x" marks.

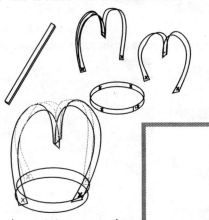

A different crown can be made by cutting away the
bottom of a margarine/sour cream container, leaving
the circular rim intact. Draw the ornamental crown
on the container before cutting, creating peaks and
crosses. Spray paint with black or white; allow to dry
and then spray a light coat of gold or silver. See
PARADE OF KINGS in the EPIPHANY PARTY.

Celebrate the Feast of Christ the King with a ROYAL
DINNER. Set a place for Christ the King at the head
of the table. Assume ROYAL IDENTITIES worthy
of being in the King's presence. Feast on fine food
with perfect manners.

Ordinary
Time

CATHOLIC RESOURCES

www.love2learn.net

Favorite Resources for Catholic Homeschoolers
A comprehensive website offering hundreds of book reviews for Catholic parents.

www.catholicculture.org

Catholic Culture is a combination of the existing site www.Petersnet.net with Catholic site reviews and a library of documents. The Liturgical Year section focuses on the seasons, feasts and saints along with suggested prayers, activities and recipes to help make the Liturgical Year come alive in the domestic church.

There are many wonderful CATHOLIC RESOURCES available. We have included only those that we have discovered personally!

www.companionscross.ca

The **Companions of the Cross** is a new and growing community of priests and seminarians founded in Ottawa, Canada in 1985.

They combine a strong community way of life with parish and other ministries focused on evangelization and renewal, under the guidance of the Holy Spirit and with full obedience to the Magisterium.

email: magnific@nbnet.nb.ca

Magnificat Ministries is a lay apostolate dedicated to the renewal of worship in the Catholic Church. Marcel Dion's music is available on several CDs.

The **Benedictine Monks** of Oxford, Michigan follow the example of St. Benedict and St. Sylvester, serving and loving God through reading, meditation and prayer. They support themselves through a printing press, farming and a retreat program welcoming thousands of teenagers and young adults each year.

The monastery has a brand new Chapel, an amazing feat of Architecture, a welcome addition to a renovated monastery and an innovative Retreat centre!

www.benedictinemonks.com

The prior, Fr. Daniel Homan is co-author of *Here I Am, Lord: A Prayer Journal for Teens, Benedict's Way* and *Radical Hospitality*.

NewCatholicHomeschoolResourcesandNews@yahoogroups.com*
Catholichh@yahoogroups.com   (Catholic Homeschooling)
TheCatholicFamilyHome@yahoogroups.com*
OurHeartsinHisHands@yahoogroups.com*
FunFaithFormers@yahoogroups.com*   * periodic e-newsletter

Yahoo Email Discussion Lists

WEB OF CATHOLIC RESOURCES

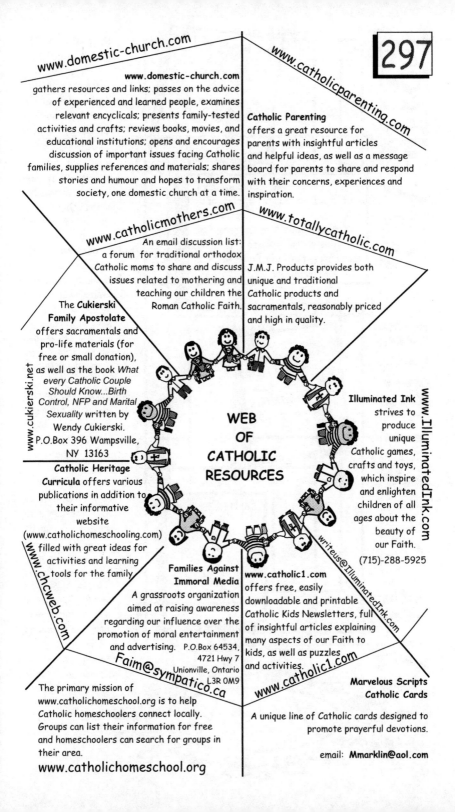

www.domestic-church.com
gathers resources and links; passes on the advice of experienced and learned people, examines relevant encyclicals; presents family-tested activities and crafts; reviews books, movies, and educational institutions; opens and encourages discussion of important issues facing Catholic families, supplies references and materials; shares stories and humour and hopes to transform society, one domestic church at a time.

www.catholicparenting.com

Catholic Parenting offers a great resource for parents with insightful articles and helpful ideas, as well as a message board for parents to share and respond with their concerns, experiences and inspiration.

www.catholicmothers.com

An email discussion list: a forum for traditional orthodox Catholic moms to share and discuss issues related to mothering and teaching our children the Roman Catholic Faith.

www.totallycatholic.com

J.M.J. Products provides both unique and traditional Catholic products and sacramentals, reasonably priced and high in quality.

The **Cukierski Family Apostolate** offers sacramentals and pro-life materials (for free or small donation), as well as the book *What every Catholic Couple Should Know...Birth Control, NFP and Marital Sexuality* written by Wendy Cukierski.
P.O.Box 396 Wampsville, NY 13163

www.cukierski.net

Illuminated Ink strives to produce unique Catholic games, crafts and toys, which inspire and enlighten children of all ages about the beauty of our Faith.
(715)-288-5925

www.IlluminatedInk.com

writeus@IlluminatedInk.com

Catholic Heritage Curricula offers various publications in addition to their informative website (www.catholichomeschooling.com) filled with great ideas for activities and learning tools for the family.

www.chcweb.com

Families Against Immoral Media
A grassroots organization aimed at raising awareness regarding our influence over the promotion of moral entertainment and advertising. P.O.Box 64534, 4721 Hwy 7 Unionville, Ontario L3R 0M9

Faim@sympatico.ca

www.catholic1.com offers free, easily downloadable and printable Catholic Kids Newsletters, full of insightful articles explaining many aspects of our Faith to kids, as well as puzzles and activities.

www.catholic1.com

Marvelous Scripts Catholic Cards

A unique line of Catholic cards designed to promote prayerful devotions.

email: **Mmarklin@aol.com**

The primary mission of www.catholichomeschool.org is to help Catholic homeschoolers connect locally. Groups can list their information for free and homeschoolers can search for groups in their area.

www.catholichomeschool.org

MAGAZINE RACK

The Bread of Life
C.C.S.O.
Bread of Life
Renewal Centre
209 MacNab Street N.
P.O. Box 395
Hamilton, Ontario
L8N 3H8

(905) 529-4496

The mission of **The Bread of Life** magazine is to promote a deeper understanding of the Holy Spirit and His Presence in the lives of God's people.

www.catholic1.com offers free, easily downloadable and printable **Catholic Kids Newsletters**, full of insightful articles explaining many aspects of our Faith to kids, as well as puzzles and activities.

www.catholicity.com Check out this site for great Catholic links, special offers and information. Subscribe to Bud Macfarlane Jr.'s always inspiring **Catholicity Message.** Bud Macfarlane Jr. is the author of great Catholic fiction novels including *Pierced By A Sword, Conceived Without Sin* and *House of Gold* (offered free on this site) and is founder and director of the Mary Foundation, producing Catholic audio tapes.

See Yahoo Email Discussion Lists and e-Newsletters listed on p. 296

CANTICLE

www.canticlemagazine.com
phone orders:
1(888)708-0813

The mission of **Canticle** is to provide a forum of reflection and insight on the *inherent dignity and unique vocation of woman.* **Canticle** is universal in scope, joyful in tone, and fully obedient to the Magisterium of the Roman Catholic Church.

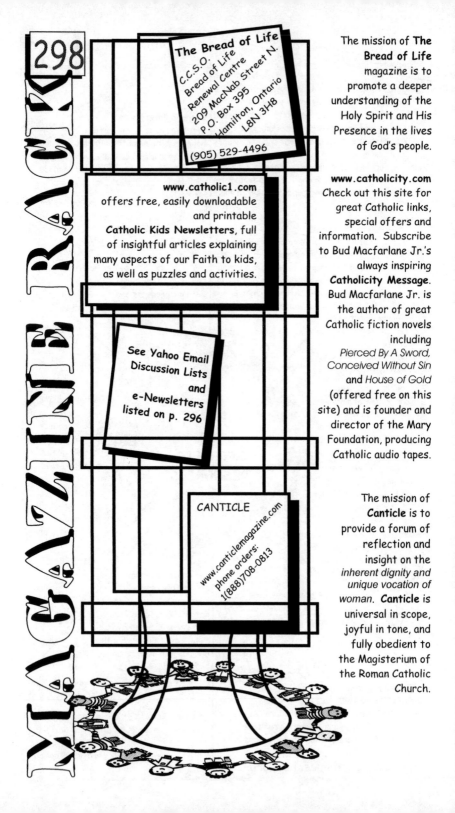

Catechism of the Catholic Church. Ottawa, ON: Canadian Conference of Catholic Bishops, 1994.

Dues, Greg. *Catholic Customs and Traditions.* Mystic, CT: Twenty-Third Publications, 1998.

Erickson, Donna. *Prime Time Together...with Kids. Creative Ideas, Activities, Games and Projects.* Minneapolis, MN: Augsburg Fortress, 1989.

Essential Catholic Handbook, The. Liguori, MO: Liguori Publications, 1997.

Fiarotta, Noel and Phyllis Fiarotta. *The Colossal Book of Crafts for Kids and Their Families.* New York, NY: Black Dog and Leventhal Publishers, 1997.

Foy, Felician, ed. *1991 Catholic Almanac.* Huntington, IN: Our Sunday Visitor Publishing Division, 1991.

Green, Victor J. *Festivals and Saint Days.* Poole: Blandford Press, 1979.

Hoever, Hugo. *Lives of the Saints.* (revised) New York, NY: Catholic Book Publishing Co, 1974.

Ickis, Marguerite. *The Book of Festivals and Holidays the World Over.* New York, NY: Dodd, Mead and Company, 1970.

Ickis, Marguerite. *The Book of Religious Holidays and Celebrations.* New York, NY: Dodd, Mead and Company, 1966.

Lang, Jovian P. *Dictionary of the Liturgy.* New York, NY: Catholic Book Publishing Co., 1989.

Loxton, Howard. *The Encyclopedia of Saints.* London: Brockhampton Press, 1996.

McCarver Snyder, Bernadette. *Saintly Celebrations and Holy Holidays.* Liguori, MO: Liguori Publications, 1997.

Saint Joseph Baltimore Catechism. (Official revised edition No. 2) New York, NY: Catholic Book Publishing Co., 1969.
Saint Michael and the Angels. Rockford, IL, 1983.

Saints and Feastdays. (Sisters of Notre Dame of Chardon, Ohio). Chicago, IL: Loyola Press, 1985.

Rufus, Anneli. *The World Holiday Book.* San Francisco, CA: Harper Collins Publishers, 1994.

Walter, F. Virginia. *Super Toys and Games from Paper.* New York, NY: Sterling Publishing Company Inc., 1993.

All scriptural references from the Saint Joseph Edition of the New American Bible. New York, NY: Catholic Book Publishing Co., 1987.

BIBLIOGRAPHY

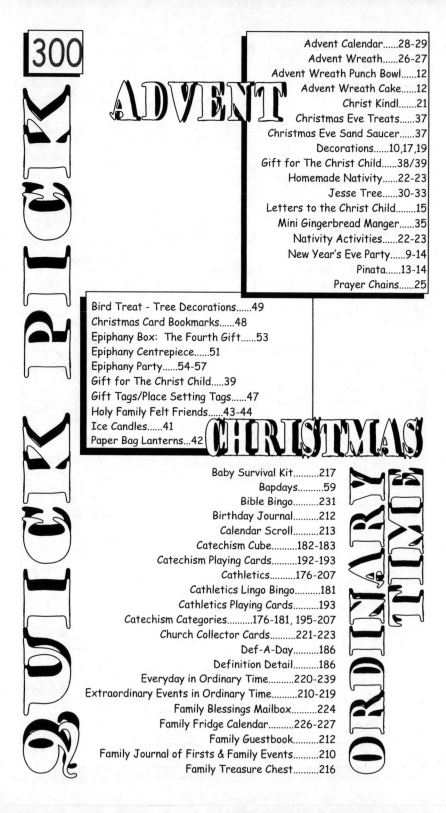

QUICK PICK

ADVENT

Advent Calendar......28-29
Advent Wreath......26-27
Advent Wreath Punch Bowl......12
Advent Wreath Cake......12
Christ Kindl......21
Christmas Eve Treats......37
Christmas Eve Sand Saucer......37
Decorations......10,17,19
Gift for The Christ Child......38/39
Homemade Nativity......22-23
Jesse Tree......30-33
Letters to the Christ Child......15
Mini Gingerbread Manger......35
Nativity Activities......22-23
New Year's Eve Party......9-14
Pinata......13-14
Prayer Chains......25

CHRISTMAS

Bird Treat - Tree Decorations......49
Christmas Card Bookmarks......48
Epiphany Box: The Fourth Gift......53
Epiphany Centrepiece......51
Epiphany Party......54-57
Gift for The Christ Child......39
Gift Tags/Place Setting Tags......47
Holy Family Felt Friends......43-44
Ice Candles......41
Paper Bag Lanterns...42

ORDINARY TIME

Baby Survival Kit..........217
Bapdays..........59
Bible Bingo..........231
Birthday Journal..........212
Calendar Scroll..........213
Catechism Cube..........182-183
Catechism Playing Cards..........192-193
Cathletics..........176-207
Cathletics Lingo Bingo..........181
Cathletics Playing Cards..........193
Catechism Categories..........176-181, 195-207
Church Collector Cards..........221-223
Def-A-Day..........186
Definition Detail..........186
Everyday in Ordinary Time..........220-239
Extraordinary Events in Ordinary Time..........210-219
Family Blessings Mailbox..........224
Family Fridge Calendar..........226-227
Family Guestbook..........212
Family Journal of Firsts & Family Events..........210
Family Treasure Chest..........216

ORDINARY TIME

Family Tree..........214-215
Father's Day..........161, 163, 168
Flash Cards..........185
Four-in-a-Row..........191
God Box..........224-225
Hallowe'en Costumes..........276-279
Hallowe'en Decorating..........274-275
Holy Card Memory Game..239
Holy Hero Album..........239
Holy Heroes Felt Friends / Folder..........234-235
Holy Heroes Puppets/Theatre...236-238
Holy Medal Bracelet..........239
Holy Rummoli!..........193
House Swatch..........218
Jell-O Box Jeopardy...189, 191
Jig-Saw Jell-O Boxes..........191
Lists and Levels..........195-207
Mass Parts and Prayers.....223
Memory Catcher Cards...211, 217
Mobile Home-Maker..........218
Momentum Builder Grid..........187
Namedays..........59
Pass the Torch Party..........229
Prayer Bank..........62-63
Prayer Carousel..........64-65
Prayer Habits..........73
Prayers..........68-79
Prayer Time and Mass Prep...220
Project: Definition..........186
Sacrament Anniversary Party...219
Summer Fun..........173
Trivia Tube..........183

LENT

Band-Aids for Christ...112-113
Blessing Eggs...96-97
Count our Blessings Book...99
Crown of Thorns...104-105
Daily Gifts to Jesus...99
Easter Story Banner...125
Easter Story Eggs...118-119
Empty Tomb Cookies...128-129
Friend of Jesus...95
Happy, Fruity, Fluffy [Pan] Cakes..83
Heart Cross Banner...111
Jelly Easter Eggs...130
Lenten Calendar...102-103
Lenten practices...85
Mardi Gras Masks...84
Offering Cross...107
Our Lenten Share...87
Paschal Candle/Votive Candle.116-117
Passion Play....126-127
Pretzels...93
Resurrection Crown...104-105
Seder Supper...120-123
Shrove Tuesday...83
Simple Suppers...91
Sin Cross...108-109
Spring Cleaning...115
Stations of the Cross...124
Thirty Pieces of Silver...89
Weight of the Cross...101

EASTER

Ascension of the Lord...152-155
Bubble Blower and Bubble Solution...155
Catch the Spirit! Wind Catcher....159
Easter Mosaic...135
Easter Sunday...131
Jelly Easter Eggs...130
Holy Spirit Sweets...158
Kite Building..152-154
Melted Wax Stained Glass..136
Pentecost Dough Doves...158
Pentecost Pinata..157
Praises Phrases..157
Prayer Petal Flower Easter Baskets..133
Prep for Pentecost...151
Resurrection Rolls...137
Wafer Cross Cookies...131

QUICK PICK

MONTH OF MAY

Family Mantle of Protection...140-141
Mary Altar.........139
Mary Collage.........149
Mary Garden.........145-146
Mary Garden Markers...146-147
May Crowning.........139
Modest Mary Dolls...149
Mother's Day.........143
Paper Dolls of Mary...149

MONTH OF OCTOBER

Crown of Jewels.........265
Crown of Roses.........262-263
Crowns and Wreaths.........265
Finger Rosary.........259
Homemade Rosaries...243-244
Rosary Gift Cards...261-263
Rosary Refresher...256-259
Spiritual Bouquet Cards.........260
Spiritual Bouquet of Prayer Petal Flowers..245
3D Rosary Wreath...265
Three-Rosary Crown/Four-Rosary Crown...264

PRAYERS

Act of Contrition.........68, 69
Angel of God.........68
Angelus.........140
Apostle's Creed......206
Bedtime Prayers.........75
Daily Offering.........69
Five Finger Prayer.........77,79
Gesture Prayers.........77,79
Glory be.........68
Grace before Meals.........71
Hail Mary.........68
I'm sorry.........68
Memorare.........52
O My Jesus......68
Our Father.......68
Prayer Habits.........73
Rosary Prayers........68
St. Anthony Prayer.........160
St. Jude Prayer.........272

SAINTS DAYS INDEX

December.........16
January.........50
February.........72
March.........90
April.........110
May.........138
June.........156
July.........172
August.........194
September.........228
October.........242
November.........280

QUICK PICK

All Saints' Day Party (Nov.1).........283-291
All Saints Solemnity (Nov.1).........281-291
All Souls Feast (Nov.2).........292
Annunciation Solemnity (Mar.25).........100
Apostle Party.........144, 170-171, 174-175,
184,208,233, 270-271, 284-291, 294
Archangels (Sept.29).........240
Assumption Solemnity (Aug.15).........204
Bean Bag Arrow Game (Jan.20).........67
Bouncy Bread (Mar.19).........98
Bread Basket (Jan.17).........61
Candles (Dec.7)....18
CD Hockey (Jan.20).........66
Christ the King!.........295
City of God (July 3).........174-175
Cookies ("Lucia Cats"-Dec.13).........34
Corpus Christi.........166-167
Dream Team Mobile (Nov.1).........282
Dream Team of Saints (Nov.1).........281-282
Family Fire Drill (Feb.5/Aug.5).........78, 200
Family Litany of Saints (Nov.1).........281
Foil Kiss Roses (Oct.1).........247
Guardian Angel Mobile (Oct.2).........254
Guardian Angels (Oct.2).........248-254
Grotto for Mary (Feb.11).........80-82
Holy Card Frame(Dec.8)....20
Holy Family (Dec/Jan).........43-45
Holy Innocents (Dec.28).........46
Immaculate Conception Solemnity (Dec.8)..20
Immaculate Heart of Mary.........165
Indoor Obstacle Course (Jan.20).........66
Jelly Bean Angel (Oct.2).........250
Jesus Tour.........166-167
Mary, Mother of God (Jan.1).........52
Our Lady (Birth -Sept.8).........230
Our Lady of Guadalupe (Dec.12).........24
Our Lady of Lourdes (Feb.11).........80-82
Our Lady of Sorrows (Sept.15).........233
Our Lady of the Rosary (Oct.7).256-259
Painting (Bubble/Etched/Squeezed).........269
Paper Mache' Angel (Oct.2).........253
Pope Postcard / Pope Trivia (Feb.22).........88
Prayer Posting Boards.........272-273
Presentation of Mary (Nov.21).........293
Presentation of Our Lord.........74-75
Profile of Jesus (Oct.18).........268
Pure White Dinner (Dec.8).........21
Queenship of Mary (Aug.22).........204
Sacred Heart of Jesus.........169
St.Abraham, St.Isaac, St.Jacob (Dec.20)..36
St. Agatha (Feb.5).........78, 200
St. Ambrose (Dec.7).........18
St. Andrew (Nov.30).........294
St. Ann (July 26).........188
St. Anthony (Jan.17).........60-61
St. Anthony Box (June 13).........160-161
St. Anthony of Padua (June 13)...160-161
St. Augustine (Aug.28).........209
St. Bartholomew (Aug.24).........208
St. Benedict (July 11).........184
St. Bernardine of Siena (May 20).........148
St. Blase (Feb.3).........76
St. Catherine of Siena (Apr.27).........134
St. Cecilia (Nov.22).........294

St. Christopher(July 25).188
St. Clare (Aug.11)...202
St. Dominic Savio(Mar.9)..92
St. Frances (Jan.24)...70
St. Frances of Rome (Mar.9)...92
St. Francis of Assisi (Oct.4).........255
St. Gerard Majella (Oct.16).........266
St. Gregory the Great (Sept.3).........230
St. Ignatius of Loyola (July 31).........190
St. Isidore (May 15).........148
St. Ita/Ida (Jan.15).........58
St. James (May 3).........144
St. James (July 25).........184
St. Joachim (July 26).........188
St. Joan of Arc (May 30).........150
St. John (Dec.27).........40
St. John Baptist de la Salle (Apr.7)..114
St. John the Baptist (June 24).....162-163
St. John of God (Mar.8).........92
St. John Vianney (Aug.4).........200
St. Joseph (Mar.19).........98
St. Joseph (the Worker-May 1)...142
St. Joseph of Arimathea (Mar.29)...106
St. Jude (Oct.28).........270, 272-273
St. Lucy (Dec.13).........34
St. Luke (Oct.18).....266,268-269
St. Mark (Apr.25).........114
St. Martha (July 29).........190
St. Matthias (May 14).........144
St. Matthew (Sept.21).........233
St. Monica (Aug.27).........208
St. Nicholas (Dec.6).........18
St. Patrick (Mar.17).........94
St. Paul (Conversion - Jan.25)...70
St. Paul (June 29).........170-171
St. Paul on the Horse Game (Jan.25)....70
St. Peter and St.Paul(Churches-Nov.18).293
St. Peter (June 29).........170-171
St. Peter (Chair - Feb.22).........88
St. Philip (May 3).........144
St. Scholastica (Feb.10).........78
St. Sebastian (Jan.20).........66-67
St. Simon (Oct.28).........270
St. Stephen (Dec.26).........40
St. Theresa (Oct.1).........246-247
St. Thomas (July 3).........174-175
St. Valentine (Feb.14).........86
St. Veronica (Feb.4).........76
St. Vincent de Paul (Sept.27).....240
St. Zita (Apr.27).........132
Sand Plate (May 20).........148
Shamrock Buns / Cookies (Mar.17)...94
Spoon Angels (Oct.2).........249
String of Guardian Angels (Oct.2)...248
Sweet Angel Treats (Oct.2).........251
Telephone Book Angel (Oct.2).........252
Tin Lanterns (June 24)....162-163
Tissue Paper Roses (Dec.12)......24
Transfiguration (Aug.6).....202
Trinity Sunday.........164
Trinity Bracelets.........164
Trinity Braid Pins.........164
Triumph of the Cross (Sept.14)...232
Woven Prayer Petition Heart...165
Valentine Cake/Cookies (Feb.14)...86
Visitation Feast (May 31)...150

SAINTS' DAYS ACTIVITIES

QUICK PICK

Armour of God...285
Baby Survival Kit...217
Bible Bingo...231
Bird Treat - Tree Decorations...49
Birthday Journal...212
Blessing of the Home (Epiphany)...56
Bubble Blower and Bubble Solution..155
Calendar Scroll..213
Candles (Dec.7)...18
Catch the Spirit! Wind Catcher...159
Catechism Cube...182-183
Catechism Playing Cards...192
Cathletics...176-207
Cathletics Lingo Bingo...181
Cathletics Competition...286
Cathletics Flash Cards...185
Cathletics Playing Cards...193
Church Collector Cards...221-223
Christmas Card Bookmarks...48
Count the Rosaries in the Jar...288
Crown of Roses...262-264
Crowns and Wreaths...54,265, 295
David and Goliath Bean Bag Toss...288
Def-A-Day / Definition Detail...186
Dough Doves...158
Everyday in Ordinary Time..220-239
Extraordinary Events
in Ordinary Time.210-219
Family Blessings Mailbox..224
Family Fire Drill (Feb.5/Aug.5)...78,200
Family Fridge Calendar...226-227
Family Fun Date...45
Family Guestbook...212
Family Journal of Firsts
and Family Events..210
Family Treasure Chest...216
Family Tree...214-215
Felt Friends...43
Felt Friends' Flat...44
Fishers of Men Coin Toss...271
Foil Kiss Roses (Oct.1)...247
Four-in-a-Row..191
Gift Tags/Place Setting Tags...47-48
God Box...224-225
Guardian Angel Mobile (Oct.2)...254
Halo Toss...288
Holy Card Memory Game...239
Holy Hero Album...239
Holy Heroes Felt Friends 43-44,234-235
Holy Heroes Halo Game...289
Holy Heroes Puppets/Theatre...236-238
Holy Rummoli!...193
Holy Spirit Sweets...158
Holy Water Font...56
House Swatch...218
Ice Candles...41
Jelly Bean Angel (Oct.2)...250

Jell-O Box Jeopardy..189
Jig-Saw Jell-O Boxes...191
Kite Building..152-154
King's Cake...55
List and Twist...287
Lists and Levels...195-207
Liturgical Chairs...285
Mass Parts and Prayers...223
Memory Catcher Cards...211, 217
Mobile Home-Maker...218
Momentum Builder Grid...187
Musical Instruments...294
Painting
(Bubble/Etched/Squeezed)...269
Paper Bag Lanterns...42
Paper Mache' Angel (Oct.2)...253
Party Drinks...11
Pass the Torch Party...229
Pinata...13-14, 284,, 290-291
Potato Stamping...263
Praises Phrases...157
Prayer Bank/Carousel...62-65
Prayer Chains...25
Prayer Habits...73
Prayer Posting Boards...272-273
Prayer Time and Mass Prep..220
Project: Definition...186
Pure White Dinner (Dec.8)...21
Rosaries...243-244
Rosary Bee...288
Rosary Gift Cards...260-264
Rosary Refresher...256-259
Sacramental Memory Game...288
Sacrament Anniversary Party...219
Saint Name Game...286
Scripture Search (Dec.27)...40
Sin Pinata...290-291
Sin Pin Bowling...270
Special Intentions Candle /
Picture Frame...267
Spiritual Bouquet Cards...260-264
Spiritual Bouquet of
Prayer Petal Flowers...245
Spoon Angels (Oct.2)...249
String of Guardian Angels(Oct.2).248
Sweet Angel Treats (Oct.2)...251
Telephone Book Angel (Oct.2)...252
Tin Lanterns (June 24)..162-163
Tissue Paper Roses (Dec.12)...24
Trinity Braid Pins...164
Trinity Bracelets...164
Trivia Tube...183
Works of Mercy Relay Race...286
Woven Prayer Petition Heart...165